Writing for Wally
My Life With a Brilliant Idea

By John G. Hubbell

ISBN: 1484913019

ISBN 13: 9781484913017

Dedication

For Punkin, the love of my life and the Queen of my world, who, under constant siege by the gang of nine, held down the fort all those years, while I was out there, having all that fun.

And for each of the gang of nine.

And the 27 (so far) grandkids.

And the 2 (so far) great grandkids.

And all those who follow.

Table of Contents

Preface

Once there was a brilliant idea called The Reader's Digest. It was conceived in the mind of a man named William Roy DeWitt Wallace; he went by the name DeWitt. With his wife, Lila Bell Acheson Wallace, and later with the help of the best editorial talent he could find, he nurtured and developed the idea, a monthly service of searching out, finding and delivering to readers the most interesting and best written non-fiction to be found in the world's public prints. He lovingly sculpted the idea until it became, arguably, the greatest print journalism institution in history. At its peak, it had a domestic circulation of some 18,000,000, which meant that it was seen by one in four Americans every month; and a worldwide circulation of some 31,000,000, which meant that it was seen by approximately 100,000,000 of the world's people every month. The Reader's Digest became perhaps the most influential print communications organ ever devised.

The idea occurred to Wallace as he convalesced in a hospital in France, recovering from serious wounds he had suffered in the late days of World War I. A voracious reader, he found himself constantly searching through the hospital's stacks of magazines for articles that captured his interest. It occurred to him that he was no different than most people, and that what interested him would also interest most people.

He was home, in St. Paul, Minnesota, after the war, and enamored of Lila, the sister of a college friend. He told her of his idea for a reader's service. She thought it was a great idea, and urged him to pursue it. He spent months searching the magazine stacks in the large Public Library in Minneapolis, looking for the most interesting and valuable articles he could find.

Lila and DeWitt were married on October 15, 1921. They moved to New York, and she went to work with him in the City's Public Library. They scoured the stacks for articles of significant interest, that would provide and enhance knowledge, entertain and have as much value years from the day they were first read. Indeed, that would be their goal, their digest magazine's motto: "An article a day of significant value and enduring interest."

Wallace ascertained early on that writers too often used too much time and space trying to impress the reader with their talent. He taught himself what would become a new art, how to condense, to revise the pieces he liked, fit them into less space and without sacrificing the author's style, while at the same time making certain that the piece retained everything that was worth knowing about the subject.

The Wallaces acquired permission to republish the articles they had chosen from the editors of the publications in which they had first appeared, with full credit to those publications; most agreed, for the free sales promotion. (In later years, as the Digest's fortunes bloomed, Wally paid them handsomely for reprint rights, and the authors of articles reprinted in the Digest were paid well for them, too.)

Then, they sent letters to every name on lists they had collected, rosters of all kinds of professional, religious and civic organizations, some 5,000 people whom they hoped would subscribe to what they promised: a Reader's Digest of compact size, small enough to carry in one's pocket, full of interesting, high value non-fiction and humor, and free of advertising. They asked the recipients of their letters if they were interested enough to send $3.00 for a one-year subscription.

Astonished at an overwhelmingly positive response, DeWitt and Lila used all of their own money, about $2,000, borrowed $5,000 more and ordered a first printing of 5,000 copies. Very quickly, it became obvious that Wallace had been correct in his view that most people would be interested in what interested him. Now, he hoped that his invention would earn them enough to live on; Lila was sure of it.

Thirty years later, Time Magazine's cover featured Lila and DeWitt Wallace, and the cover story was entitled, "The Common Touch." The article led off with the observation that the Digest "… is read in foxholes in Korea, in the cockpits of transatlantic planes, by Swedish farmers, Brazilian housewives, Japanese coal miners, Igorots in G strings…one of the greatest success stories in the history of journalism…unique proof that circulation alone can turn the trick, with no help from advertising revenue. In its thirty progressively successful years, the Digest has run not one line of paid advertising in its domestic edition (9,500,000 copies). This year the Digest should gross between $25 million and $30 million and net about $1,500,000…." (That was small potatoes compared to the amounts the Digest would earn in the years that followed.)

I remember reading the Time piece with admiration and a modicum of pride. I had just sold my first article to the Digest. It was still basically a "reader's service," a reprint magazine, but had for some time been accepting original articles and paying high rates, which meant that many of the world's best writers kept Digest editors under constant siege with their proposals. The competition for space in the magazine was formidable. It was something of a feat to break into it.

My first article appeared in the April, 1952, issue, and was the beginning of a beautiful 41-year relationship. After publishing a few more of my articles DeWitt Wallace brought me on as a Staff Writer. A few years later I was listed in the masthead as a Roving Editor. It is to vastly understate matters to say that mine was an interesting, exciting career.

I was also fortunate enough to spend more than four decades of my life working with many of the most talented journalists in the business, Digest Editors and other Roving Editors who also happened to be the best, brightest and nicest people I would ever know.

Wally died in 1981, a victim of Alzheimer's Disease, complicated by cancer. Because of the arrogant, ignorant cupidity of those who were able later to seize control, his beloved magazine lasted in the form he conceived it only a few years longer. The company has since been through bankruptcy twice, and the Digest, now minus the collection of great editors and writers who helped Wally make it the success it became, struggles. Peter Canning, who was once a Digest managing editor, recounts the details of the original's glorious history and tragic demise in his 1996 book, "American Dreamers: The Wallaces and Reader's Digest, An Insider's Story."

I retired in 1993. This is my story, about DeWitt Wallace's Reader's Digest and me, and how much interesting fun it was to have been a part of it during its glory years.

1
A Stupid Decision

In the summer of 1949 I did the dumbest thing ever done by any graduate of a School of Journalism. I turned down the offer of a good reporting job from a really good newspaper and took a job instead as a billing clerk for an air conditioning company. The job I took paid so well that I sometimes had to hitchhike to and from work, get my lunch out of a vending machine in the factory and dinner at a drug store lunch counter.

Sixty-plus years later I still wonder at my stupidity that summer, and wonder even more at the incredible good fortune that followed.

Here's what happened: The School of Journalism at the University of Minnesota was then in the top tier of such schools, along with those at Columbia, Northwestern and Missouri, so enjoyed a great deal of success in placing its graduates with good newspapers; not big city dailies, most of which were not interested in neophyte reporters, but dailies and weeklies in smaller towns and cities, from which emanated the now experienced reporters who manned (and, to be sure, womaned) the editorial staffs of the big city dailies. The newspaper that I turned down was an excellent daily in a nice, sizable Midwestern city not far from Chicago and St. Louis, and a number of journalists who had started there had, within a few years, moved on to the newspapers in those big cities.

The job I was offered was a great opportunity, and any would-be journalist would be crazy not to take it and make the most of it. The Editor-in-Chief, a very nice gentleman, had introduced me to the staff, showed me around the plant and the town and made it clear that he wanted to hire me. I thought hard about it for a couple of days, then finally admitted to myself that I was crazy, that I did not want to be a newspaper reporter.

The prospect of reporting on the mundane events of daily life didn't thrill me. I had long harbored dreams of a more glamorous career, of being a big-time correspondent for a big time magazine, a writer who dealt with national and world events. That's where the glory was in those days, just as it later became television. Magazine writers were out in the big wide world, not just reporting, but writing, capturing thoughtful readers with displays of their own styles, analyzing, infusing their work with their own brilliantly thought out opinions, *expressing* themselves.

That's what I would do, and how stupid was that? Why in the world would anyone care about some 22-year-old dumbbell's style, ideas, opinions?

The air conditioning company needed someone to type up invoices and I could type, so became a billing clerk. I don't think anyone else applied for the job.

It wasn't quite what I was looking for.

One day about six weeks into my career as a billing clerk I called in sick and went job-hunting. It turned out to be a pivotal day in my life. I was thinking in terms of public relations, blowing some company's horn. It was a field that paid well, and if I could find that kind of a job I could spend nights and weekends free-lancing, finding and writing articles in which I could display my work to major magazines.

Things were not going well that morning. A couple of major corporations had no interest whatever in employing a totally inexperienced Journalism graduate. Then, I wandered into the personnel office of the Minneapolis-Honeywell Regulator Company. At the time it was one of the state's biggest employers. It designed and manufactured all kinds of electronic controls for all kinds of things, its basic product being the thermostat that controlled the temperatures for most of the buildings in the universe. I knew nothing of electronics or controls. I didn't know why I had taken the time to come here. I had no idea what I could do for such a company. I was surprised when the lady in Personnel got on her phone, talked to someone, then sent me upstairs to see Mr. Ainsworth.

W. Hale Ainsworth was the manager of the Publications Department of Honeywell's Aeronautical Division. The Division designed and produced all kinds of "gee whiz" stuff for airplanes, like automatic pilots, fuel gauges, guidance systems for missiles. The Publications Department produced the technical manuals necessary for the installation, use and care of the Division's products. Mr. Ainsworth explained to me that the Division now planned to publish an institutional house organ, a magazine, not for its employees but for it customers and prospective customers. It would deal with all subjects of interest in the aeronautical field. An editor was already at work, and needed help. Did I think I might be interested in such work?

I think I almost shouted that I was a graduate of the University of Minnesota's School of Journalism, that as a student I had already sold magazine articles (true: I had sold *one,* to a minor golf business publication). I pointed out that I had been trained to interview, how to think through ideas and subjects and write editorials. I said that there was a Professor of Creative Writing at the University who would vouch for my creative sensibilities and capabilities, that I had been an Aviation Radioman in the Navy and could type sixty words per minute. I may have mentioned that I had been writing (i.e., typing up invoices) for an air conditioning company for approximately six weeks.

Mr. Ainsworth was grinning. He called in the man who was the Editor-in-Chief of the new publication. His name was Merrill Jones. He was tall, slim, crew cut, smiling, soft-spoken, perhaps forty years old. Mr. Jones asked me a few more questions than Mr. Ainsworth had, and seemed okay with my answers. Mr. Ainsworth said, "Let's go to lunch and see how we all fit together."

We drove to a restaurant in his Cadillac. At the time eating in a nice restaurant was an unusual and pleasant experience for me. What made it especially pleasant was that it was found that we all fit together nicely. I had a new job. The air conditioning company did not seem overly upset at my abrupt departure. I was soon at work at Honeywell, in a job that paid me well enough to provide for bus fare to and from work and to eat in nice places three times every day.

Hale Ainsworth and Merrill Jones would remain two of the most important figures in my life. We got a glossy magazine produced called Flight Lines. We filled it with material of interest to the industry, and the industry gave us rave reviews. In time, Merrill and I were traveling throughout the aeronautics industry, acquiring new material. I learned that in the Pentagon, each of the different military Services had "Book and Magazine" offices whose whole purpose for existing was to steer people like me to stories about the wonderful things that were going on in their Services. I made contacts, some of which evolved into close friendships that would last for decades.

In the few years that followed the Industrial Editors Society conferred many awards upon Flight Lines for layout and content, and upon me personally for writing. I was not getting rich, but was prospering. I was driving a new convertible and living in the plushest area of the city, on the very comfortable upper floor of a home whose owners, a fiftyish lady and her elderly mother, wanted a young male in residence for security purposes. They were very pleasant people who kept my bed made and my lodging immaculate. And I kept looking for the big chance.

Meanwhile, I found myself really awed at some of the people who had made Honeywell the great company it had become.

Willis Gille, for example. He had been a sales engineer, making his living by selling the company's electronic heating controls. One day in the spring of 1941 he was demonstrating his wares at Wright-Patterson Air Force Base, near Dayton, Ohio. Following his presentation one of the officers who had been listening brought him into a room with a "No Admittance" sign on the door, swore him to secrecy and showed him a device called a bombsight. A New York inventor named Carl Norden had devised it, and claimed it could place a bomb within 100 feet of its target from an altitude of four miles. It was explained to Gille that it should allow for high precision bombing from high altitudes, but it needed help, something that would hold a large aircraft steady during a bombing run. Could the principles involved in electronic heating controls be applied to this problem? Could a system be produced that would allow a pilot to turn his aircraft over to his bombardier during a bombing run?

Gille went home to Minneapolis and worked the problem on a ping pong table in his basement. A few months later he returned to Wright-Patterson with what he called "a stabilizing device." It worked. By December, 1941, Honeywell was delivering the first of some 30,000 electronic automatic pilots it supplied to the Army's Air Forces during World War II. In addition to providing stability during bombing runs, the C-1 made it possible for hundreds of bombers that had been all but destroyed by anti-aircraft fire to limp back to their bases.

Gille's C-1 autopilot took Honeywell into the aeronautical industry, where it continues to thrive, making all kinds of marvelous systems for military and commercial aviation.

Gille became the company's Director of Research, a Science Advisor to two Presidents, the holder of 93 patents and the first member of Minnesota's Inventors Hall of Fame.

One of my early stories for the Digest was about the Niagara of amazing devices that continued to pour out of the company. I entitled it, "Honeywell's House of Magic." A Digest editor retitled it, "They're Wizards at Control."

But I'm getting ahead of myself.

2

I *Did* Need the Marines

One evening in late 1949, only a few months after I had started working at Honeywell, a friend proposed that we join the Marine Corps Reserve Unit based at Wold-Chamberlain Airport, serving the Twin Cities. He had discovered that the Marines would admit us at ratings equivalent to those we had held while on active duty in the Navy during World War II; we would both enter the Corps as sergeants. He was now married and had two children, and a Marine Corps obligation would *require* him to leave the house for an entire weekend once each month; think of the fun we could have. I declined, pointing out that I was not married, had no children or, at the moment, any personal attachments whatever, that I was comfortable with the way things were and did not need the Marine Corps to get me out of the house at any time. He joined, attended one meeting, was issued a uniform and never attended another.

At length, he received a registered letter from the Corps advising that if he would return the uniform he would be issued a discharge. He didn't get around to it.

The Korean War erupted on June 25, 1950. He learned to fire a rifle off the fantail of the ship that carried him to the war.

In November, he was among a crowd of Marines who were captured by Chinese forces at the Chosin Reservoir and were imprisoned in a camp above the Yalu River, in Manchuria.

For several months the prisoners, when they were not being mistreated and underfed, were subjected daily to endless lectures on the wonders of Communism and the glories of China's leader, Mao Tse Tung. As time passed, my friend and several of his fellow Marine prisoners began trying to convince their captors that they finally were sold on communism, ready to return to America and preach Mao's gospel.

It worked. One day nineteen of them were told that they were to be released so that they could "return to America and carry out your plan."

A handful of Chinese troops escorted them south, toward the United Nations' lines, where they were to set them free. They had nearly reached freedom when the U.N. forces unleashed a massive offensive. The Chinese guards chattered, excitedly, among themselves. One of the Marines who understood some of the chatter explained that their escorts were debating whether to shoot them or return them to the prison camp. Neither option was attractive; the Marines fell upon the escorts, killed them, returned themselves to U.N. lines and were forthwith returned to their homes in America. None was ever known to preach Mao's gospel.

I spent several hours listening to my friend describe his experiences.

I thought it had the makings of a great magazine article. I suggested that I write one, and that if a magazine bought it we split the proceeds sixty-forty – sixty percent for me, because I had done all the work of organizing, writing and selling the story, forty percent for him, for telling me about it. He argued that since he had gone to the trouble of living the horrific experience the split I proposed should be reversed, sixty percent for him, forty for me. We compromised at fifty-fifty.

I spent several evenings writing it, getting everything just right.

Then I composed a page and a half outline. No outline has ever been more carefully crafted. Not only did I want to sell the story, I wanted to sell myself as a writer. I addressed it separately to the Editors-in-Chief of the major American magazines of the time: The Saturday Evening Post; Collier's; The Reader's Digest; Look; Life; True; Argosy.

They all wanted it. The Reader's Digest wanted it most. I had sent the proposal to DeWitt Wallace, the Digest's Founder and Editor-in-Chief. The response came from an Associate Editor named Hobart Lewis, who offered $300 just to look at it. Having not seen such an amount in one piece in a long time, I sent the manuscript to him "Special Delivery Air Mail" – other than the telephone or a telegram, that was as fast as anyone could communicate in those days. I fully expected that he would return it along with a regretful note and a check in the amount of $300. He sent me a check in the amount of $3,000, along with a congratulatory letter, saying the piece would be published in the April, 1952, issue of the Digest.

Holy Moses! I don't know what $3,000 is worth today – probably nothing like $3,000, but in early 1952 it was worth a lot, maybe $3,000.

It occurs to me that I *did* need the Marine Corps, not to get me out of the house, but to get my friend out of his house and go collect an experience that would provide me with the opportunity to write my way into the world of major magazine journalism.

When the story appeared my ex-POW friend and I were both local celebrities. The Minneapolis Sunday Tribune got permission from the Digest and used an entire page to reprint it. Popular local columnists wrote about the story and about both of us, and we were interviewed on radio and television shows.

It was fun, exciting. I was walking on air! I couldn't help thinking how great and how lucrative it would be to be writing all the time for a major magazine.

3
The Fun Begins

I had broken through, but how to make the most of it? In my spare time I kept exploring newspapers and magazines for germs of ideas, finding them, proposing them to my new friend at The Reader's Digest, Hobart Lewis. He always responded, but negatively; one story idea was too similar to one that was already scheduled for publication; another just didn't "fill the Digest's needs right now," another is good, but "unfortunately", I'm too late with it, another writer has the assignment.

Then, one day, the phone on my desk rings, and I am astonished to find myself talking to Lewis; we had corresponded a lot, but had never spoken to each other before. I had sent him a copy of Flight Lines. He is very complimentary about it and about my writing; he is impressed with the aviation material, and has an idea he thinks I might like to pursue: As the Korean War rages on, U.S. Air Force fighter pilots are confronted with Soviet-made

Mig fighter aircraft that can climb higher and are faster and more maneuverable, in other words, superior to the U.S. Air Force's best fighter aircraft, the F-86 Sabrejet. It is known that a lot of the Migs are being flown by presumably well-trained Chinese and Soviet pilots. Yet, the Americans thus far have racked up a 14 to one win ratio. Thus, the reason for American air superiority must be found in the Air Force's pilot training program. Would I be interested in finding the answers for a Digest article on the subject? The research would involve a good deal of travel through the Air Training Command but it might also yield some useful material for Flight Lines, and the Digest would be happy to cover expenses.

Merrill Jones and Hale Ainsworth love the idea. Hale arranges a leave of absence for me.

I spend weeks roaming through the Air Force. It starts with briefings in the Pentagon, where I am impressed at how quickly doors open when the name of The Reader's Digest is invoked. Then, there are interviews at Maxwell Air Force Base, Alabama; Lackland Air Force Base, Texas; San Angelo Air Force Base, Texas; and finally at the Tactical Air Force's Gunnery School, at Nellis Air Force Base, near Las Vegas. There, I meet some fighter aces, men whose names have been in headlines and whose faces have been on the covers of newsmagazines, like Jim Kasler and Robbie Risner, who have shot down five or more Migs and are now training newly winged fighter pilots en route to war. (20 years later I will engage Kasler and Risner again, in several day-long interviews, following their return from prison camps in Vietnam.)

The story of how U.S. Air Force pilots achieve air supremacy in Korea's "Mig Alley" appears as a lead article in the Digest, and a shorter version runs in Flight Lines. Everyone is happy. Especially me.

4
Mediterranean Excitements

I n December, 1953, I took what I thought would be a two-week vacation to spend the Christmas holidays with my parents, who now lived in retirement in Asbury Park, New Jersey. My brother, Les, who was now the Skipper of a destroyer, the U.S.S. Owen, came up to spend a few days with us.

"You should write a story about the Navy's anti-submarine warfare capabilities," Les told me. "We're pretty good at it now, and people would like to know that if we ever have to go to war again no enemy's submarine force is going to be able to do to us what Germany's U-boats did in the early 1940's. They sank millions of tons of allied shipping. They were sinking ships within sight of the east coast. People actually stood on the shore and watched it happen. They almost cut our supply line to Britain. We didn't have much of an anti-submarine capability then. But no one will be able to do that to us again. We're leaving Norfolk on January 4 on anti-submarine warfare exercises that will take us all the way to Athens, Greece, and back again. Why don't you join us? It would make a good story for you."

It sounded good to me. We were locked in a bitter Cold War with the Soviet Union, which was known to be constructing a formidable undersea fleet. We certainly could not allow the Soviets to do what Hitler's submarines had done during World War II. The world's sea lanes had to be kept open, and it was up to the Navy's Hunter-Killer task forces to see to it. I called Hobart Lewis to ask if the Digest might be interested.

"Absolutely!" he said. "That sounds like a great story. Do it."

In a frantic couple of days Lewis got some expense money to me, I called Merrill Jones, who agreed that the trip likely would yield a good story or two for Flight Lines. He talked to Hale Ainsworth, who quickly got me another leave of absence from Honeywell. Les got the Navy's approval to take a civilian correspondent aboard, and I acquired a passport.

I spent the next several weeks watching a seagoing ballet that started the morning after we left Norfolk and stretched all the way across the Atlantic and through the Mediterranean to Athens, Greece. It involved a number of destroyers, a light aircraft carrier and some submarines. I studied operations from all the ships, from the carrier, during operations from the back seat of one of the carrier's aircraft – when I complimented the pilot for his skill after a *night* landing in choppy seas he replied, "I'm terrified every time I do it!" I decided that if he was terrified, so was I, in retrospect. I made a few more flights, but none at night.

I spent a lot of time aboard a submarine in the depths of the Mediterranean. Its job was to conjure up different ways to attack the surface force, then do its best to defend itself and hide when the force turned the attack back on him.

A bonus to the cruise was that I was able to explore a lot of the Mediterranean, to visit Algeria, as far south as an oasis in the Sahara, then Sicily, Naples, Athens, and to spend several days in Cannes, Nice and Monaco and some of the surrounding villages. There were some exciting moments. I was walking alone down a nearly empty street in Algiers one day, at about the time when Algeria, then a department of France, which meant it was integral to France, just as the state of Kansas, for example, is integral to the United States, was agitating to secede from France. Suddenly, I was aware that the only other man on the street had a gun in my ribs. He shouldered me into an alley. He identified himself as a cop and searched me. I was sure that he was sure that I represented the De Gaulle government in Paris, which was treating Algeria's demand for independence with De Gaullian contempt. He examined my passport and my wallet, handed them back to me, confiscated my cigarettes (I smoked then), and waved me on my way. It would be many years before I would be able to wean myself off of cigarettes, but I was glad I had them to give that day.

One evening I was dining alone at a small, highly recommended restaurant in the hills behind Cannes. Not only was the food as good as reputed, but a strolling violinist moved about playing requests. When he came to my table I requested the ballad, "Lili Marlene." He did not want to play it. I had always liked the song, and insisted, forcing a five dollar bill upon him. He played it. Suddenly, I was aware that the room had gone silent, and most of the people in it were looking at me; in fact, seemed to be glaring at me. A gentleman rose from another table and came to sit with me. He explained to me quietly, in fluent English, that in case I was unaware of it the ballad I had selected was of German origin, that it had been the favorite of the German forces that had occupied this region during World War II, that this area had been "a very active hotbed" of the French resistance, which doubtless included some of the people who were present in the restaurant this evening. He added that while he meant no disrespect he felt compelled to point out that I had a full head of blond hair (at that time, I did), blue eyes, fair skin and that I would easily fill the bill as Adolf Hitler's ideal Aryan youth. I thanked the gentleman, asked him to explain to whomever would listen that I, too, had despised Hitler, that I was of Irish and Welsh extraction, that I had served in the U.S. Navy during the war, that I was unaware that Lili Marlene had been a German favorite, that I felt stupid about it and would never listen to it again. I thanked him profusely. It occurred to me that my waiter was a tough looking guy who may well have been a member of the resistance. I paid my bill, left a huge tip on the table and departed.

The anti-submarine warfare story looked good in Flight Lines, and my time on the submarine suggested another story. Soon, I was on my way to New London, Connecticut, to learn how the Navy transformed young Americans into men who could live and fight in very close quarters for long periods of time inside of dim-lit tubes beneath the surfaces of the seas.

5

The Making of a Submariner

"No can do," the officer in charge says. "Not a chance."

"Why not," I ask.

"You're a civilian."

"That's my thing. I only change out of it when there's a war on."

"We can't let civilians go into the training tank. For one thing, we're busy with students. For another, there's an element of real danger. If you don't know what you're doing you could make a mistake, you could suffer an embolism that kills you."

"There's no chance of that."

"Yes, there is a good chance. Why do you say there's no chance."

"Because you are going to teach me how to do it, the same way you teach your students. I'm a good listener. I pay attention. I'll take instruction along with your students. I'll be just as good at it as any of them. Maybe better, because I have already been in the Navy and know how important it is to listen when officers speak."

He wasn't buying it.

"You're not in the Navy now," he pointed out. "They are. They volunteered for the Submarine Service. I don't even want to think about the kind of trouble we'd be in if we let a civilian do this and…"

"I'm volunteering. Get out a piece of paper that says so and I'll sign it. I will absolve you, and the Navy and the entire government of any responsibility."

"Forget it. Go away."

I am in Groton, Connecticut, across the Thames River from the city of New London; I'm at the site of the Navy's Submarine Service Training School. I am here because Hobart Lewis and I have been discussing the fact that World War II ended ten years ago and that zillions of great war stories have yet to be told. One untold story: how the U.S. Navy was able to assemble a force of men who were able to spend years of their lives working under the seas in very close quarters with a lot of other men and a lot of torpedoes and literally strangle the Japanese empire, sinking 56 percent of all its shipping. Incredible!

The first thing that happens to volunteers for the Submarine Service is a week of exhausting physical and psychological screening. They are almost turned inside out in a search for their ability to think and react with lightning speed and coordination to a seemingly endless variety of situations, because every Submariner must be able quickly to do any and every job on the boat – the submarine, by the way, is the only Navy man o' war (combat vessel) called a boat; all the others are ships.

One of the first things Submariners learn is that when their boat is submerged their ears become their eyes, that in order to man the sonar system one must have a keen sense of pitch and loudness, listen for the enemy, find him, keep track of him; and if the sonar man becomes a casualty someone else must take over instantly – an Engineer, a Torpedo Man, an Electrician, a Bosun's Mate.

The last thing the new recruits do on Friday of the first week is learn whether or not they are claustrophobic; you can't be claustrophobic and be a Submariner. An important part of this is to learn how to escape a downed boat, and how to deal with the pressures of the deep on one's ears. All of which is learned in an 11-story high brick silo containing a quarter million gallons of water and a number of recompression chambers.

To the extent possible, I want my readers to know the rigors of the training tank. I want to go through it myself and describe a first-hand experience.

And the officer in charge won't let me.

What to do?

I find a telephone and call a friend in Washington, a senior Naval officer. "Go see Slade Cutter," he tells me.

Captain Slade Cutter is the school's commanding officer – Slade Cutter. What a name! It almost seems to describe a fictional hero, like Captain Marvel. But there is nothing fictional about this guy. He is an authentic Naval legend; in the Navy's pantheon of heroes he ranks right up there with John Paul Jones. During World War II he skippered a submarine named Seahorse and sent 19 Japanese ships to the bottom of the Pacific. By the time the war ended he had been decorated with four Navy Crosses, the Navy's highest award for combat valor; the only thing higher is the Medal of Honor. On one patrol in June, 1944, he found a strong Japanese battle group headed for Guam, then a major Japanese stronghold. Clearly, its purpose was to help defend the island against oncoming American forces which by then were sweeping through Micronesia, intent on establishing bases from which aerial assaults could be mounted against Japan's home islands.

The intelligence provided by Cutter enabled Admiral Raymond Spruance, commanding Task Force 58 and guarding the Fleet Marine Force's back, to meet the oncoming enemy force in the Battle of the Philippine Sea. The meeting cost the Japanese three aircraft carriers and some 400 aircraft. In Naval lore the event is remembered as The Marianas Turkey Shoot.

"Don't try to talk to Cutter about what he did in the war," my advisor warned. "He won't want to talk about it, and he always gives credit to the crew, as though he had nothing to do with it. Talk to him about the really important things in life. Like the field goal he kicked that beat Army."

A light went on in my head. I had been a football fanatic since about age one-half. My fanaticism had been at its steamiest in the 1930's. I had forgotten that I had hero-worshipped many of the great players of the era, had read every sports page article and every magazine piece I had been able to find about them; memories flooded back. The football heroes of the era had all been my heroes, and, to be sure, included Navy's Slade Cutter, whose field goal in 1934 had ended Army's 13-year winning streak over Navy.

"I knew that!" I almost shouted over the phone. "Thanks for reminding me, and for the advice."

I called Cutter's office, and a secretary said I could see him at "1100 hours" (that's 11 a.m.) the next day.

He's tall, over six feet, well built but trim. He gets up from behind his desk and walks toward me, smiling broadly. His handshake feels like he means it when he says he's glad to meet me.

"I've wanted to meet you since you kicked that field goal that beat Army," I tell him. "I'm from a Navy family, and you were one of my heroes."

His smile broadens; he laughs. "You *remember* that? How old were you then?"

"Seven. But I've been a football fanatic since before I was born, and my family is all Navy, and I knew that was the first time in years that Navy had beat Army."

"Thirteen years," he says.

"Wow! What a thrill that must have been."

"It was great. I've played that game over in my head a thousand times."

"You must have been nervous getting ready to kick."

"Yeah, we were all excited, but I knew I could make it. That's one of the great things about the Naval Academy. You learn to rein in your emotions and focus on the job at hand."

The interview slips into reverse. He wants to know where I grew up, went to school, notes that, "Minnesota had some really great football teams back in the '30's, when he played. He wants to know how I got into, "the writing business." I tell him about my friend, who tried to get me to join the Marine Corps Reserve. He can hardly believe the story. He summarizes: "So he forgot to return the uniform, and that got him a trip to 'Frozen Chosin,'[1] and he got to enjoy Mao's hospitality for a while, and then he came home and helped you launch your career."

"That's one way of putting it."

"He's a friend in need. I want to be your friend, too. Tell me how I can help you."

"Tell me about this job."

"I like it a lot. It's one of the most important jobs in the peacetime Navy. There is no shortage of kids who want to be Submariners. We have a waiting list of volunteers. The task here is to indoctrinate them and start making them into the best Submariners they can be."

"That's the story I want to write. How you do it. How you take ordinary young Americans and turn them into skilled practitioners of undersea warfare. It seems to me that this is a major element of deterrence, of keeping wars from happening."

"Boy," he laughed, "you *are* a writer! I couldn't have said that better. I couldn't have said it at all."

"I would like to experience some of it myself, so that I can give the reader a realistic feel for it. I don't want to just *tell* the reader about it, I want to *show* him how it's done, give him a feeling for what happens."

He smiles. "Well, we're always open to volunteers. You want to enlist…"

"How about if I write a dramatic story showing how it's done, show the world's largest circulation what these young guys go

---

[1] Korea's Chosin Reservoir, where my friend was captured on a bitterly cold November day in 1950, was often referred to as, "Frozen Chosin."

through to become Submariners. I think the most effective thing I can do is go through the training tank, take the reader through it, let him experience it with me. Do you think that could be arranged?"

"Sure. I'll call the officer in charge and set it up."

I'm wondering to myself how the officer in charge will react to my going over his head. Will he talk his commanding officer out of it? But I have the feeling that when Cutter makes a decision it's made, and that he doesn't abide backtalk. And I had been in the Navy long enough to know that the commanding officer of any facility is like God; what he says goes, and there is no argument. The flip side is that if anything goes wrong, he pays the damages.

"Can I take you to lunch?" I ask.

"Not if I take you first."

We go to his table in the Officers' Mess. The officer in charge of the training tank is at another table. Cutter calls him over, asks him to include me in the next group going through the tank. The officer looks at me, looks anxiously at his commanding officer, says, "Sir, I tried to explain to Mr. Hubbell…"

"Relax, Tommy," Cutter says, patting the young man's arm, "we all know the rules. Mr. Hubbell is intelligent, strong and a Navy veteran, and he'll sign a disclaimer and follow your instructions to a T, and his article will be helpful to the Navy and the Submarine Service. Everything will be fine."

Tommy relaxes and smiles at me. "Mr. Hubbell, if you could be in my office at 0800 tomorrow we'll set everything up."

"I'll be there."

In the following two days I learn enough to instruct the reader on how to escape from a downed submarine, something everyone should know.

Shouldn't they?

Who knows what the fates have in store?

With a group of 15 other volunteers I learn how to use a breathing device. All 16 of us learned that we could be stuffed together into a chamber little larger than an ordinary coat closet, that enough warm water could be let in to cover the tops of our heads and that none in this group were claustrophobic; anyone who shows the slightest sign of claustrophobic panic is immediately let out of the chamber and out of the Submarine Service.

Early the next morning we are all in a chamber at the bottom of the training tank, with 100 feet of water between us and the surface. It is emphasized to us that the last 33 feet to the top are the most dangerous, that in that stretch of water pressure decreases rapidly and the gases in the lungs increase so rapidly that if we forget to exhale for five feet our lungs could burst, death could be instantaneous. A line has been floated to the surface. We exit the chamber one by one, encircle the line with our hands and feet, arch our backs and float upward. We keep our eyes open and keep a safe distance from the man above, so as to avoid panic.

Nobody dies.

We all reach the surface in quick time.

I am not aware of anyone exiting the program because of claustrophobia, but I am informed that it happens, and not infrequently.

I can't provide the reader with the experience of the next eight weeks: I can only tell him that the candidates learn the names and locations of more than 50 ballast tanks in a submarine's hull. Each will take his turn again and again at a formidable looking bank of valve handles called a trim manifold, learn to operate the bewildering maze– they will be very awkward about it at first, but then will operate it with increasing confidence and speed, learning to take on seawater for a dive, blow the tanks to surface, transfer fuel or seawater from any tank to any other to give the boat proper trim.

By the end of the first week 28 of the 255 who entered with this class are washed out for various reasons.

The others move on, learn where the diesels are and how they work, learn all about the generators, the electrical systems, all about torpedoes and how to make the tubes ready for firing. They learn how to light off the engines, rig them for dive, rig them for battle, rig them for patrol quiet, for ultra quiet. They take frequent written exams. Some fear that they are failing, and voluntary night classes fill– an instructor tells them, "Every time I look at you I am wondering whether I want you on my boat, at sea, at war. Any time you even *look* like you want out, we'll help you out the door."

A training boat takes us down the Thames River, to the ocean, for a first experience. The students see what happens when we reach the sea and the Captain orders, "Take her down." Someone shouts, "Clear the bridge!" Lookouts on the bridge come flying through a hatch, one of them stops to lock it shut, then leaps behind the other down a ladder to the control room. A discordant horn blares, "AH OOGA...AH OOGA! A voice cries, *"Dive! Dive! Dive!"* The crew moves in what seem a thousand different directions in a quick, sure dance of knowledgeable action, whirling valve handles, pulling and pushing levers, pressing buttons, looking for signals to flash from red and green lights until finally someone shouts, "Green board, pressure in the boat!" And we are cruising in the subsurface.

The students seem stunned; most can't believe they will ever learn to do what they have just seen.

The training effort seems endless but the weeks pass in a flash; they include more training cruises, and the recruits spend a lot of time talking to the crew, men who have been through all this and have actually become Submariners. They become increasingly comfortable with the notion that they can do it, too. Finally, there is a searching three-hour exam requiring a great deal of written description and pages of minutely detailed colored pencil sketches of every system in the boat. The next morning they are back in class, tense and hollow-eyed from a sleepless night of worry – *"after all this, did I make it? I can't believe I made it. That exam was too much...I know I screwed it all up....."*

The instructor enters the classroom, looking at a paper in his hand, his face glum. "I can't believe this," he says. Then, the glum visage is replaced with a big, smiling face, and he informs them that they all have passed. A loud cheer rattles the building. The candidates leap around, slapping backs, shaking hands, chattering. Their boats are waiting for them, they are told, here, in New London, at Norfolk, Key West, San Diego and Pearl Harbor. Each man would receive his orders following noon chow

What they know now is that they still must prove themselves to their new shipmates, and that it will be six months to a year before their boat's leading petty officer will check them out on a submarine's every job and tells them to pin on their Dolphins, a brooch warn on the chest with two small dolphins flanking a submarine hull, a symbol of achievement similar to the wings worn by military aviators and the hard-won insignias worn by other special forces operatives, proof that the wearer has mastered a vital military profession.

And I was able to show the Digest's readers that there are plenty of young people who volunteer to guard the country, who are anxious and able to learn how to do all the complicated and often dangerous things that must be done.

6

"He Has No Enemies, But..."

Hobart Lewis called one day in the late winter of 1955 to remind me that it was now 25 years since the great golfer, Robert Tyre Jones, Jr., had won his amazing "grand slam," victories in the same season in the world's four major tournaments, then the U.S. and British Opens and the U.S. and British Amateurs. By this time Hobe and I had become good friends who shared a deep interest in golf, and had played some golf together. He was well aware of my passion for the game.

"I think," he said, "that it would be a good idea to run a profile of Jones in the Digest. The nation reveres him, and I think it would have a lot of appeal for our readers, and I think you would be just the guy to do it. What do you think?"

"I can't tell you how impressed I am with your judgment." I said.

"Well, The Masters is coming up soon, so why don't you go on down to Augusta..." he started to say, and I interrupted to say. "I'm on my way!"

But suddenly it occurred to me that we had no idea whether Jones would want to involve himself in such a story. He had been famous most of his youth and had retired when he was only 28, having won every golf event in the world that was worth winning. He had been worn out by the pressure of being expected to win every tournament he entered. He was 53 now, and reportedly not in the best of health. Maybe he didn't want to be brought back into the limelight; maybe he just wanted to be left in peace. I had to find out, and I had no idea how to reach him.

I went to the editorial offices of the Minneapolis Star, presented myself to the Sports Editor, a man much older than I named Charlie Johnson. I explained my problem to him and asked if he knew how to contact Jones. "Go see Wally Mund," Charlie said. "I think he can help you."

Wally Mund was the head professional at the Midland Hills Golf Club, just on the other side of the Mississippi River, in St. Paul. I found him in his office and explained myself. Without a word, he picked up the telephone on his desk, called the Augusta National Golf Club, in Augusta, Georgia, and asked to speak with "Mr. Roberts."

Clifford Roberts was a financier who had, with his friend, Bobby Jones, bought the property and founded and built the Augusta National golf course. For twenty years they had been hosting The Masters, the tournament, which signaled the start of each new golf season. It was an invitational event to which the invitation had to be earned – the contestants had to have distinguished themselves with their play in previous seasons. The Masters had become the golf world's most prestigious annual event. It was, indeed, a gathering of the Masters of the Game.

"Cliff," I heard Wally Mund say, "there's a young fellow in my office who needs to talk with you." And with that, he handed me the phone.

I was nervous. Cliff Roberts was a legend, the real power at the Augusta National, its Chief Executive Officer and, literally, its policy dictator. The club's elite international roster included some of the world's most important people, but none so important as to flout the rules of behavior Roberts had imposed; he told CBS-TV how it was to cover the action, he was known to have expelled members who complained openly about the condition of the golf course, or the prices in the dining room, or who persistently drank too much, or who failed to wear their green jackets at the Club's special events. As I introduced myself, I recalled that the current President of the United States, Dwight Eisenhower, was an active member – I doubted that Roberts would expel him for anything less than a devastating international disgrace that reflected badly on the Club.

I explained that I represented The Reader's Digest, that it had occurred to us that this was the twenty fifth anniversary of the Grand Slam, and that our readers would enjoy reading a profile of the great golfer and..."

"That's a *great* idea," he enthused, "and I know that Bob would love to work with the Digest. I'm a great fan of your magazine, and so is Bob. I love the pocket size, I'm able to carry it with me wherever I go, and the articles are wonderful. When do you want to come?"

"As soon as it's convenient for all of you. Tomorrow? The next day?"

"Good. The tournament starts next Thursday. Come tomorrow. I'll reserve a room for you at the Bon Air Hotel. You can spend all the time you need talking to Bob. A lot of his contemporaries always come down for the tournament, Gene Sarazen, Jess Sweetser, Walter Hagen, and you will want to talk to them, I'm sure, and lots of others who know Bob. And you can see the tournament."

I checked in at the Bon Air late the next afternoon, rented a car and found the Augusta National. The guard at the entrance had my name. He directed me down Magnolia Lane, to a parking spot near the clubhouse, and then to the Jones' residence, a lovely white house facing the tenth tee, and not far from it.

Bob Jones and his wife, Mary, greeted me warmly, made me feel truly welcome and at home. This was one of the nicest couples I was ever to meet. He wanted to know that my accommodations at the Bon Air were satisfactory, offering to make a phone call if I felt the need for a larger or more comfortable suite. I reassured him on the matter. Cliff Roberts was there, too, telling me to make full use of the clubhouse and its bars and dining rooms. I mentioned that I had seen someone who looked a lot like Gene Sarazen in the Bon Air lobby.

"Yes," Jones replied, "Gene is at the hotel, and you will meet him in a few minutes; we're all having dinner here. You will like him. He's a grand fellow, and has been a good friend for many years."

I learned that evening that Jones' friends called him Bob, not "Bobby." The latter was what the sportswriters, hence, the public, called him.

He was confined to a wheelchair now, and had been in constant pain for many years. He told me that it was the result of a hard practice swing he had made during the 1926 National Amateur Championship at The Country Club, in Brookline, Massachusetts, near Boston. He had felt and heard something snap in the back of his neck. It had not prevented him from winning that tournament and a number of others thereafter, including the four majors in 1930, the only one-year Grand Slam in golf history. But the pain had lingered and slowly increased. It was diagnosed as syringomyelia; a cavity in the spinal cord had filled with fluid. This had caused the pain, and eventually paralysis. From 1935 through 1948 he had made ceremonial appearances in each Masters Tournament, but by the time he reached the final hole of his last round, he had had to literally drag his right leg up the fairway. He had never been able to play again.

He was now 53 and overweight. Not obese, but heavier than such an outstanding athlete should have been at his age, the result of all the years in a wheelchair and being unable to get any exercise. And he smoked a lot of cigarettes. But in 1955 about the only one in the world who was truly focused on the notion that cigarettes were bad for you was DeWitt Wallace, who, in a few years, would publish articles that would help to devastate the tobacco industry.

I couldn't resist asking both Sarazen and Jones questions they had answered probably thousands of times. Sarazen about the 235-yard three wood he had sent into the hole on the par five fifteenth green of the 1935 Masters for a double eagle two. He laughed. "It was a good shot, well struck," he said, "but it was a lucky shot. The greatest eleven shots I ever hit were the pars I made on the next three holes to tie Craig Wood and force a playoff. I still don't know how I managed that."

He had won the playoff.

I asked Jones about the famous incident during the final round of a U.S. Open in which he had been leading when he called a penalty on himself for an infraction no one but he had seen; he had insisted that when he addressed the ball on one shot, he had caused it to move. No one, none of his playing partners nor anyone in his large gallery, had seen it move. The officials he called to assess a penalty on himself interviewed his playing partners and members of his gallery, and tried to convince him that it had not happened. His response had been the same then as it now was to me: "*I* saw it move, and I *knew* that I had caused it to move. Who would want to win a U.S. Open knowing that?"

He had lost the Open by one shot, but his integrity had won the admiration of the nation, which still perplexed him: He said, "You might as well congratulate a man for not robbing a bank!"

I asked Sarazen about his good friend and rival, Walter Hagen. He laughed. "Walter enjoyed being thought of as a fellow who loved a good party, and who could party and then play better golf than anyone else in the world. There were many stories of how the night before a major golf event, while all his competitors were sleeping, Walter would be out on the town partying, drinking and having a great time. Then would show up at the golf course and win the tournament. It was all show business. Walter wanted to win, and he was never out on the town during the nights of a tournament. He was in bed, getting a good night's sleep. Then, he would get up in the morning, lay out his tuxedo, sprinkle it with bourbon, then put it on and go to the golf course, acting as though his evening was just ending and smelling like a still. It made for great copy!"

The next morning I joined Jones in his golf cart for a tour of the course; Cliff Roberts accompanied us in his own cart. It was a gorgeous day and layout, and large crowds of azaleas and cottonwoods were exploding into bloom everywhere. Roberts and Jones were justifiably proud of what they had wrought.

Off in the distance we could see a lone golfer on the thirteenth fairway, a 500-yard-plus par five that runs along Rae's Creek to the left and doglegs left to a green framed with flowers on the hill behind it. He would hit a shot, study it, then hit another, study it, and finally a third. We drove out to meet him. His name was Arnold Palmer. A nice looking young man, he had a winning smile and personality. He told us what a privilege it was to meet us, and assured us that the invitation to play here was absolutely the greatest thing that had ever happened to him, and that he could not be more grateful. As we left him to his tune up round and continued our tour, Jones asked Roberts, "Cliff, what did that young man do to get here?"

Being a fanatical golf fan, I knew why Palmer was here, but decided not to be a know-it-all and appear to be educating these two historic figures in their game's modern history. Cliff Roberts ruffled through some papers in his cart and then said, "Arnold Palmer, United States Amateur Champion, 1954."

I cherish the memory of having been present when two of the game's greatest champions, whose names are stamped on different eras of golf history, met for the first time.

Twenty odd years later I was a guest at Palmer's golf resort, Bay Hill, near Orlando, Florida. Arnold enjoyed people, and spent a lot of time on the putting green, talking to his guests. I asked him if he remembered the first time he met Bob Jones.

"I sure do," he said, "it was at Augusta, and he was just wonderful to me…"

"Do you remember who was with him?" I asked.

He thought about it. "Well," I said, "Cliff Roberts was with him., and…"

Arnold was nodding his head now, and I continued, "There were three of us. *I* was there, too." I explained why I had been along.

Palmer's face lit with a broad smile. "I remembered that Cliff Roberts was there when you mentioned his name," he said, "but I had no idea who the other guy was. It was *you*!" He laughed, and we shook hands. "Well, I'm very happy to meet you – *again*! And I'm glad you're here, and I hope you're enjoying your stay." And he sounded like he really meant it, and I'm sure he did. And I did enjoy my stay.

And my thoughts went back to my visit with the Jones – and others.

In the next few days all the contestants arrived, Ben Hogan, Sam Snead, Tommy Bolt, Lloyd Mangrum, Byron Nelson, Jimmy Demaret, Cary Middlecoff, Bob Rosburg, the whole roster of golf's best players. Jones introduced me to each of them. Typically, he said to Ben Hogan, "This young man has the unenviable task of writing a story about me for The Reader's Digest, so when it is convenient, Ben, I would appreciate it if you would sit down with him and tell him some pleasant lies about me."

Hogan flashed me a bright smile and said that he would be available "any time to talk to you about this great man."

This was fantastic! Hogan ranked at the pinnacle of my pantheon of heroes. Indeed, he was everyone's hero. A few years earlier he and his wife, Valerie, had been driving home to Texas after some tournaments in California and, while making their way through a virtually impenetrable fog, had collided head-on with a bus. At the last second, and when he knew it was too late to avoid a collision, Ben had thrown himself across the seat to protect Valerie. She had escaped with minor injuries. Police at first reported that Ben had been killed. He had survived, but nearly every bone in his body had been broken.

He had hung on, in a coma and at the edge of death for weeks. At first, his doctors couldn't believe he would survive, but he kept hanging on. He regained consciousness, and eventually it became clear that he would survive, but his doctors were certain that he would never walk again. But he began making himself get out of bed and walk, and it was decided that while he might walk, he certainly would never play golf again. But after a while he began hitting practice shots and even playing, at first a few holes at a time, then more holes and then more – but certainly he would ever be able to come close to the level at which he had formerly played. But bit by bit, by sheer, unbelievable, overpowering strength of will he rebuilt himself and his golf game. Despite all the medical predictions he returned to the tour. In his first event, the Los Angeles Open at the Riviera Country Club, he tied for the championship, but lost to Sam Snead in a playoff.

Circulatory problems in his legs prevented him from playing in more than six or seven tournaments per year, but when he played he won more than his share. He was surely one of the greatest object lessons imaginable for anyone who had ever suffered any kind of severe setback.

He had displayed a distinct affection for Jones when the latter had introduced us, and his thoughts about Jones, who still was widely regarded as the best who had ever played the game, would be a highlight of my article. I could hardly wait to talk to him.

But I didn't want to bother any of these contestants while they were on the practice tee or the golf course. Every one of them had established himself as one of golf's best, and was convinced he could win the storied Masters. I wouldn't think of breaking anyone's concentration. I had to time my approaches carefully, when they were relaxing.

I knew that Hogan was not beloved by his colleagues, but I took that as envy. His mental toughness was legend. He had been quoted as saying, "I play golf with friends, but we don't play a friendly game." A later biography would describe him as "aloof, brusque, even rude." Years later Arnold Palmer would recall for a golf magazine that during a practice round at Augusta with Hogan, Hogan had never called him by name, always called him, "Fella"; and he overheard Hogan asking another contestant, seriously, "How did that Fella get into this tournament?"

That was the year Palmer won the first of his four Masters championships.

But Hogan's bright smile when Jones introduced us and his assertion that he wanted to talk to me about "this great man" had inspired confidence. I approached him in the locker room one evening after he had completed one of his famous marathon sessions on the practice tee, after he had showered and was finishing getting dressed. Did he have time for some conversation about Bob Jones?

The bright smile was not on display now. *"What?"* he said in a loud voice. He sounded offended. He was incredulous. "Why *should* I?" he asked. Everyone else in the room was staring at us. "Why should *I* spend any of *my* time helping *you* write a story about somebody else?" he said, nastily. "What's in it for me? What are you going to do for me?"

I was embarrassed, crushed. I mumbled something to the effect that "it couldn't hurt to be involved in an article about Bob Jones in the world's most widely read magazine."

He stared at me as though he couldn't believe what I was saying. He looked as though he had just eaten something distasteful. "Forget it!" he said, disgustedly, waving me away. "I haven't got time for this."

I wanted to disappear. As I reached the door of the locker room an arm went around my shoulder. It belonged to tall, dark-haired Cary Middlecoff. "Lemme buy you a beer," he said.

Middlecoff had been a practicing dentist in Memphis, Tennessee. A top-drawer golfer, he had decided that he loved the game and the competition more than dentistry, and could make more money at it. He joined the PGA tour and during his career would win forty of its tournaments, including a Masters and two U.S. Opens. He led the tour in wins in three different seasons. Now, he took the time to sit with me at a bar and soothe me. "Ben's never easy to deal with," he said.

"I can tell," I said. "I bet if I came to write an article about him he'd be easy to deal with."

Middlecoff didn't disagree, but said, "I think he's still in a lot of pain, from the accident."

We visited. Middlecoff asked me to call him "Doc," pointing out that all his friends did so. He actually wanted to know how I had become a writer, which he thought was "outstanding!" He wanted to hear about stories I had written that had appeared in the Digest. He thought I was living a *fantastic* life.

A couple of beers and some pleasant conversation were all I needed to shrug off Hogan's behavior. "Who looks good to you for this tournament, Doc?" I asked.

He stared into the distance, thoughtfully, for a long moment. Then he said, "I have to say that the way I've been playing, I don't see how anyone in the world can beat me."

In the next few days he proved it. On the par five thirteenth green of the final round, he rolled in an 82-foot-long putt for an eagle three. He was leading the field, and had an enormous gallery. From the slightly elevated fourteenth tee he surveyed his huge gallery, then spotted me. He called me by name, waving me up to the tee. Spectators opened an aisle for me. He whispered, "Do you think you could get me a Coke?"

I got him a Coke; I would have gotten him a turkey dinner if he'd asked for one. People stared at me and whispered, and acted as though they should throw rose petals in my path.

"Doc" had it figured right: the way he played, no one could beat him. He won the tournament. Life was good.

In the years that followed I was lucky enough to play in a number of pro-ams (professional-amateur events) around the country in the company some of the game's other luminaries. Mostly, they were genuinely nice people. They shared an awed reverence for Hogan, especially for his astonishing achievements after the accident that had so brutalized him – 13 more wins, including six majors; in fact, in the single season of 1953, four years after the accident, he won The Masters, the U.S. Open and the British Open, and had his game at such a level that he might well have won the PGA (Professional Golfers Association) championship if it had not been scheduled so close to the British Open that he didn't have time to reach it. The game's other most accomplished practitioners were agreed that he was among the greatest of history's athletes.

On the other hand there were lots of Hogan stories that put me in mind of a quote attributed to Oscar Wilde with reference to an acquaintance who could not seem to be anything but rude, that, "He has no enemies, but his friends dislike him intensely."

7
Meeting Mr. Wallace

Early on Friday, the second day of the Masters tournament, Dorothy Kavanaugh, Hobart Lewis's secretary, called me at the Bon Air to say, "Mr. Wallace would like to meet you. He wonders if you could be here Tuesday afternoon."

I had never met Mr. Wallace, and the idea excited the dumbo reflexes in my response mechanism. I said. "You mean, Mr. DeWitt Wallace?"

"Yes. That's the one."

"Um, ah, yes, I think I can do that."

"Good. Try to get here as early in the afternoon as you can."

Hobe Lewis met me in the rotunda, the impressive entryway into editorial headquarters. He was all smiles as he escorted me down a couple of long corridors to the corner office where DeWitt Wallace worked. Two quick knocks on the door, then he opened it. The Editor-in-Chief was bent over a desk strewn with manuscripts.

"Mr. DeWitt Wallace," Lewis said, "May I present Mr. John G. Hubbell."

I was trying not to look dumbstruck; I was standing inside the office of one of history's most remarkable men, the inventor of the most widely read publication in the world, the most successful journalistic enterprise ever conceived. I had seen his face on the cover of Time Magazine and elsewhere and had read all about him. And he was walking toward me with a broad smile on his face and his hand out. "I've been looking forward to this," he said. "You've been doing some great work for us."

He was sixtyish, a shade over six feet tall, well proportioned, his thinning hair graying. He was in shirtsleeves and a tie. He waved me to a comfortable chair beside his desk. He turned to Lewis and dismissed him: "I'm sure you can find a more productive way to spend your time," he said.

Lewis exited, closing the door quietly, and Mr. Wallace sat down at his desk.

"I'm looking forward to seeing a lot more of your work," he said. "You do an excellent job of engaging the reader. Your piece in the current issue, about the training of the Submariners, is just terrific."

He wanted to hear more about it. He pointed out that in my article I had said that I was the first civilian ever to undergo the rigors of the training tank. The Digest's Research Department, its fact checkers, had found this to be so. How had I managed it? I told him.

Mr. Wallace was laughing. "That's very impressive initiative!" he says. "The officer in charge tried to chase you away, but you found a way to get to the commanding officer and talk your way into the training tank. And then you passed all of the tests. That's wonderful! I enjoy your adventurous spirit."

"I even got him to buy lunch," I said.

He laughed again, then said, "What are your plans for the future?"

I was disappointed; I had expected him to invite me to write for his magazine throughout my future; was this all he wanted to do, talk?

"I have a good job," I said. "I get to write a lot, which is what I like to do, and it gives me time on nights and weekends to look for articles for major magazines, like The Reader's Digest."

"Then perhaps you would consider coming with us full-time?"

I wanted to say, "I thought you'd never ask!" I could hardly believe what he had just said. I said, "I certainly would."

"Good," he said, "then it's settled. What about your present employer? You will probably want to give notice."

"I would like to give Honeywell a month's notice," I said. "The company has been wonderful to me, granting me leaves of absence so I could pursue Digest assignments."

"Seems appropriate," he said, nodding. "I'm sure they'll have a tough time replacing you. What ideas do you have in mind for the Digest?"

I was trying to make myself understand that no less a figure than DeWitt Wallace had just entered me into major league magazine journalism.

I pulled myself together and told him what I had just been doing in Augusta. He was not enthusiastic. He thought it might have worked had it been in the magazine's inventory and published during the month the Masters Tournament was being played, but it hadn't been written yet, and could not now be scheduled for publication for many months, by which time the glow of the 25th anniversary of the Grand Slam would be gone. I listened; he made sense. I learned later that he was not a golf aficionado. I deduced that he was not excited at the idea of an article about a golf legend who had retired from the game a quarter of a century earlier. I would learn later that he liked baseball and rodeos, and often attended the Calgary Stampede. And he liked stories that inspired. I made a mental note to keep all my notes on Jones intact; maybe they would prove to be of some value later on. I moved on:

"There has been a lot of public attention on the Strategic Air Command's Survival Training Program," I said. "A number of people who have been through it have been quoted as calling it 'cruel and unusual treatment.' I don't understand why people who are constantly flying over a lot of the world's most inhospitable terrain would not want to know how to survive if they went down in it, and would not want to know how evade capture and how to escape. I think it's worth investigating."

"I think that's a wonderful idea. I think you should pursue it."

"I'll wind up things at Honeywell and get at it."

"Good. That sounds great. It's obvious that you have a feel for the kind of stories that our readers enjoy."

Then, he said the most remarkable thing anyone ever said to me: "Now, of course, you'll have an expense account, I want you to feel free to go anywhere in the world where you think there is an article that will work for us, that will interest our readers. If you have to go to Timbuktu to get a paragraph to make a story right, you don't have to ask anyone's permission. Just be sure that when you bring a story in that it is definitive, that it has everything in it that is worth knowing about the subject."

With such a charter, I thought, one would have to work very hard not to succeed. This was one of the big thrills of a lifetime.

The meeting lasts a little more than half an hour. He walks me to his office door, a hand on my arm. "You're going to be very successful, a strong addition to our staff," he says, "I'm very pleased."

I can't imagine that he can imagine how pleased I am!

We shake hands as we exit his office. He steps into another nearby office to talk with someone. At the same time, Hobe Lewis is emerging from his office, also nearby, and we stand in the hallway, talking. "How did it go?" he asks.

"I don't know how it could have gone better. I am now 'a strong addition to the staff'."

He grins, broadly. "That's terrific, John, that's wonderful!" he says. Then, laughing at himself, "I thought I was supposed to be an important guy around here, but did you see how he dismissed me, telling me that he was sure I could find a more profitable way to spend my time? Anyway, this is *great*! You *are* a strong addition."

We both assume that Mr. Wallace will want me to live in the neighborhood. That is not a problem for me; my family is now scattered from New Jersey to Virginia, and I am a bachelor and have no personal attachments remaining in Minneapolis. Hobe says. "There are a lot of nice apartments in White Plains and Mount Kisco. Edie and I will help you find…" Edie is Hobe's wife, another new friend.

Just then Mr. Wallace comes by and overhears us. He interrupts: "You don't want to move out here, do you John?"

"Well, I..."

"If you move out here you'll have all these editors looking over your shoulder and telling you how to write. If they could do what you do they would all be doing it. Don't you like Minneapolis?"

"I love it. I grew up there. All my friends are there..."

"I think a writer ought to live where he's happy. You'll be traveling wherever the stories are that you're going to be after, so it makes no difference where you live. If you're happy in Minneapolis, I think you should live there. You can come in here any time you want to."

"I think I'm going to live in Minneapolis," I say to Hobe.

"I think so," he says.

I knew that this had been the best day of my life so far, but would not understand for a while how really wonderful it had been.

Think of it: If DeWitt Wallace hadn't come by at precisely that moment and overheard the conversation, I would have moved east, never would have met my beloved Punkin, never would have participated in a happy marriage that has so far lasted nearly 60 years, which produced nine wonderful children who so far have produced 27 grandchildren, and the great grandkids have begun to arrive.

God works in His own ways.

8

"If It Walks, Crawls, Slithers, Swims..."

"How many reporters have actually taken the course? I asked.

"Are you kidding?" he asked. This was Air Force Captain Mike Connolly. He handled press relations at Stead Air Force Base, near Reno, Nevada. It's called, "Home of the Walking Air Force," the place where the Strategic Air Command teaches its airmen how to survive if they go down in hostile terrain, how to evade capture and how to escape.

"You're getting a lot of bad Press," I pointed out, as though he didn't know that. "Some of these reports must be based on first-hand knowledge."

"Look," he said, "most of the people who have gone through this program have understood and appreciated it. A few have been real outdoorsmen and have really enjoyed it. And a few have found it uncomfortable enough to complain that it is 'cruel and unusual' treatment. It's this last group that's been getting all the media attention."

"But no one from the media taken the course, examined it up close and personal?"

"That is correct. There have been a lot of telephone calls, and a few have visited the base and talked to the commanding officer, but none have had any first hand experience with what they have been writing about."

"I would like to take the course. Can that be arranged?"

Shortly, I was at Stead, where I became the 11th member of a ten-man crew of a B-36 bomber, then SAC's primary weapons delivery system. I was in a classroom listening to an instructor explain, "If it walks, crawls, slithers, swims, or flies, you can eat it."

I could think of lots of creatures that did all those things that I could never imagine eating.

For example, he said, "All reptiles except the toad are edible. Most snakes, frogs, lizards and turtles are delicacies. Most of a lizard's meat is in the tail. To make a poisonous snake or lizard good to eat, simply chop off its head, skin it, cut the meat into thin strips and dry it on a rock in the sun."

I was right. I was finding the thought of eating these examples repulsive.

But he was talking about staying alive, how to survive in severe circumstances. He laid it on. "Don't turn up your nose at grubs, worms, locusts, grasshoppers and maggots. If you go down somewhere and are hurt, lost and hungry you will be very glad to eat them, they will provides you with protein…"

Now, I thought, we're getting past repulsive, we're getting close to 'cruel and unusual…'

"…and you would insist that under the right circumstances they can be delicious

I wasn't sure I wanted to know what he meant by, "the right circumstances."

I reminded myself that I did want to know, that's why I'm here.

Now, he talked about water; water is okay with me, it's not repulsive, like grubs, maggots and worms, which he said could be delicious. He said, "You don't have to go to school, do you, to know that when you are faced with a long hike across a hot, barren desert you have to ration your water very carefully? Common sense tells you that you must be economical with your water, to just allow yourself the occasional sip, slake your thirst. Doesn't it?"

No one said anything, but I felt certain we all agreed that common sense is never to be ignored.

"Well," he said, "let me tell you something that you had better believe: Common sense is *wrong*."

Rationing your water, he explained, is the route to death by dehydration. Do that, you allow your blood to get hot, and the water level in your body will keep slipping. Drink your whole canteen as soon as you are down. It will cool the blood and keep you from sweating so much and lowering the water level in your body. If you ration yourself, all you will be doing is quenching your thirst periodically. You sweat, your water level will keep slipping and soon there won't enough left to bring it back up.

Then, the blood starts drying up. You will last longer if you drink it all right away."

What to do if you go down in Sahara-like desert: "Build some shade. Use your parachute, or airplane parts. Get under the shade and don't do anything. You know that the Air Force keeps track of its people and its aircraft, and that if you go missing someone will come looking for you." Meanwhile, he said, "No coughing, no sneezing, no blowing the nose, don't even breathe hard. Each time you do any of these things you dehydrate yourself a little more. If you are convinced that you can use the stars to navigate your way out of the desert and decide to walk, walk at night and in slow motion. Eat nothing unless you have plenty of water to drink with it, because any food needs water to absorb it. You can live a long time without food in that kind of desert, but you can only live 22 hours on a single quart of water, and you need three quarts per day to live efficiently."

We learn that if we're going down, the jungle is a good place to do it. It teems with edible food, fish, animals, vegetation, and there is plenty of water. What there is also plenty of is malaria, typhoid, typhus, fungi, all kinds of parasites; the slightest scratch will quickly become infected, so treat it fast. It's important to blouse sleeves and pant legs against insects, and each day to rinse all clothing and bathe to prevent skin disease. Make your way out of the jungle by following rivers; they lead lo larger rivers, clusters of habitation and seashores.

Another instructor advises that survival in the Arctic is a piece of cake. There is food and water everywhere, he explains. Frozen sea-weed is edible, raw or dipped in boiling water. The moss that grows on rocks is full of life. There is abundant fish and game, including fox, caribou, seals, rock ptarmigan, musk ox, shrimp, polar bears.

Someone says that while the notion of grappling with a shrimp doesn't frighten him, he tends to be less confident about polar bears, musk ox, caribou, even foxes.

The instructor says that all these creatures usually avoid or run away from a lot of noise, so make lots of noise. This is met with a room-sized sigh that seems to say, *"And good luck with that!"*

But the instructor points out that when airborne we will be equipped with survival rifles that are up to the hunt. We won't have them here, on our ten-day trek through the Sierra Nevadas, because at the start of the program some aircrews equipped with survival rifles had taken deer in the early stages of their treks and their luxurious meals had denied them the opportunity to learn how to really live off the land.

We rode in the back of a truck for a couple of hours, into the mountains for what is called, "The Starvation Trek." Night was falling as we debarked. We followed three instructors a mile or two through heavily forested mountainside, to a clearing they judged to be, "A good campsite. Find a place to sleep. Make camp in the morning."

We climbed into our sleeping bags and spent the first night under the cold Sierra stars.

We spend the next morning making camp. Using our parachutes and long, thin pieces of timber which were lying all over the place, and build five paratepees. We drag heavy logs inside the tepees, frame out beds with them, fill the interiors with pine boughs and wrap our ponchos around them. We will sleep atop them in our sleeping bags.

Not far from our campsite we find a lovely mountain stream; it looks like a picture in a magazine. We fill cans with water, boil it over a fire for 20 minutes, then let it cool while we boil more water. This will make it drinkable, cleanse it of liver flukes, infused from the excretions of sheep upstream. It's worth doing, because liver flukes can eat 15 years out of your life.

The instructors teach us how to make snares and traps, and how best to affix them to dead timber, which won't hold our scent. By midafternoon hunger pangs are gnawing. "When do we eat?" someone asks.

An instructor smiles. "Whenever you want to. You're going to be out here for ten days, and you've got two days' rations. How you use them is up to you. It's best to pretend you got up too late for breakfast, were too busy to eat lunch and went to bed too early for supper. Soon, your stomach will shrink and the hunger pains will end."

They hadn't ended by late afternoon. I'm famished. I eat a one and three-quarter ounce candy bar, look longingly at the rest of my rations and put them away. I see others doing the same.

The mountain has a large porcupine population, and we catch two; they don't fire their quills at you, that's nonsense, and they are easy to catch – simply tap them on the head with a club and they're dead. Then, slit the belly and empty the entrails into a hole in the ground. Fill the hole with its own dirt, so there's no odor to attract bears or mountain lions. Boil the meat in three changes of water,

15 minutes each time. Then, bake it in a rock oven for six hours. It tastes like pine bark. It tastes wonderful.

What? You're still hungry? Dig up the entrails, find the livers, slice them, fry them, eat them. Wow! Tasty.

A couple of days and we dismantle the campsite, leave it as pristine as we found it, and begin the trek. We darken our faces and hands with dirt, and camouflage ourselves with pine boughs and foliage. We keep quiet unless it is absolutely necessary to talk, then whisper; we enunciate, very carefully, so that there is no need to repeat ourselves. As taught, we practically tiptoe through forest areas, taking care not to snap twigs. We don't expose ourselves atop ridgelines, we walk around them, not over them. We do not cross open spaces in daylight; we wait until dark, then cross them on our bellies.

Near the end of a hot day when we have hiked across high desert, when there is not a drop of water left among us, we come to a sheep trough brimming with water. The bloated body of a dead chipmunk floats on it, and little black snakes swim in the recesses. It's a beautiful sight. We boil cans of the stuff, let them cool while we boil more cans and let them cool, and it's the best drink any of us have ever had.

We fantasize about favorite meals, and the fantasies vary wildly. One man revels, almost wallows in the memory of Thanksgiving Dinner, stuffed roast turkey, cranberry sauce, mashed potatoes, candied yams. Another dreams of peanut butter and grape jam sandwiches and huge pitchers of cold milk. My dream is of Sunday breakfast, a plate full of bacon and fried eggs, hash brown potatoes, English Muffins and lots of coffee.

Ten days, and all that stands between us and freedom is a heavily forested nearly 10,000-foot mountain that is full of aggressor troops. We go in pairs, in darkest night, using every evasive trick we have learned. Anyone who is captured will have to sit and watch as those who are not caught are trucked back to a fabulous steak dinner at Stead. None of our crew is captured, although there are a couple of close calls.

Back at Stead we all shower for a long time. We all have lost weight; for me, eleven pounds. Then, remembering incredible hunger, we go at our steaks with a will. After a few of the most delicious bites imaginable, I'm done – my shrunken stomach won't accept any more food. Most of my crewmates eat more than I, but few are able to finish.

I shake hands with my crewmates and wish them well. We had shared an experience that none of us ever would ever forget. They will return to Fairchild Air Force Base, near Spokane, Washington, and will continue to fly missions that will help to keep the world at peace.

"You are part of this team," someone tells me. "You've got to come with us. If we go down in dangerous territory, we'll need the whole team."

"I have a better idea," I said. "Don't go down in dangerous territory. Ever."

So far as I know, they never did.

I return to my hotel room in Reno, where I remember how to sleep in a bed. My wristwatch says it is 3 a.m. when I get up. I dress, go down to the hotel's coffee shop and order the meal I had fantasized about on the trek: bacon and eggs, hash brown potatoes,

English Muffins and coffee. I eat eight or ten bites before I am stuffed and have to quit.

I go back to bed, awaken about 10 a.m., go to the coffee shop and order bacon and eggs, hash brown potatoes, English Muffins and coffee. This time I am able to eat all of one of the eggs and half of an English Muffin.

I have to train myself to eat like a civilian.

I go home and write my story. I make it clear that it would be 'cruel and unusual' for SAC not to equip its aircrews with the survival skills they learn at Stead.

Wally loves it. Life is good.

9
A Flight to Remember

"Good Luck and don't worry," the Air Force sergeant says, "the ocean is warm this time of year."

It's 1957, the dawn of jet travel. I'm at a Boeing Aircraft field in Redmond, Washington, putting on a flight suit and pulling a parachute harness over my shoulders. An Air Force sergeant is helping me don a flotation device in case I find myself in the water.

I have been cleared by both the Air Force and Boeing to make a jet-to-jet refueling flight, the first non-Boeing civilian ever permitted to do so. The idea of two giant aircraft flying close enough for one to refuel the other is a fairly new development, and has me a bit nervous.

I climb into a brand new Boeing KC-135, brute of an aircraft that is designed to refuel the Strategic Air Command's bombers, its jet-propelled B-52s and B-47s, then the Free World's primary weapons systems, without requiring them to deviate from course, speed and altitude. Until now both bomber types had had to descend as much as 30,000 feet to rendezvous with non-jet tankers. Sometimes the tankers could not climb above bad weather, where the bombers were, and the bombers had to waste time and fuel hunting for them between cloud layers. Sometimes the tankers had to really hustle to refuel the bombers, because even when the tankers were at full throttle the bombers were flirting with stall.

Soon, we're at high altitude over the Pacific. I accompany my new friend, Hank, back through the barn-sized interior of the -135 to a hatch beneath the tail. Hank is a veteran boom operator; the boom is the pipeline through which we will transfuse a whole lot of highly volatile jet fuel into a B-52 bomber to extend its range. I follow Hank down through a hatch and we lay on leather pallets, looking out a big window. The world, six miles below, is something to see. So is the B-52 bomber, another brute, 200 tons of aircraft with a 185-foot wingspan and a huge tail assembly, which is soon behind us and much too close for my taste. This is called a rendezvous. I have experienced rendezvouses I thought much more fun. How did I ever get into this one?

I find myself envisioning a fiery conclusion, silently praying that there will be no such thing. Can't happen, I tell myself. It's clear that these guys know their business; they are competent.

Hank seems unconcerned. He tells me, "Depth perception and voice clarity are essential to handling the boom. You have to be able to judge, almost exactly how far behind you the receiver aircraft is because you are handling a 45-foot-long steel boom that telescopes in and out like a pile driver. You've got to lay it in gently. If you hit him hard bad stuff could happen. And you have to speak clearly so everyone will understand you the first time. You might not have a second chance."

He releases the boom, which has been stashed in the underside of our aircraft; it streams out behind us, a long steel pipeline. Hank explains that a couple of small, black vanes near the end are "ruddervators," – they perform as wings and elevators as the boom operator literally flies the boom into the bomber's fuel receptacle.

The B-52 moves closer and closer to us; this is getting what military guys call "hairy," but the voices I am hearing are calm. Hank speaks to the B-52 pilot: "Forward 60." He wants the bomber to advance 60 feet closer to us. Then, "30". Then,. "To your right nine," The bomber pilot complies. "Forward 15," Hank says. Then, "To your right four." The bomber keeps complying

There may have been incidents when I felt more tense, I just don't remember any.

With his control stick, Hank is aligning the boom with a V-shaped alley atop the B-52's fuselage.

"Keep coming," Hank coaxes, "easy… easy."

It appears to me that the bomber is about to crash into our underside.

I'm checking my parachute straps and my flotation gear. I am hoping I can escape before the fiery explosion.

Hank eases his stick forward, and the end of the boom slides smoothly into the receptacle atop the B-52, fastens itself there.

"Contact." Hank says.

"Roger," the bomber pilot answers. I can see him clearly, 12 yards away, can actually see his eyes moving across his own panels and a director panel on bottom of the tanker. I am nervous. I know that it's cool up here, but I am sweating. We fly like that, quietly, for a very long 30 minutes. I am told that's about the average time a refueling takes

At last, the pilot says, ""Receiver ready for disconnect." Hank works his controls. We feel a slight jolt as the boom jumps out of the bomber's receptacle. Hank works controls, draws it back into the lower half of our fuselage. The bomber drifts away in another direction. I feel myself relax.

"That was easy," I assured Hank.

"Nothin' to it," he said.

Minutes later we are on the ground, the blessed, blessed ground, at Boeing Field.

The story appears in the Digest under the title, "Join Me in One of the New Jet Tankers."

And don't be nervous. These guys know what they're doing.

10

Your Basic All Around Special Operations Writer

When the Survival article appeared in the Digest, someone in the Army's Book and Magazine branch called me and got me interested enough to go spend some time at Fort Bragg, North Carolina, with a group of "special forces" soldiers. In 1957 I didn't know what the term "special forces" meant; I was curious as to their specialty. They turned out to be paratroopers who wore green berets, and were called "The Green Berets."

I had never heard of them, and at the time I don't think many people had.

All of them had volunteered for "special forces" duty, and had been very carefully chosen from the Army's Airborne Infantry. In addition to a continuing physical training program that honed their bodies to razor sharp condition and kept them there, they learned various languages well enough to operate effectively deep inside countries where the United States' vital interests are concerned, and which might become the scenes of armed conflict. They developed an eyes-closed expertise in all of the weapons used by the armed forces of virtually all of the world's nations; they could take them apart and reassemble them blindfolded, and most of all, they knew how to use them, and were trained in how to provide locals with the weapons and training they needed. Like SAC's aircrews, they learned to live off the land, to the extent that other Army people, called them, "The Snake Eaters." They were not yet well known to the general public, but they would be soon.

It was another good story for the Digest. As I completed my research and was leaving Fort Bragg I was presented with a Green Beret of my own. I was proud of it, and kept it on display in my study. Then, as the years passed and the Green Berets became increasingly famous, my kids began growing up, and when I was absent, chasing a story, decided that they wanted to go out into the woods and play "Green Beret." I never saw my beret again.

Then, someone in the Navy's Book and Magazine branch suggested that a visit to Little Creek, Virginia, would be interesting. There, the fabulous Frogmen, the Underwater Demolition Teams (UDT), were trained. During World War II these undersea warriors actually swam in and dismantled the obstacles America's enemies had constructed beneath the waves before every Allied invasion beach from Sicily to Okinawa. Forty One percent of the UDT force had been lost to enemy fire. But there was never any shortage of tough-minded, courageous new recruits.

I wrote a piece entitled, "Hell Week at Little Creek," which described the unbelievably hellish introductory week of UDT training. One result, a dozen years later, was that the Navy first made known, exclusively to me, the existence of a then six-year-old supersecret special operations force of its own called the SEALs, for the methods in which they entered their operational areas: SEaAirLand. All SEALs had proved themselves to be extremely highly skilled UDT operators, had learned their stuff at each of the other Services special forces schools. They were well rounded warriors. SEAL Team One already had been effectively active in the jungled wetlands of Vietnam. I spent a lot of time visiting with them at their headquarters, in Coronado, California. In fact, one of the most rewarding moments of my life as a writer occurred when one of them, a young Navy lieutenant named Ron Campbell, who had led 40 missions into Vietnam, told me that years earlier my article, "Hell Week At Little Creek," was the reason that he was a SEAL, that he had been finishing school and looking for a challenge when he read it, and decided that the UDT life was for him.

I filled the story on SEAL training with details of their operations in the Vietnam War. Entitled, "Supercommandos of the Wetlands," it ran as a lead article in the Digest.

I could not have been more admiring of the Green Berets, the UDT teams or the SEALs. I could not imagine myself learning languages, living off the land while organizing and training guerrilla fighters, swimming into hostile beaches and removing obstacles for invasion forces, dealing with all kinds of dangerous wildlife as well as enemy guerrillas in places like Vietnam's Rung Sat – the words refer to the killer jungle that lies between Saigon and the sea. In the Rung Sat one day SEAL Chief Petty Officer Joe Churchill, had hid himself in thick foliage a few yards from a Viet Cong (communist guerilla) encampment and was listening to them make plans when something heavy fell from a nearby tree; it shook the ground when it landed five or six feet from Churchill. It was a monster Burmese python. If he had to kill it he would give away his position, and almost certainly would be killed or captured by the enemy. Churchill and the snake stared at each other for a couple of hours. Then the giant snake, which must have sated its appetite earlier, slithered off in another direction.

During the Vietnam War I learned of more incredible American war fighters. There was Air Force Colonel George E. "Bud" Day. I wrote extensively about him in my book, "P.O.W. – A History of the American Prisoner of War Experience in Vietnam, 1964-1973".

Three days after the December 7, 1941, Japanese attack on Pearl Harbor, Day, then 17, dropped out of high school in Sioux City, Iowa, to join the Marine Corps. He served 30 months in the Pacific. After the war, he enlisted in the Iowa National Guard. He was awarded a direct commission in the Army 39 days prior to the eruption of the Korean War. He transferred to the Air Force, was trained as a pilot and served two combat tours in Korea flying a fighter-bomber.

Between wars he earned a law degree.

When the United States entered into the Vietnam War, he volunteered. A major by then, he took command of a Fast FACs (Fast Forward Air Controller) squadron, flying F-100s. All FACs were veteran pilots and volunteers, because the job was so very dangerous: Finding enemy missile sites, ammunition factories and troop concentrations and directing high performance aircraft in attacks against them. This involved flying low and slow enough to search the triple-canopied jungles below. Day was brought down by enemy fire on August 26, 1967. During ejection his right arm was broken in three places. He was captured and subjected to grueling and extensive torture. His behavior as a prisoner of war is the stuff of legend. He escaped, was recaptured, escaped again, was again recaptured, subjected to gruesome tortures and gave his captors nothing but contempt. Upon returning to the United States he was honored with the Air Force's highest award, the Air Force Cross, and the nation's highest award, the Medal of Honor. He died on July 27, 2013, at age 88.

Eventually, more than 150 Air Force pilots volunteered for FAC duty.

I went to Hurlburt Field, at Eglin Air Force Base, Florida, to talk with some who had been doing the job and had returned to train others. One of them took me aloft in the kind of airplane he and many other FACs had been flying in Vietnam, a small, single engine Cessna. Camouflaged in earth tones, it was a 90-mile-per-hour county airport-type. In addition to its slow speed, it stayed at low altitudes and had no protective armor, so was extremely vulnerable to ground fire.

My pilot explained that like some other FACs he had taken up residence, alone, in a Vietnamese village. On a number of trips to supply depots on big U.S. bases on Vietnam's east coast, he had loaded his Cessna with food, medicines, all of life's necessities and made them available to the villagers where he lived, and made friends of them. After a while, villagers, who were terrified of the

Vietcong (VC) nevertheless began to provide him with information as to the locations of VC concentrations. He explained, "You can't act directly on such information. You have to convince the enemy that you found him all by yourself. Otherwise, he will know it came from the village, he will raid it, he will subject the inhabitants to unspeakable tortures and will kill a lot of them. So you spend days, maybe weeks, flying low and slow over the suspect areas. You meander this way and that way, then back again. You know that down below, you are being watched, but the people down below won't give away their position by firing at you. But if they decide that you have discovered them they will do their best to bring you down. So you keep overflying the areas at different times every day, at different altitudes, and you keep coming from different directions. You always fly a single straight and level pass; nothing tricky. You want to convince the watchers on the ground that this is a routine air patrol; you don't want them to think that you have discovered anything."

It takes days, sometimes weeks, but there came a time when he had seen through openings in the green canopy the corners of buildings, the glisten of gun barrels, the movements of lots of people. During several overflights he had found a big plant where the enemy was manufacturing weapons and ammunition.

He had returned to a major air base near the coast and briefed American and South Vietnamese air intelligence people. A strike was planned. The FAC would lead them to their targets.

"I went at sunrise, with the sun directly behind me," he said.

He put me in the back seat of a Cessna and took me aloft. We flew to a target area in a remote, jungled part of huge Eglin Air

Force Base. We were at an altitude of about 1000 feet. "When I got directly over the target," he said, "fighter-bombers were orbiting high above me. I told them that I would mark the target with with 'willie-peter" (white phosphorous), and did this:" Whereupon, he rammed his throttle forward and we plunged down at the target. We were at an altitude of 500 feet when he fired his rocket. I watched it streak ahead of us, then explode on the target in a cloud of white phosphorous as we jinked away, climbing an erratic path as fast as we could.

We repeated the maneuver several times, firing "willie-peter" rockets.

When we landed, the pilot explained that the instant you begin the maneuver, the enemy on the ground knows that you have found him, and the air all around you is alive with ground fire. But if you prepared properly in the previous days and weeks you have taken him by surprise, and his fire isn't very accurate, but occasionally you hear little thunderclaps, which means that bullets are hitting your aircraft. But they don't have much time to shoot at you, because all of a sudden the airpower above comes roaring down on them."

After one such target was marked by my pilot ground troops found that 12 buildings had been obliterated and counted 104 enemy bodies.

More than 150 veteran Air Force pilots volunteered for this duty. Nearly 25 percent were shot down. Captain Lance P. Sijan, went down on November 9, 1967, a month and a half after Bud Day. Like Bud Day, he suffered a number of severe injuries. He evaded capture for weeks, until Christmas Day. Weak from starvation, he still overpowered a guard and escaped again. Recaptured hours later, he was tortured for information, but yielded only name, rank and serial number. By the time he reached other Americans he was unable to stand or even sit up without help. His compatriots worried about his untended injuries, but he pleaded only to be kept in a sitting position so that he could exercise his muscles preparatory to another escape attempt. He died of pneumonia on January 22 1968.

Along with Jim Stockdale and Bud Day, Lance Sijan was awarded a Medal of Honor, posthumously, for his inspirational example of courage.

11
Unforgettable Sister Kenny

Hobart Lewis asked if I would be interested in ghost-writing an "unforgettable character" piece on Sister Elizabeth Kenny, the Australian nurse who had developed successful methods for helping victims of poliomyelitis regain the use of affected limbs. Her approach had triggered a great deal of controversy among orthopedists, but when she visited the United States in 1940 she was well received by the University of Minnesota Medical School, so had made her American headquarters in Minneapolis. She had died in 1952, but the Kenny Institute, still headquartered in Minneapolis, and continued to operate under the directorship of Marvin Kline, for whom I would be ghosting the article.

Kline was a former Mayor of Minneapolis; in winning the office, he became the only person ever to best Hubert Humphrey in a political contest. I found him to be an agreeable man, perhaps six feet tall, slim, balding, bespectacled and full of interesting anecdotes spotlighting how Sister Kenny, when he was Mayor, had bullied him and gotten him to find ways that the city could provide for all the things she needed. Her every demand, Kline recalled, was followed by a challenge: "What are you going to do about it?"

"Most of the time I had no idea what I was going to do about it, or could do about it, but somehow she got everything she wanted. When my service as mayor was over, I knew what I had to do about it. I had to do what she and everyone else wanted me to do, become the Kenny Institute's Director." As Director, fund-raising had been his primary task.

I drained him of his memories of her at several meetings, in his office in downtown Minneapolis, and at his home, a plush suburban place equipped with stables, horses and all that goes with horses – he showed me one saddle that he said had cost $25,000. There was also a very large party room, in fact, more like a dance-hall, complete with a bar and a stage. I told Punkin that running a charitable organization appeared to be very lucrative. I thought no more about it.

I interviewed several others who had known Sister Kenny well, some of them polio victims who, under her tutelage, had recovered enough of themselves to pursue successful careers. The stories they told me enabled me to "get inside her thinking," to show her as the intensely committed, truly heroic person that she was. I wrote the article, a story of how the young Australian girl who had studied anatomy and had learned on her own how to treat effectively with the effects of infantile paralysis, and how, through sheer, persistent force of personality, she won out in the face of powerful medical opposition, got her methods accepted, helped countless polio victims regain the use of affected limbs. Kline signed it without changing a word. I sent it to Hobe Lewis. He called to say, "This is the greatest magazine article I've ever read!"

Sister Kenny died in 1952, but she remains a monumental figure in the history of effective physical therapy. Her innovative thinking and her intense faith in her own demonstrably sensible ideas has been responsible for the restoration of function in crippled limbs and better lives for millions of people. I was proud to be able to tell her story to Digest readers. My only lament, and it was to myself, was that it had Marvin Kline's name on it instead of mine; I had to remind myself that it was his story.

What I don't like to remind myself is that later Marvin was convicted of stealing millions of dollars worth of the Kenny Institute's funds and was sentenced to ten years in a penitentiary. Sister Kenny deserved much better than that.

But the Kenny Institute continues to flourish.

12

I Owe Rosie Big Time

Some golf pals and I were spending a long weekend at a lovely golf resort by a lovely lake in central Minnesota, which calls itself the "Land of 10,000 Lakes." One of the guys had brought along his beautiful girl friend, Rosemary, who had persuaded an unattached girl friend of hers to join them. We golfers were on the course playing the game and the girls, were walking along behind us.

"Whaddya thinka Punkin?" said Rosemary's guy.

Was he speaking in code? "What? Punkin?" I was confused. I looked around for a large, yellow orange fruit.

He pointed to the girls. "The girl with Rosie," he said. "Whaddya think?"

I had never before heard of her or seen her. I couldn't see her now. She wore a white sailor hat with the brim pulled down to cover most of her head, a tattered gray sweatshirt, a pair of blue jeans with holes in the knees and tennis shoes, also with holes in them so that some of her toes stuck out. Aside from her toes, I had not seen enough of the rest of her to feel qualified to offer a judgment.

"I don't think anything about her," I said.

"Isn't she a doll?" he asked, then answered himself. "She's a *doll*!"

"How can you tell?" I asked. "In case you haven't noticed, girls, especially girls who are dolls, usually care a lot about how they look. She obviously does not care how she looks."

"Maybe she cares so much that she doesn't want one anyone to see her the way she looks now," another guy mused.

I did not realize that my friend and Rosie had brought her here. I thought she might work here. "Is she a waitress? A caddy? How does Rosie know her?"

It turned out that Rosie and Punkin were best friends, that they had gone all through school together, that at the moment she had no romantic attachments and that Rosie had talked her into coming with them for "a fun weekend," explaining that some of her boy friend's bachelor friends would be on hand.

I said that was okay with me, and thought no more about it.

Until cocktail time in the resort's lounge. She showed up with beautiful Rosie, but I only had eyes for Punkin. She was stunning. She wore a blue cocktail dress, perfectly coiffed dark hair that lay in a gentle curl all the way down to and around her shoulders, blue eyes that truly sparkled, red lips that smiled a breathtaking smile and high heels supporting a pair of lovely legs. "Holy Smokes!" I thought.

"I told you on the golf course," my friend laughed. "Punkin's a *doll*!"

I demanded an introduction. Instantly. "What kind of name is Punkin?" I asked, taking her by the arm and steering her to the bar. "Let me buy you a drink."

"It's short for Punctuation," she said, "and I'll have a glass of Chablis."

"Nobody is named Punctuation," I said."

"Only me. I am unique."

"Yes, you are! Let's dance."

We danced. We talked. *I* talked. I couldn't stop talking. I wanted to know everything about her, like how did she get a name like Punkin, and where had she been all this time, certainly not where anyone had been able to see her, or I would have heard. Then, another friend cut in. "You *louse*!" I whispered to him, as I left the dance floor.

I sat down next to Rosie. "I'm in love," I told her.

She laughed. "Why not? She's lovely."

I waited a minute or two, then couldn't wait any longer. I got up and cut in on my former friend who had cut in on me. He called me a bad name as he left the dance floor.

"Let's get married," I suggested.

She smiled that smile. "I want twelve children," she said.

"Of course you do. Who doesn't?" I wanted her to know that I could go along with a gag.

"I'm not kidding," she said, still smiling.

"Who would kid about as thing like that?"

When my rival who used to be my friend cut in again I sat down with my other friends and their wives. I announced, "I'm gonna marry her."

"Well," said one of the wives, "you've known her for 45 minutes. I was wondering if you were ever going to make a decision."

I spent all my free time that autumn and winter trying to convince her that we were meant for each other, learning that her first name was Katherine, that her father had called her Punkin the day she was born and the name had stuck, everyone called her Punkin, and if you called her Katherine she probably wouldn't answer because she wouldn't know you were talking to her. She was studying Nursing at the University of Minnesota. I didn't know that I had made my case with her until one day just before Christmas when I was chauffeuring her to a final exam at the University and she said, "This is a waste of time. I'm not going into Nursing. Let's go to a movie."

We were engaged by Christmas, married in June. That magical thing would not have happened if DeWitt Wallace hadn't advised me to live where I was happy. We didn't have the 12 children she said she wanted, but we did have nine. We did the best we could; they all have grown up to be really good, really nice people. They are all each others' and our best friends. They have created 27 grandchildren so far. Our great grandchildren have begun to arrive, and we are looking forward to many more. They will be welcome.

And I owe Rosie big time.

13
How I Became John G....

Maybe you want to know who I am, a background check: I was born in New York City, in the borough of the Bronx, on July 14, 1927. I was the fourth and last child born to Lester Sprague Hubbell and Margaret Malia Hubbell. My three siblings all were much older than I. My brother, Les, had been born in 1916; my brother, Woody in 1917; and my sister, Peggy, in 1922.

We were a Roman Catholic family, and I was baptized John Gerard in the Church of St. Martin of Tours, in the Bronx, and everyone called me Jerry. Except my mother, who all her life called me Gerard; she had named me after the patron saint of childbirth. It was okay with me that my mom called me Gerard, but I didn't care for the name because it was so different from the names of every one I grew up with, kids named Billy, Jimmy, Eddy, Joey, even Fletcher. I changed my name to John G. when I began writing for a living.

I had opted with what I thought good reason, for a career as a writer, the reason being that as I went through school I greatly enjoyed reading history and writing. I thought people who liked to read would find John G. more dignified and impressive than Jerry, or Gerard. Besides, what sense did it make to have a terrific name like John and never use it?

Was that wrong?

We were a close-knit family, but strangely I know virtually nothing of my parents' antecedents. All any of us kids knew of our father was what our mother had told us, that he had been an only child, that he was born in Albany, New York, in 1890, and that he had lived with his parents in an apartment somewhere in New York City. When he was 12 years old he had returned home after school one day and found the door to the apartment locked, and no one answered his knocks. He had waited patiently for his father to arrive, and when they got inside they found that his mother had died, apparently from a heart attack. After that, as far as any of his children were concerned, his life was a blank. We knew nothing of it, where he lived, who looked after him, how or even if he was educated, how he survived. He would never discuss it. About all we knew was that at one time or another he took a number of college correspondence courses, and that he met and fell in love with our mother, a stunningly beautiful brunette, and married her on May 23, 1915. He never spoke to any of us of the intervening years except to say that he had started out in Manhattan on the loading docks of the National Biscuit Company (Nabisco), helping to fill the trucks that carried the company's delectables to those who retailed them. If our mother knew anything about Dad's growing up years she never mentioned it.

All I can say is that my siblings and I lived with our parents for many years, and never discovered anything remotely disgraceful or even exciting about their early lives. I think we all concluded that they were just a normal couple, and that there wasn't much to discover that we didn't know.

A cousin who knew more than I ever did told me that her mother and mine, who were sisters, were members of a very large Irish Catholic family, with many children who had immigrated from Ireland and settled in Scranton, Pennsylvania. When they left Ireland the family name had been O'Malley, but by the time they all got past all the illiterate bureaucrats at Ellis Island, and notwithstanding the fact that they were all sisters and brothers, their names were Malia, Mulroy and Malloy; there was not a single O'Malley among them. Two possibilities occur to me:

1) On the day the family O'Malley arrived at Ellis Island there were no admitting officers there who were familiar with apostrophes and simply could not make sense of O'Malley. The admitting officers that day may all have been Chinese, or Afghans, or Hottentots, or

2) Some members of the O'Malley family had no wish to be found by the English authorities who might be hunting them.

In Scranton, Mom's Dad became a coal miner; apparently it was much better than anything he had been able to do in Ireland, and he had a lot of mouths to feed. Every Saturday night the adults all would go to a saloon trailing a red wagon, which was needed to transport Grandma home when the joyous evening ended.

I never knew any of my grandparents. They all died long before I was born.

Unwilling to settle for lives in the coal mining milieu, Mom and two of her sisters, my Aunts Kitty and Julie, migrated to New York City, where Mom got a job as a telephone operator. She was the Central in "Hello, Central," when people made a call. The sisters stayed close, physically as well as emotionally, and I saw a lot of my Aunts Kitty and Julie as I grew up.

When I was born my parents decided that the six of us could not remain in the two-bedroom apartment in the Bronx. My first awareness of a locale was a pleasant four-bedroom house in Teaneck, New Jersey, across the Hudson River and approximately eight miles due west of Times Square, in New York City. There was a walk-in playhouse in the yard behind the house, and a one-car garage at the end of a gravel driveway on the south side of the yard. Beyond the driveway was another house, occupied by a family named Sullivan.

My Aunt Kitty and her husband, my uncle, Jim Earle, who doted on me, became some of my favorite people, as did their three sons, Frank, James and Bill. These brothers were all nice people, but much older than my brothers, They lived in Paramus, not far from Teaneck, and there was a lot of back and forth visiting.

During the deep of the Great Depression, in the 1930's, my Uncle Jim, who was very good at carpentry and plumbing, actually built a house next to his own and rented it out. He had a lot of help from his son, Bill, who was also good at carpentry and plumbing.

My Dad, by now was a Nabisco salesman and doing well enough not only to buy a house, but also a new Buick. One Sunday afternoon he took my Mom, my sister, Peggy and me out to Paramus to show off the new car. Uncle Jim sat in the driver's seat with a sour look on his face, got out, opened the hood, stared at whatever was inside, kicked the tires, walked around it a couple of times and said, "Y'know, they slap a few panels over a setta tires, connect everything to a flyspeck of an engine and call it an automobile. Comes the revolution they won't be selling this kind of stuff anymore!"

I was too young to know how tough the 1930's were for a lot of people. All I remember about my Dad's reaction to Uncle Jim's reaction to the new car is that he was not pleased, and muttered something about Uncle Jim being a bolshevik, whatever that was. All I had to know about my Uncle Jim was that he was always buying me ice cream cones and candy bars, and taking me to a lot of baseball games around northern New Jersey, and he was always fun to be with. So he was a bolshevik and thought our new Buick was junky. Big deal.

When I grew up I understood that he was not a bolshevik, that like a lot of people in the 1930's he was just unhappy at the way things were going.

Aunt Julie's husband died before I was born; if I ever knew the cause of his death, I don't any longer. He left Julie with two children, Arthur and Catherine. During the Depression years Julie had no choice but to put them in a Catholic Orphanage in New York City. I remember when I was very young going with my parents to visit them there, and that they seemed happy. I never saw them again. I know that during World War II Arthur joined the Marine Corps, and was killed in action at Iwo Jima.

Sometime in the late 1990's Catherine tracked me down; I had heard nothing from her or of her in 60-plus years. She now lived in Oceanside, California, and was the adored Queen Mother of a sizable and successful family. We corresponded for a while. Once, I mentioned having visited her in the orphanage in New York City. She said that it had been a wonderful place for kids to live and grow up, that she and Arthur both had loved the place and the nuns there who had cared for them. That's nice to know.

One of my earliest memories is of seating myself on the curb outside the house in Teaneck one warm, sunny day and being joined there by the boy who lived in the house on the corner across the street. There was so little traffic in those days that no one thought to caution us. The boy's name was Vinny. He was two years older than I, so he was six, and we liked each other a lot and agreed to be best friends.

14
The Catch

I idolized my big brothers. Les was eleven years older than I was, and he always demonstrated a lot of enthusiasm for me. Woody, who was only ten years older than I, was not as outgoing as Les, but he also made clear his opinion that I was right out of the top drawer, and both of them played a lot of catch with me with baseballs and footballs. There was no question in my mind that they were the two greatest people in the world.

Les and Woody both played football for St. Cecilia High School, which was in Englewood, another nearby town. My parents took me to see every "Saints" football game, against teams from schools named Ramsey, Tenafly, Hackensack, Bogota, West New York, Cliffside Park and some others. St. Cecilia always won; I could not imagine them not winning. The last game of the season was against Ridgefield Park, the next town to the south of Teaneck. The boundary line was Mann Avenue, about five blocks south of our house.

The game was in a stadium at Veterans Park, where my friends and I played a lot, and where every Fourth of July there were spectacular Fireworks shows. Both teams were undefeated, the game was for the conference championship and the crowd overflowed the stadium. St. Cecilia won 7 to 6. Life was proceeding as it was supposed to. I was a sports fanatic. At night, I lay awake in bed dreaming of the days in the future when I would be running wild on football fields for the glory of St. Cecilia.

One day when I was six years old my best friend Vinny and I were watching my brothers and a group of their friends play touch football in the street in front of our house. The game reached a point where the contestants negotiated an agreement that the team that scored next would be the winner. During the negotiation Vinny and I asked if we could play. I was assigned to my brothers' team, and Vinny to the opposing side. The opposing side kicked off, someone on our side caught the ball and advanced it toward the goal line, but we still had a long way to go. In the huddle, my brother Woody suggested that no one on the other team would take Vinny or me seriously, but that he and I played a lot of catch with the football, and he gave strong assurances that I could catch a pass. He proposed that the ball be centered to him and that he lateral it to Clemmie de Quintal, one of his best friends, that Clemmie would make it appear that he was running around the right side, drawing all of the defenders to that side of the street, that Jerry – that was me – should run as fast as he could down the left side of the street, that no one on the opposing team would pay any attention to him, and that when Clemmie saw that Jerry was in the clear he should throw him the ball. Clemmie threw it. Jerry caught it.

Touchdown, we win! My teammates hoisted me on their shoulders, cheering me. My brothers carried me into the house, telling my parents what a hero I was!

Later that day, I stood in our yard, back near the garage, trying to understand my best friend, Vinny. He was standing on the street side of the low hedge along the front of our yard, throwing rocks at me. He had a nasty look on his face, and kept yelling at me, calling me names. It turned out that he was very angry with me for catching the pass that won the football game, and for being treated like a hero by all the big guys. He shouted that I wasn't such a big shot as I thought I was. Then he threw some more rocks. I went inside, deciding that we weren't best friends anymore.

Life moved on.

15
Flunking Kindergarten

I remember reflecting on all the complex things candidates for the Submarine Service must learn, and thinking about the unpromising beginning of my own education.

Eddie Oakley, who was almost exactly my age, lived across the street from me, and one day in 1932, when Eddie and I were five years old, we both were enrolled in the kindergarten in Longfellow Public School, which was a mile or two from our homes. Our mothers walked us to the school together a few times. Each time, they carefully explained to us to look both ways for traffic before crossing any streets; we were to be especially careful at Fort Lee Road, which was the most trafficked thoroughfare in the area. Thereafter, they left it to Eddie and me to find our own ways to and from the school; the world was a safe place for five-year-olds in those days.

Our kindergarten teacher was a Mrs. Sullivan, who was no relation to the Sullivans who lived next door to us. She was beautiful, and Eddie and I both instantly fell deeply in love with her.

But we both thought that the school building looked and felt like a prison. Neither of us had ever seen a prison, but we were sure that this was what prisons looked like and felt like, and we wanted out in the worst way. We were Americans, and wanted our freedom back! School started at 8 a.m., and there was a mid-morning recess at 10 a.m., when we all went out on the playground to do the kind of stuff goofy kindergartners do. Mrs. Sullivan came out with us, but became preoccupied in conversation with another teacher whose class was also at recess. When Eddie and I realized she was not looking, we sneaked away, recaptured our freedom. We ran almost all the way home, but not quite, because we knew that our mothers would want to know why we were home so early, and would probably take us back to the school. So we went to the woods on Teaneck Road, about three blocks from home. I can't remember what games we played in there, only that they had to do with the World War (the first one; the second was still years away), which we knew about from someone or maybe some "horrors of war" comic book, and I think we played something involving Daniel Boone, the "Kentuckian," which also probably came out of some comic book, and I remember that there was a "Black Ace" of an aviator who did fantastic things during the war on behalf of America. Neither of us had learned to read yet, but we both had older brothers who either read this stuff to us, or just told us thrilling stories about them and showed us pictures.

Since kindergarten only lasted half a day, we could safely return home at noon for lunch, then spend the rest of the day enjoying our recovered freedom. It did not occur to us that the teacher, Mrs. Sullivan, would contact our mothers, and that there would be a great deal of anxiety on all sides. Eddie's mother and my mother both were at our house when we arrived. They were not happy. They were about to call the police and report us missing, and where had we been?

We both conjured up some tears and explained that we hated kindergarten, that it was "dumb", and "a lousy place," and never wanted to go back. Ever!

We were told that it was too bad that we didn't like it because we were going back, and we had better not ever run away like that again.

The next morning we were back in kindergarten, and Mrs. Sullivan made it clear that she was not happy with us, either. She told us that we had "better behave" or we might be "expelled," and "that would look very bad on our records." We learned that to be "expelled" meant to be kicked out of school. Instantly, we decided to go for it.

Eddie and I skipped out enough so that Mrs. Sullivan spent much of her time that school year on the phone with our mothers. Our mothers spent a lot of time discussing our absenteeism in very stern tones with us, and so did Mrs. Sullivan. There were angry lectures. There were threats: "Wait 'til your father hears about this!"

Our fathers never mentioned it; I don't believe they ever heard about it. There were penalties, days when we wanted to be outside playing, but were not allowed to do so – in a later era, this penalty would be called, "grounding."

At the end of the school year neither my mother nor Eddie's was shocked to receive a message from Mrs. Sullivan that we had missed so much kindergarten that it was not going to be possible to award us graduation certificates. Our mothers feared the worst: If we wouldn't go to a half day of kindergarten what could be expected now that we were going to start first grade, where we would have to be in school until mid-afternoon?

That summer Eddie and I terrified each other discussing what appeared to be a miserable future. We planned, schemed, plotted. But in the end our escape team was sundered and our plans, if we had any, were scuttled. In the Fall, Eddie was entered into the first grade at Longfellow School, and I was moved to St. Joseph's, a Catholic school in Bogota, the next town to the west of Teaneck. We both were made aware that if we ran away from school now that we were in first grade there would be serious consequences, we would be *breaking the law*, we would be picked up by police – truant officers, they were called – *and would go to jail!*

St. Joseph's was about the same distance from home as Longfellow School. It was a much brighter, nicer looking place, it was full of a lot of my neighborhood friends and I didn't mind being there at all. My sister, Peggy, was in the seventh grade, and both of my brothers had graduated from St. Joseph's. A lot of us from the neighborhood walked to and from school together.

We were taught by nuns, and I remember being amazed on the first day at St. Joseph's when our first grade teacher, Sister Cornelia, started things off by saying that we were going to "learn a lot of wonderful things," and that the first thing we were going to learn, which was "going to help us to learn everything else", was how to spell. She asked if anyone knew how to spell the word "see." Nobody raised a hand. The only thing I had taken the trouble to do in kindergarten was learn the alphabet, and I knew very well that the way to spell "see" was simply the letter "C." But I didn't say a word, either, because I was too shy. I just sat there thinking how smart I was, and enjoying condescending thoughts about all the dumb bunnies around me when Sister Cornelia went to the blackboard and, explaining that when the word was spelled "s-e-e" it meant vision, "to see something or someone with your eyes," or, when spelled "s-e-a" it meant a big body of water that separated the continents of the earth.

I was shocked. I didn't know that. And I had no idea what a continent was. I was concerned. For the first time, it occurred to me that there was a lot to learn.

16
Bad News

The bad news came in late winter: When the school year ended, in June, we were going to move away, to a place called Atlanta, Georgia. My Dad was a good salesman, and was now the company's Sales Manager for a district that encompassed New Jersey, Delaware and eastern Pennsylvania. He was headquartered in Newark, which was perhaps a 30-minute drive from our house. There were twenty five districts in the country, and every month the company sent out a sheet rating them in terms of sales performance. The sheet always had the district manager's picture on it. My Dad was always Number One. It was as predictable as the sunrise. Now, with things going well in the MidAtlantic and with the company's fortunes at a low ebb in the Southeast, he was being transferred there.

My oldest brother, Les, graduated that June from St. Cecilia, so the move was not too terribly disruptive for him, although he was pretty sweet on a beautiful girl named Norma Keyes, who lived in Bogota.

For Woody, the move was catastrophic; he was going into his senior year at St. Cecilia, had already been elected President of the senior class and was a star running back on a championship football team. Efforts to keep him at St. Cecilia were discussed, the possibility of his staying in the home of a family friend, but nothing worked; I didn't know it at the time but in those Depression years no one could afford to keep him, and as well as our father was doing in comparison with most men he couldn't afford to support a family member who was not under his own roof. Beyond that, I don't think our parents ever seriously entertained the notion of moving far away and leaving one of their kids behind.

Peggy and I were sad to leave all our friends in New Jersey, but to me, at least, it was an adventure. I remember awakening one morning in a very comfortable sleeping berth in a bedroom on a train, then sitting next to a big window at a table in a dining car, looking out the window at the passing countryside, having a wonderful breakfast of pancakes, then stopping for a little while in a place called Spartanburg, South Carolina. I was dazzled. Then, later, we got off of the train in a big station in Atlanta, which turned out to be a big city, and rode in a taxi cab to the Cox Carlton Hotel. It was on Peachtree Street, and right next door to another, big, fancy hotel called The Georgian Terrace. Across the street was the huge Fox Theater.

We lived for a short time at the Cox Carlton, then moved into a beautiful house above a long, broad lawn on Peachtree Circle. Actually, we were on the lower floor of a duplex, but it was big and as lovely as any house we would ever live in, and the neighborhood at that time was one of Atlanta's nicest. The family upstairs was named Mitchell, and the father owned an automobile dealership. The governor's mansion was not far away, and the great golfer Bobby Jones and his family lived in the neighborhood. I was entered into the second grade at Sacred Heart School, and his son, Bob, was a classmate of mine. I would meet the Jones family again, 20 years later, at the Augusta National.

My brother Woody entered Marist College, which was not a college at all, but a Catholic military prep school for boys. Sacred Heart and Marist occupied a considerable campus together in downtown Atlanta, a few miles from home. Which meant that Woody, my sister, Peggy, who entered the eighth grade at Sacred Heart, and I had to walk several blocks to Peachtree Street and catch a trolley car which took us almost to the schools' front doors.

Having spent my entire life until now in the New York metropolitan area, I spoke New Yorkese – like a Noo Yawka. At first, my classmates and teachers had difficulty understanding me. They all had grown up here, in the deep south, and spoke in accents I could not understand, that sometimes made me think that they were falling asleep, and they used funny words that were meaningless to me, words like "reckon," and "yonda" (yonder), and "y'all" (which had both singular and plural meaning). And they called me, "Yankee." None of which bothered me; in fact, which made me think of the New York Yankees, and thus induced in me a feeling of pride, although I was a fan of the New York Giants because the Giants had an All Star pitcher named Carl Hubbell, who was a distant cousin of ours. Looking back, I think that in those days many southerners were upset that any of us Yankees had the gall to come and live among them. I knew nothing yet about the Civil War; I didn't even know there had been one. Southerners called it, "the war between the states." Only about seventy years had passed since General William Tecumseh Sherman had burned Atlanta to the ground and scorched a 60-mile-wide path from Atlanta to the sea, and angry scars remained on cultural and family memories.

I was oblivious to all this. I missed my friends in New Jersey for a short while, but soon enough I was enjoying many new friends in Sacred Heart School as well as in the Peachtree Circle neighborhood. I attended school and did my homework assignments. For some reason I learned to read more quickly than any of my classmates, so well that our second grade teacher, Sister Therese, was soon sending me with my reader, which was full of Aesop's Fables, to the eighth and seventh grades to demonstrate my prowess as a reader. In each of these classrooms the teachers would tell me how wonderful I was, and would award me a religious medal or a holy card, with a picture of Jesus or His Mother or a saint on it, and a prayer on the back. I would deliver these medals and cards to my mother, who would show them to my father, brothers and sister, and everyone would heap praise upon me.

Life in Georgia was good.

I devoured sports magazines, particularly those having to do with football. I loved going to movies with my parents, mainly for the brief newsreels that always included short visual reports of recent college football games. At home I would go out in the yard with a football and run up and down the lawn, mimicking the great radio sportscaster Bill Stern, as I described to a mesmerized America the incredible feats of Jerry Hubbell before hundreds of thousands of roaring, adoring fans. Sometimes I would be compared favorably to Alabama's great halfback, Dixie Howell, other times to the incredible Ken Kavanaugh, LSU's "glue fingered receiver," sometimes to Tennessee's George "Bad News" Cafego, another great broken field runner. This Jerry Hubbell was really something!

I had a great deal of confidence in him, perhaps induced by that touchdown pass he had caught in the street in front of our house in Teaneck. In any case, he was good enough on the playground during second grade recesses that his classmates were soon selecting him first when choosing up sides for a football game: "Ah take *Yankee!*"

As for my brother Woody, his heart may have been broken when he had had to leave St. Cecilia, but the move had no effect on the rest of him. His single year at Marist was unbelievable, except that it happened. He played football for the school in a fashion that kept his name prominent in the Atlanta's sports pages and earned him all city honors. And the following spring the city also learned that he was quite a baseball player. In one very important game with a team from Boys High School Woody started in the outfield, then, when the catcher was injured, went behind home plate to catch for a few innings, then, when the pitcher weakened, was sent out to pitch. I can't remember how many innings he pitched, but I do remember that he denied the Boys High team any hits. Finally, in the ninth inning, he hit a home run to win the game. The next day, there were big headlines calling attention to his performance.

I also remember that after that game Woody and one of the Boys High players stood for a long time near home plate talking to a man who had been watching the game. I went out to Peachtree Street and took a trolley home. Woody came home later, and we learned that the man he had been talking to was a major league baseball scout who wanted to sign both boys up for the Cleveland Indians system. Woody had declined, explaining that he meant to go to college. Not many people had college degrees then, and our parents wanted that for their kids. Moreover, Woody had demonstrated that he was college material. At Marist's graduation exercises that spring, he was awarded almost all of the academic honors the school had to offer.

Holy Mackerel, what a guy!

Meanwhile, Les was completing his freshman year at Georgia Tech. I don't know how expensive college was in those days; certainly nothing like today. But a lot people were having trouble paying for food and shelter, and had nothing left for college. Dad was making a good income, and Les told me many years later that when he was transferred to Atlanta the company agreed to pay some, maybe all, of college tuitions.

Tech was a military school in those days, and all male students were required to enter a Reserve Officers Training Corps (R.O.T.C.), either the Army's or the Navy's. Les opted for the Navy, and during the summer following his freshman year spent a couple of weeks on a training cruise to Puerto Rico. He probably spent most of the cruise swabbing decks, painting things and running errands for officers, but he returned home full of excitement over the experience and full of tales about shipboard life and Puerto Rico. He was a very happy, engaging guy, and we all always loved listening to him.

I was shocked and disappointed when Woody decided to enter Emory University. I had looked forward to him leading Georgia Tech to a national football championship. Instead, he was going to Emory, a school that did not participate in intercollegiate athletics! *What kind of a place was that? What did they do there?* I wondered at Emory's reason for existing, and my adored brother's sanity.

But that's what happened. He went to Emory, and enjoyed it every bit as much as Les enjoyed Georgia Tech.

One day as I rode the trolley home along Peachtree Street I noticed that the console the driver used in the front of the trolley was replicated in the back, so that the trolley car didn't have to be turned around when it reached the end of the line; the driver simply had to go to the back, which then became the front, and drive it from there. I got up and went back to sit at console at the back of the car, to pretend I was driving. The trolley stopped in the middle of a block. I looked toward the front, and saw the driver, or conductor, or whatever he was, bearing down on me. He took me by the hand and explained to me that I was not sit back here, in the "colored" section. He escorted me up to the front of the car, to the "white folks" section. That was the first time I noticed that there were differences as to where "colored" and "white" people did things. I don't remember what I thought about that, or if I thought about it at all. I do remember that I never saw many "colored" in the neighborhood where I lived. I probably thought that was just the way things were; I certainly did not know why. We had a "colored" maid named Lily; she and my Mom were always talking and laughing and cooking and gossiping together, and seemed to be close friends, and Lily never hesitated to whack me where I sat when she thought I had it coming.

My Dad hustled the Atlanta district to the top of Nabisco's standings saleswise. A couple of years passed, and sales were flagging in the district headquartered from Richmond, Virginia. So now we were living in an apartment building on Davis Avenue, a block and a half south of Monument Avenue, in Richmond. Monument Avenue was a beautiful wide two-lane boulevard, and at every intersection stood a monument to a confederate hero of "the war between the states." At the intersection of Davis and Monument Avenues, our intersection, stood an impressive tribute to a man named Jefferson Davis, who had been the first and last President of the Confederate States of America.

Made me proud, but I still wasn't clear on what it was about.

17

Good News

My beloved big brothers had remained in Atlanta, having moved into their fraternity houses, on the campuses of Georgia Tech and Emory. Les was a member of Sigma Phi Epsilon, and would be elected President in his senior year. Woody was at Kappa Alpha, a fraternity rooted in the glory of the old Confederacy; it had no chapters in any schools north of the Mason-Dixon Line, the demarcation line between the North and the South.

In Richmond, I attended Cathedral Boys School. I think it was the only Catholic school in the city, and it was a long walk from our apartment, a couple of miles. But I walked it, and made very sure to be there before the school day began at 8 a.m. because the Christian Brothers who taught there were utterly intolerant of tardiness, and the latecomer, unless he could prove a genuine emergency, always was required to bend over and take a painful switching, usually five strokes. And you certainly never wanted to smart off or get caught misbehaving in class or in any way on the playground, because these Brothers were big, tough guys, and they felt no need to consult with any authorities, including parents, if they judged that a student needed to be slapped around. Moreover, in the America of those years, it was generally inadvisable to complain to parents of punishment by a teacher, because often as not one would find one's parents to be in sympathy with the teacher, and there would be additional punishment at home.

We were not in Richmond long before the sales effort in the MidAtlantic had slumped, and the new good news was that my Dad was transferred back to Newark. We moved back into the house in Teaneck. I was back in the first house I had ever lived in, where I belonged, and I was able to be with all my old friends, who were most welcoming. I was joyful. Life was good.

Except that my friends couldn't understand me when I talked. I had a lazy drawl and kept using funny words, like, "reckon," and, "yonda," and, "y'all," and they couldn't seem to make sense of them, the dopes.

We all wanted to be altar boys at St. Joseph's, because everybody who was anybody, including our heroic older brothers, had all been altar boys, and our parents wanted us to be altar boys. So after school we would meet in the church with Father Boniface, the pastor, who taught us Latin, and we didn't serve until we proved to him that we could respond to the priest's Latin prayers without reading from a card. It didn't take long. Father Boniface was a hard driver, a taskmaster who got quick results. All of us were soon serving mass. Schedules were drawn up for the 6:30 a.m. and 8 a.m. masses every weekday, and four masses on Sundays.

Father Boniface was a native of Germany. He had a pronounced German accent, and he was a no-nonsense guy, an old-fashioned, pulpit pounding, dictator of a pastor, a real force in the parish and the town. He made things happen and not happen. One Sunday morning he expounded in the pulpit about a movie entitled, "Ecstasy," starring an extraordinarily beautiful actress named Hedy LaMarr, that was scheduled to open at the Queen Anne Theater, on Queen Anne Road, in Bogota. In the movie, the breathtaking Miss LaMarr's character was unhappily and inexplicably married to a dolt who paid her no romantic attention. She dumped him and returned to her parents' home, then engaged illicitly with a handsome stranger who lavished her with the treatment such a beauty had every reason to expect. The Legion of Decency had condemned the movie, and religious leaders across the nation were denouncing it. All of which guaranteed that it would be a smash hit at the box office. But Father Boniface pounded his pulpit and asserted that this infamous film would "never open in this town."

And, doubtless to the intense disappointment of many, it did not.[2]

I had never been happier than when I returned to Teaneck, where I was with all the friends with whom I had begun. I vowed to all who would listen that here I would stay forever. Forever ended three years later, immediately as I completed the sixth grade at St. Joseph's. In early 1939 Nabisco's sales fortunes were flagging in

---

[2] Years later, when I was in the Navy and aboard a ship anchored off of Bremerton, WA, I discovered in a newspaper that the forbidden movie was playing in a Seattle theater. A group of us hustled to the theater and, to our intense disappointment, found "Ecstasy" to be less interesting than many of today's TV commercials.

the Upper Midwest, so when the school year ended we would be moving to Minneapolis, Minnesota, a place of which I knew nothing and could scarcely imagine. I found it on a map; it was way up north and way out west. My brother Les told me that Henry W. Longfellow – for whom that lousy place where I had gone to kindergarten was named – had written a poem about it called, "The Song of Hiawatha." What came close to making it okay was that it was the home of the University of Minnesota Golden Gophers football team, which had been making a habit of winning Big Ten and national championships.

In June, before we moved, my brother Woody graduated from Emory University and returned home, to Teaneck. But it didn't feel like home to him anymore. For one thing, he was not the despondent lad who half a decade earlier had been denied his senior year at St. Cecilia High School, had been robbed of his senior season of athletics there and had been forced to forego the Presidency of its Class of 1935. Many of his friends of those years had scattered, and in any case he was now a confirmed Atlantan. A year of high school and four years of college and all of the concomitant friendships and activities involved had made him a genuine, out-and-out Georgian. He thought of Atlanta as his home town now, and he missed the city and his college friends and wanted to be there with them, and not in northern New Jersey. He had become a southern gentleman, who spoke softly and who, when he used words like "reckon," "yonda" and "y'all" infused them with a soft gentility not to be found in the coarse environs of the Noo Yawk metropolitan area.

Moreover, the Depression was at its nadir and there were no jobs to be found in Atlanta, nor anywhere else, not even for college graduates – especially college graduates who had majored in Philosophy, as he had; in 1939 there was no market at all for newly minted philosophers.

But I was deeply impressed when he explained to me all about the intensely competitive intramural athletic program at Emory. He had played four years of football, basketball and baseball. The yearbook was full of his exploits, and an impressive gold plaque awarded at the graduation ceremony was inscribed to him as the school's "Best All Around Athlete." I remained certain that he would have made All America if he had gone to Tech, or Alabama or Duke, or any of the major schools in the region instead of dumb Emory, but he was still my hero.

My brother Les had graduated from Georgia Tech a year earlier. By this time he was a great big guy, well over six feet tall, and husky, and he was very happy and gregarious, and people loved him. He had found a job in Brooklyn as a collector for a loan company. I don't recall that he ever had acquired a southern drawl, but if he did he shed it quickly. Apparently he had no trouble collecting loan money that was due. He was living at home, in Teaneck, which was only a couple of nickel bus rides from Brooklyn. He spent his free time romancing Norma Keyes. I was enjoying their romance a lot, because Norma was so pretty and as much fun to be with as Les, and often when they went to the movies they took me along. When we left for Minneapolis, Les found an apartment in Brooklyn.

A train took the rest of us to South Bend, Indiana, where we collected a brand new Studebaker automobile from the factory in which it had been manufactured. We toured the lovely campus of the University of Notre Dame, then motored up to Minnesota, where I would live for the rest of my life.

18
A Good Place to Be

Minneapolis was impressive, a beautiful, lively place that called itself the "City of Lakes." There were eleven of them, all of them large and attractive, many of them with inviting beaches, and surfaces crowded with colorful sailboats. In the center of the city rose a 32-story office building called The Foshay Tower. Modeled after the Washington Monument, it was named after its builder, a man named Wilbur Foshay, and was then the tallest building between Chicago and Seattle. Today, it is difficult to find in a forest of skyscrapers.

We lived most of that first summer in a comfortable apartment in the Curtis Hotel, then one of the city's best, and which no longer exists. By late summer my parents had found a house they liked in a suburb called Edina. It abutted the southwestern corner of the city, in what was called the Country Club section. The neighborhood was a collection of mansions and near-mansions; our house was handsome and comfortable.

We had been renting it for about a year when the owner decided to sell it. He offered it to my Dad for $5,000. I heard my Dad tell my Mother that the man was "out of his mind," that he would never get anything approaching that amount,[3] I later learned that the house in Teaneck had been sold, and that we had taken a financial drubbing. My Dad had decided not only that real estate was a terrible investment, but also that we moved too often to get tied down to a house anywhere. Years later he told me that the rent for the house in Edina had been $65 per month.

We moved into a beautiful lower duplex on Linden Hills Boulevard, which looked like Norman Rockwell's vision of middle America. In southwest Minneapolis, the street was wide, and curved very gently this way and that way, and was lined with a profusion of Linden trees and attractive houses facing broad green lawns. The streetlights were distinctive, big, white globes. The boulevard was situated directly between two of the prettiest lakes in the "City of Lakes," Lake Calhoun and Lake Harriet. We were about a block and a half from each lake, both of which had numerous swimming beaches and hosted large numbers of sailboats. Lake Harriet had a wonderful big bandstand, and every night all summer long crowds from all over the city came to enjoy great concerts. Nearby stood a confectionary where ice cream, popcorn and hot dogs were available, and the area was always crowded with high school and college boys and girls eyeing each other.

---

[3] As this is written, houses in Edina are selling from approximately $800,000 into the many millions.

In the autumn of 1939 I was enrolled in the seventh grade at a brand new Catholic grade school called Christ the King. My new schoolmates included two boys whose friendships I would value for the rest of my life. They were first cousins named Bob White and Bill Hedrick. They lived together with their mothers, who were sisters, and two younger brothers, Jim White and Pat Hedrick. The White boys' Dad supervised a camp for the Civilian Conservation Corps (CCC), and occasionally was able to come home on weekends.[4] The Hedrick boys' Dad had been killed in an automobile accident some years earlier. The mothers had decided that it made sense to merge into one family. Bill's mother was a dental hygienist, and Bob's mother stayed home and looked after the boys. All four boys contributed to the family economy, working newspaper routes every afternoon after school and every weekend morning.

Bill would become prominent in Twin Cities medicine, and would become my personal physician until he retired, more than fifty years later.

Bob would become a world renowned neurosurgeon, an innovative neuroscientist, an advisor to Popes Paul VI and John Paul II, he would be biographied in virtually every important Who's Who-type book in the world, there would be a section devoted to him in a book entitled, "Giants of Neurosurgery," and he would be the

---

[4] In the months prior to the eruption of World War II Bob's father was commissioned an Army infantry captain, his CCC unit was mobilized and sent to the Philippines. Captain White was among those captured when the Japanese invaded. Imprisoned in Manila's Bilibid prison, he did not survive the war.

recipient of many of neurosurgery's most prestigious honors. More on him later.

Meanwhile, life in Minnesota was good. Cold in winter, hot in summer, but always good.

19

A Last Summer in Jersey

Woody found a job in a warehouse in St. Paul. It took well over an hour on streetcars to reach the place, so he moved into a YMCA not far from the job. He came home on weekends.

My parents, my sister, Peggy, my brother Woody and I all returned to New Jersey in June, 1940, for Les's and Norma's wedding, at St. Joseph's. I remember a lot of muted conversation between my parents about the fact that Norma had developed Bright's Disease, a serious inflammation of the kidneys that might well shorten her life. But Norma and Les were crazy in love, and decided to bet that with proper medical attention she would get through it.

Father Boniface performed the ceremony at St. Joseph's, Woody was the best man and I served as an altar boy. A few days later, Norma and Les left for Dayton, Ohio, where Les now worked as a salesman for Nabisco. Our Dad had recommended him to the company's sales vice president, who had thanked him for the favor, offering the opinion that Les was "an irresistible salesman".

My Dad returned to his job in Minneapolis. Woody returned to his warehouse job in St. Paul and my mother, my sister Peggy and I stayed in New Jersey all summer. My Mom and Peggy stayed with Aunt Kitty and her husband, Jim Earle, at their home in Paramus. I spent the summer living with the Hill family, in their house on Beechwood Avenue, in Bogota. Ironically, the Hills had migrated from Minneapolis to Bogota years earlier. There were ten kids in the family, they all had gone to St. Joseph's School, and Billy and Jimmy, who were right in the middle of the lineup were my good buddies. My Mom and Mrs. Hill had long been very close friends, and Mom dropped in every week or so and they would visit for hours, and she also wanted to know that I was still alive.

It was a great summer for me. Mr. Hill took us twice to the New York World's Fair, in Long Island, twice to see the New York Giants play, at the Polo Grounds. We played a lot of baseball games we organized at Martin's Oval, a few blocks from our old house, in Teaneck, we went swimming a lot, and we just hung out around the old neighborhood. The worst thing that happened was that one day in September, when all the Hill kids were returning to school, my Mom showed up and said it was time to go back to Minneapolis.

More than 40 years would pass before I would see Teaneck and Bogota again. I was researching a magazine article that required an interview in Hackensack, which was adjacent to Bogota. I visited the old neighborhoods, which hadn't changed much. The first house I had ever lived in was still there, and looked as nice as I remembered it. St. Joseph's Church was still there, but the school was gone. I didn't try to find anyone I had once known; my closest friends, the Hills, had long since moved to Dallas, and I only saw them once again, many years later, when I was in Texas gathering information for a magazine article.

The school year at Christ the King had been underway for a week or so by the time I returned. I was greeted as a celebrity – after all, I had been to the World's Fair, had even seen the New York Giants play!

20

A Great School

My friends, Bob White and Bill Hedrick and I left Christ the King School in different directions. Bob and Bill went to De La Salle, a Catholic High School in downtown Minneapolis taught by Christian Brothers. I went to St. Thomas Military Academy, in St. Paul.

What impressed me about St. Thomas was its long tradition of championship football teams; every week during the football season I would read on the sports page of, "the powerful St. Thomas Cadets." A number of Cadets lived in my neighborhood, in Minneapolis, and I thought they looked splendid in their uniforms. I wanted to be a "powerful St. Thomas Cadet." It meant a streetcar trip of several miles, across the Mississippi River, followed by an eight or ten block walk up a hill to the school – if you took the streetcar to the top of the hill, it cost an extra token, which was worth seven and a half cents, and who could afford that? And classes started at 8 a.m., and you had better be on time. And after football and basketball practices you had that long ride home, and you could count on a couple of hours of homework every night.

When I attended the school its name was St. Thomas Military Academy. It now goes by the named of St. Thomas Academy, but it's still Military. When I entered as a freshman, in the fall of 1941, the school was 55 years old, and still in its youth. Today, it stands impressively in new buildings on a new campus, is approaching its 130th birthday, appears to be much younger than when I matriculated and has so far graduated two of my grandsons. In the next few years it will graduate two more.

Three months after I entered St. Thomas the Japanese eviscerated the U.S. battleship fleet at Pearl Harbor., and the United State was entered into World War II.

Some seniors who graduated the following June and had achieved age 18 went to Fort Benning, Georgia, for several weeks of intensified training and then placed in command of infantry platoons and shipped off to war. They were teenagers, and they fought everywhere, from North Africa, through Sicily, Italy, Central Europe and the Pacific.

Some who had graduated earlier reached combat sooner. Like Richard E. Fleming, of the class of 1935. He led his Marine fighter-bomber squadron against a strong enemy naval force in the Battle Midway, in June, 1942. He decided to take out the Japanese heavy cruiser Mikuma. He went down through such heavy defensive fire that he was in flames by the time he impacted the ship. The Mikuma and Fleming went down together. President Franklin D. Roosevelt awarded him a posthumous Medal of Honor.

Each year, The Fleming Saber, the highest military honor the school has for its Cadets, is awarded to the senior who is selected to be Cadet Colonel, the leader of the corps. In the 1934-35 school year, Richard Fleming had himself been Cadet Colonel.

Another alumnus, Alfred E. Gruenther, of the class of 1919 who then had graduated from the United States Military Academy at West Point, became one of the brightest lights in the World War II U.S. Army, a four-star general who was a close advisor to General Eisenhower, and in the immediate aftermath of the war Supreme Commander of Allied Forces in Europe.

From my own era, Joe Bratton, two years ahead of me, who played on the football team, also went on to graduate from West Point, and eventually became Lieutenant General Joseph K. Bratton, Chief of the Army Corps of Engineers.

Some Cadets didn't survive the war. The one that sticks in my memory was James "Jim" Grant, who was my company commander when I was a freshman, and a really nice young man. I looked up to him. The whole school was devastated when word came that he had been killed in action. His younger brother, John, was a classmate of mine, and a very close friend.

In other words, there is a lot of proud tradition, glory and heart-ache connected with the school.

21
A Teacher for the Ages

I loved everything about St. Thomas except the English classes conducted by Mr. Arthur Martin. Mr. Martin was relatively short in stature, trim, well groomed and of serious demeanor. He was a no nonsense gentleman, a taskmaster, a severe man. He did not seem much impressed with me, nor with any of my classmates. One quarter he awarded me a grade of 79, and I was ranked first in the class. I had been anxious to impress my parents by earning an Eagle Award. The 79 ruled that out; an Eagle Award, required a grade point average of no less than 86 and no grade below 80. This award was a classy looking medal shaped like a shield, with red and white stripes down the shield, a blue banner emblazoned with white stars across the top and a golden American eagle atop it all. Not only did it look great on the dress jackets of all of the upper classmen who had earned it, but it was dramatically good looking evidence that the wearer was one of the smartest guys in the world. But no one with a 79 on the books was going to wear it.

With trepidation, I approached Mr. Martin with the slip of paper containing all of my grades, all of which were in the 90's except English, which I thought was my best subject. I explained that the 79 was going to cost me an Eagle Award. He immediately notified the Academic Office that he had erred, and that Hubbell had earned a grade of 80, and not 79.

Thus was my Eagle Award secured.

I felt better about Mr. Martin after that, but I never got my medal. The country was involved in the greatest war of all time, and no one had the time or the metal to manufacture medals for high school academic performance. Metal was reserved for the construction of war materiel. So at the end of the school year I received a certificate, a piece of paper attesting to the fact that I had indeed earned an Eagle Award. I tried pinning it to my dress jacket, where the medal should have been, but it looked out of place there, so I unpinned it and, God forgive me, hoped fervently that the bullet that had been made of my Eagle Award had been lodged effectively in the heart of one of my country's enemies.

But Mr. Martin went on with his taskmastering. He required the writing of lots of essays. I found that I enjoyed writing, and always put some effort into it. Usually, he awarded me a good grade – good relative to the grades he awarded most others. Often after class, he would ask to see my work again and would go over it, marking out areas with a red pencil and saying, "This is all right, but it could be much better. Finally, he would hand it back saying, "Write it again, and rewrite the areas I have marked."

The first time this happened I was bewildered, inasmuch as he had given me a much better than passing grade. I asked, "What do you mean, Sir? What should I write?"

"Think about it," he said.

"About what?"

"About what you have written there, of course. I want you to *think* about exactly what you are driving at, *think* about the thoughts you want to put in the reader's mind, *think* about how you might convey them most effectively. And then I want you to do it."

I was to take my time of course, and really *think* things through. He would not require the revision any time soon, not until, say, the day after tomorrow!

This happened a few times before I made bold to wonder why such extra work was required of me but not of my classmates. He replied that I need not be concerned with what was required of others, only with what he required of me.

He had no tolerance for sloppy thinking or sloppy writing. He certainly got my thinker going, and when I turned in a revision he would read it carefully and sometimes nod and say, "Yes, very good, this is much better, you have done a good job of developing these thoughts." But sometimes that didn't happen, and I would find myself revising the revision until it did.

I was not happy with Mr. Martin, but what he knew in those days and I didn't was that that was not what he and I were about. What we were about was imposing upon a student a needed creative discipline, teaching me how to communicate a thought or an idea until I got it just right, ultimately teaching me the sheer joy of delivering to *myself* the best that was in me, that such an approach would inform everything I did. I didn't understand that then, and, of course, Mr. Martin knew that I didn't, but he cared enough about me and my future to not care whether or not I liked it or him.

Meanwhile, the high school years dragged on, as they seem to for everyone, except for the football and basketball games and dances, until suddenly – in a flash – they were gone! It had been a wonderful place and way to spend those years, and a great preparation for college. It had been great to play on championship football and basketball teams, on actually becoming a "powerful St. Thomas Cadet," and developing many close friendships that I would cherish for the rest of my life.

Years later, after I had achieved some success as a magazine writer, I wrote an article about Mr. Martin and his influence on me for the high school edition of The Reader's Digest. I sent him a copy and a thank you note for what he had done for me. He replied with a cheerful invitation to come visit. I never got around to it. He died shortly after our class celebrated the 50th anniversary of its graduation. Following his death, I paid him a late but heartfelt tribute as a great teacher and a great man.

Nearly 40 years after I graduated, the school graduated another writer, a far more accomplished storyteller than I. His name was Vince Flynn. In a series of 14 gripping, super-best selling novels— more than 12 million books sold in the United States alone – he taught America and the world how the Central Intelligence Agency (CIA) was fighting the War on Terror. So authentic were his tales that President George W. Bush is known to have pressed him for information as to where he was getting his information. Vince was a football teammate and good friend of my son, Bill, at the College (now University) of St. Thomas. Tragically, Vince died from prostate cancer in July, 2013, at the age of 47.

22
God Helps the Navy

One night in December, 1940, my brother, Les, called from Dayton to say that he had received a letter from the Navy reminding him that along with the diploma awarded him when he graduated from Georgia Tech had been a commission as an Ensign in the Naval Reserve. It advised that he was now being summoned to active duty, and that he was to report to a Navy office in Dayton, where he would receive orders to proceed and report to the U.S.S. Fox, a destroyer, currently in port at Bremerton, Washington. He told my Dad that he planned to drop by the Navy office the following day and decline the invitation to active duty; he would explain that he was now married and had a good job which he did not wish to give up. He didn't think there would be a problem.

There was no problem. A few days later he was on a train headed for Bremerton, and Norma was packing things up in the apartment in Dayton. She would drive to Seattle by herself.

Decades later Les would confide to me that he had not been a good NROTC student at Georgia Tech, that in fact he had been so disinterested that the Professor of Naval Science who ran the program informed him just before graduation that so poor had been his performance that he had not earned a passing grade. Which would mean no commission. Which would mean, in those days, at least, no diploma. If he wanted a degree he would have to stay until he delivered a satisfactory performance in NROTC. He was panic-stricken, until the officer said, "But I'm going to give you a passing grade anyway, because I don't want you around here again. I don't want to have to deal with you. I want you gone. So you're going to get your commission, and get out of here, and God help the Navy and all of us in it if it ever has to activate you!"

Years later Les would recall, "The minute I stepped aboard the Fox I knew I was home; I was where I wanted to be. I loved being aboard ship, I loved the sea. I loved the Navy, the life."

The greatest war of all time ensued. He served with distinction in the Pacific, aboard the Fox. A lieutenant commander by July, 1944, he was in Orange, Texas, taking command of a brand new destroyer escort, the U.S.S. Rolf. He fought her through numerous battles in the western Pacific.

On Christmas night, 1944, Norma and Les lost their bet on her longevity. She died in her parents' home, in Bogota. She was 26 years old. One of the officers who had been aboard the Rolf, then somewhere in the Far East, later told me that when word reached Les he went into his stateroom and stayed there, alone, for three days. He never spoke of it again. Ever. Not to Woody, nor me, nor anyone.

A couple of years after the war ended he married Kay Bush, a lovely Red Cross worker from California whom he had met in the Far East. They had two sons, Lester and Michael, and a daughter, Kathy.

Les stayed in love with the Navy. When the war ended he applied for a commission as a regular, which was not easy to come by, especially during the frenzied demobilization. But so impressed with his wartime performance was the Navy's hierarchy that his petition was quickly granted. He was a professional Naval officer now, and over the years, in a series of assignments at sea and ashore and in wars in Korea and Vietnam, he became one of the Navy's bright stars. He was the first non-Naval Academy officer ever to be selected to the rank of Rear Admiral from "below the zone", i.e., before he had the seniority automatically to be among those under consideration. He was Georgia Tech's first Admiral, and was invited back during commencement week to be honored, to stand at the podium in Grant Field, the football stadium, and "take the review" as the NROTC midshipmen and Army cadets marched by, saluting him. It had been thirty three years since his NROTC instructor at Tech had hoped that God would help the Navy if it ever had to activate him. And indeed God had helped the Navy in no small measure when it did so.

Once, in late 1940, Les made a short visit to Minneapolis for some reason I don't recall. Woody was still working in the St. Paul warehouse. Les told him about the Navy's flight training program, and soon Woody, too, was in the Navy. He took to it just as Les had. He was awarded his commission and wings at the Pensacola, Florida, Naval Air Station on December 8, 1941, the day after the

Japanese attack on Pearl Harbor. He came home on a brief leave, and with orders to report to the "Commander of the Western Sea Frontier," in Hawaii. Our parents didn't like the sound of it, but all the young men were going somewhere. We were not to see Woody again until March, 1945, a few months before the war ended. He had spent his war flying dive bomber missions in a number of battles off of a number of aircraft carriers in the western and southwestern Pacific. He had also flown out of Henderson Field, on Guadalcanal, in the Solomon Islands. But the main thing for his family was that he had survived. When he arrived in Minneapolis that March he surprised us with a wife whom he had met and married in Hawaii. Her name was Budhi (pronounced Buddy), and she was most attractive and frightened to death to be foisted on her new husband's family. Mom was a bit standoffish at first; maybe we all were, having never heard of her. But she did her best to fit in, and it worked. Budhi and Mom became best friends, and we all loved her.

Like Les, Woody loved the Navy, and loved flying. Like Les, he sought a regular commission after the war, and like Les his World War II record stood him in good enough stead to receive one. Through the years he was a flight instructor at Pensacola, served in several different office jobs in the Pentagon, served as commanding officer at a couple of different naval air stations, made numerous sea duty tours on various carriers – when the Korean War erupted he was involved in launching history's first jet air strikes, as the Air Operations Officer on the aircraft carrier U.S.S. Valley Forge, while Les, by then a captain (the Navy's equivalent of a bird colonel), was the Fleet Operations Officer on the U.S.S. Helena and directing the strikes.

Woody and Budhi enjoyed foreign duty, serving several years in posts in London and Naples. He retired from the Navy as a captain. The Navy turned out to be the right place for this particular philosopher.

Budhi died from cancer in 1966. Woody remained alone for five years, then married vivacious, blond Helen Monroe, the widow of a State Department official and a take-charge, highly successful businesswoman. She and Woody were crazy about each other, and she fit right into our family. Les died in 1994, at the age of 78. He is buried in Arlington National Cemetery. Woody died in 2005, at the age of 88, and is buried in Arlington Cemetery, not far from Les.

23
My War

I was a a 17-year-old high school graduate when the war in Europe ended in May, 1945, with Germany's surrender. But the war in the Pacific raged on, the military draft was still operational and I would become 18 in July and eligible for the draft. Navy life, and even death in a naval situation, struck me as more attractive than infantry warfare, and death in the muck. I enlisted in one of the Navy's specialty programs, a school that would make of me an Aviation Radiomen. I would learn everything knowable about Naval Air radio communications, including how to operate radios, how to take care of them, how to construct them in survival situations and how to send and receive code at 60 words per minute. Eventually, I would take such knowledge to my work place, probably the back seat of a Douglas SB2C dive bomber.

The training was at Millington, Tennessee, near Memphis. It began with six weeks of boot camp. Shortly after dawn on the day of arrival, 180 of us from all over the country stood in front of Barracks 38, and the very first thing that was made clear to us was that we were no longer at home, that our mommies and daddies and brothers and sisters and girl friends and everything we had known and loved were gone from our lives, that henceforth our posteriors belonged to a particularly nasty Gunner's Mate First Class named Sheffield. He was tall, lanky, dark-haired and plainly disgusted at what he was looking at – us. His language ranged from profane to obscene to unspeakable, and he spoke it eloquently and very loudly. Among our company were some who were able to translate his harangue and explain that not only were we despicable specimens, Sheffield desired that we all go into the barracks and make it fit for human habitation, even though in his opinion we were less than human. We were still in civilian clothes, and most of us were carrying suitcases. We assumed that we would be issued some work clothes. We assumed wrong. We were instructed to place our suitcases in a large storeroom. Then, we set about cleaning the place, which appeared to be spotless, in fact, gleaming. And indeed we would later learn that it had just had a very thorough cleaning by the class that had just graduated. No matter. Sheffield ordered us to, "Get this goddam *pigpen* cleaned up! *Now!*"

In our civilian clothes we were ordered to steel-wool the floors, which we learned were "decks;" steel-wool the walls, which we learned were "bulkheads;" clean the windows, which we learned were "portholes;" clean the toilets, which we learned were "heads;" dust the dustless ceilings, which we learned were "overheads;" wash with mops, which we learned were "swabs," the decks we had just steel-wooled. Then we did all these things all over again, until

Gunner's Mate Sheffield was satisfied that we had the place in 4.0 condition, (perfect) which meant it was acceptably clean. Twice in the middle of all this we were marched to a chow hall, once for lunch and once for dinner. Another time, we were marched to a building where we were issued our Navy clothing, sheets, blankets and pillows. Back in Barracks 38 we were taught how to make up our bunks, the Navy way, so that "a goddam dollar bill" would bounce if dropped on the "goddam" sheet. We were told that we didn't want to know what would happen if the barracks and our bunks didn't look like this at "every single goddam inspection," which would occur "every single goddam morning." By this time it was about oh four hundred (4 a.m.) the day after we arrived. We were still in the civilian clothes in which we had arrived; the clothes were ruined, we all were exhausted and we were told how badly we stunk, which was unnecessary because we could smell each other. We were advised that no incoming recruits ever had stunk this badly, and were ordered to take showers and "hit the sack."

No one had any trouble going to sleep. We had just finished showering and climbing into our bunks when at 0500 reveille came blasting through the loudspeakers in our ceiling – excuse me, the overhead – and someone was stomping through the place banging a nightstick on the metal frames of the bunks shouting, "Hit the deck! Hit the deck! Time to *rise* and *shine*, let's *go*, let's *go*, form up outside in *five minutes*, let's *go*, let's *go!*"

We all *knew* that we had died and gone to hell.

Outside, we found that Sheffield knew all he needed to know about us.

For example, that a half dozen of us had attended military schools. He summoned us forward, by name, told us we were to teach military drill to the others; *now*! He wanted this "collection of dumbass goddam misfits" organized and marching in platoon formations by noon. "How the hell else" were they going to get to "the goddam chow hall?"

We made it happen. Under Sheffield's obscene guidance we made all the things happen that were supposed to happen in boot camp and by the end, six weeks later, we were marching like West Point cadets, feeling very superior for having weathered the horror of Sheffield's boot camp, and shouting, "You'll be *sorry!*" at the truckloads of new recruits who were just arriving.

Of course, everyone of the many millions who entered military service in those years had some such entry level experience, most of them far longer and tougher than ours. Sheffield had explained to us, often and with what struck me as unseemly glee, the reason for our short boot camp: In combat the life expectancy of the Aviation Radioman, the communicator, was eight seconds; he explained that to the enemy the communicator was more important than the pilot, because he was sending and receiving important information, so they went for him first. Thus, there was a continuing shortage of Aviation Radiomen, thus, the Navy was anxious to get us out to the fleet to fill all those fast emptying seats. (I suspected the validity of this.)

Two really wonderful things happened that summer: The first was that we finished boot camp in August, and went home on a week's leave. The second was that Japan surrendered that very week. The war was over, and Sheffield's guarantee that I would die in eight seconds was no longer operative. When word of the surrender came, I happened to be in downtown Minneapolis in my Navy uniform, obeying my mother's command to have my picture taken. She had made an appointment at a photography studio. That done, I strolled out into a city exploding with joy. The streets and bars were jammed with celebrants. In my uniform I attracted a great deal of affectionate attention. People insisted on shaking my hand, patting my back, buying me beer, and girls actually stood in line to hug me and kiss me. On the lips. I was treated as though I had won the war all by myself. I did not disabuse anyone; I may have told one or two people that it had been "tough, but it's over." It had been a long war, and Americans had earned the right to relax and have fun and love each other to pieces.

The world was all bright and shiny again. The thought crossed my mind that in the next few days I might well receive a telegram from the Navy saying that it had no further need of me, and that I might as well stay home. The telegram never came.

I was back in Millington and eight or ten weeks into radio school before the Navy, which was demobilizing, discovered that it didn't need Aviation Radiomen anymore. I soon found myself in Puget Sound, in the bowels of the U.S.S. Biloxi, a light cruiser which had been badly mangled by Japanese kamikaze attacks at Okinawa. I was helping to mothball it, wrap it up and put it in storage for the next war. It was a horrible business. The workday started shortly after dawn every morning in the very bottom of the ship, in the bilges. The bilges were dark, damp and dirty; in fact, filthy, and coated with rust. The job was to scrape and chip away the rust, then paint the cleansed areas with a rust preventative.

Those of us assigned to this task never saw daylight except for a 30 or 40 minute break in mid-day when we went above decks for chow (that's lunch). And even then we never saw sunshine or blue sky because during winter, that winter at least, there were no such things in the Pacific Northwest; it rained almost constantly, it was always gray and gloomy. I yearned for the good old days in radio school, and even boot camp, where Sheffield kept assuring me that I would soon die in eight seconds.

After some weeks of this, three of us who had been together since boot camp quietly mutinied and sent a letter to the Commander of the Eleventh Naval District charging that our skills were being misused, that surely we, who had almost completed what the Navy designated a Class A school, could be put to better use than as bilge rats on the Biloxi. A few days later all three of us were summoned from the bilges to Biloxi's quarterdeck, where the ship's executive officer, pale with anger, handed us our orders to the U.S.S. Dionysus, a repair ship anchored offshore at Bremerton. In a sort of tight-lipped way the Exec let us know that we really needed to Thank God that he hadn't known what we were up to.

The Dionysus was a fun place to be. We all were assigned to the Supply Officer, who was in desperate need of people. We worked in the ship's supply office, keeping records, and went topside when supplies were being taken aboard to muscle them down into the storerooms, or muscle them out of the storerooms and take them topside when they were going to another ship, which was often. Whatever we did we did well enough so that the Supply Officer soon saw to it that we all were advanced from Seaman First Class to

Storekeeper Third Class; a third class petty officer in the Navy is the equivalent of a sergeant in the Army or Marine Corps.

We spent most evenings in a waterfront bar in Bremerton called The Service Club, where we all drank too much beer, declaimed, expounded, argued, disagreed and occasionally went outside to settle differences. Then we would go back inside to drink more beer.

On a morning in early April, 1946, we all went topside on Dionysus to enjoy a magical sight: there was not a single cloud in a blue sky sparkling with sunshine, and majestic, white capped Mount Rainier, nearly 80 miles southeast of Seattle, which was several miles east of Bremerton, appeared to be right next door. It was terrific, inspiring; I hadn't felt this good since VJ Day, when all the girls wanted to kiss me. On the lips. I had happy memories. Someone who was native to the area said that the weather would stay like this until next winter. So that morning we weighed anchor and headed for San Diego.

The San Diego area in the mid-1940's, just after the war, was one of the nicest places on earth, so we only stayed there for a few weeks before moving to Terminal Island, the Navy port at Long Beach, a few miles up the coast.

In the days right after the war people had no qualms about picking up young hitchhiking sailors, and on weekends it was always easy to get to fabulous Hollywood. We did a lot of gawking at famous sites, Grauman's Chinese Theater, the Brown Derby Cafe, the stars embedded in the sidewalk on Hollywood Boulevard. We went to the Palladium, a marvelous ballroom where famous orchestras played and there were girls who were happy to dance with us to music provided by such as Woody Herman and Vaughn Monroe. One Sunday, three of us were standing in a crowd outside a radio studio where a show was about to begin. A gorgeous convertible arrived, and out stepped Gene Autry, the famous cowboy vocalist. He was spectacular, dressed in bright white from the top of his Stetson hat to the tips of his boots. He smiled and waved at the applauding crowd, looked around, spotted three of us together in our white sailor hats and instructed someone to, "Bring those young sailors in first, sit them right up front." It was a great show.

A section of Long Beach's beach was occupied by a fabulous amusement park called, "The Pike." I still don't know why it was so named. I was 19 years old that summer, and I found "The Pike" to be a lot of fun. It had a great roller coaster and all kinds of other rides, places that sold all kinds of good stuff to eat and drink and there were always a lot of pretty girls there who seemed anxious to make friends and take roller coaster rides and dance with sailors.

One day several decades later I was in Los Angeles working on a magazine article and decided to drive down to Long Beach to take a nostalgic look at the Pike. I found a few broken remnants of the amusement park that used to be, but the place had been long abandoned, and never really cleaned up.

In mid-August I was handed my discharge at the Naval Air Station in Minneapolis. My Naval career was over, and unlike my brothers I wanted out. I gloried in my return to civilian life, but was pleased to receive a letter from President Harry S. Truman explaining that along with several million of my countrymen, I had simultaneously defeated two enemies on opposite sides of the world, and he offered me "the heartfelt thanks of a grateful nation."

Good to be appreciated.

Home was no longer on lovely Linden Hills Boulevard, where it had been when I left. The crazy person who owned the place had tried to sell it to my Dad for some "crazy" price, about 1/60th of what it would later sell for – but who knew? – and so we had moved. We now rented on Penn Avenue, about a block and a half south of Lake Harriet.

24
College

Prior to World War II a relatively small number of Americans were college graduates; an educated elite ran the country – its government, the professions, its business communities, just about everything that needed educated leadership.

On June 22, 1944, 16 days after the Allied invasion of Hitler's Europe, The Servicemen's Readjustment Act, known as the GI Bill of Rights, became the law of the land in the United States. It would enable the returning veteran of World War II at government expense to go to the college or university of his choice, to pursue an undergraduate or graduate degree, or to attend a trade school, or take correspondence courses, or take flight training, or do virtually anything he wanted to do in terms of education. It was a grateful nation's thank-you to those young Americans who had given up years of their lives and risk their lives to defend their country and who had survived history's bloodiest war; it was also the most brilliant investment any country ever made in its future. By the time it ran its course, 12 years later, nearly 8,000,000 veterans had taken advantage of it; they now were filling the leadership and the ranks of the nation's political, professional, business and media communities. They proceeded in every conceivable way to make their country the wealthiest, the best informed, the strongest, the most vibrant in world history.

I was lucky enough to be among them. In September, 1946, I entered the University of Minnesota as a recipient of the GI Bill. The University occupied a huge campus sprawled across the northeast side of Minneapolis (although it post office address indicates that it is in the city's southeast quadrant, which, apparently, it once was). The campus included a big time football stadium. Its football teams had won several Big Ten and national championships. There was also a huge basketball field house, a baseball facility and numerous athletic fields for varsity practices and intramural athletics. The school was well attended; in a report that year on burgeoned college enrollments, Fortune Magazine led off with an interesting simile: "In the jungles of higher education, the Golden Bears of California are outnumbered only by the Golden Gophers of Minnesota…" California had enrolled about 30,000 students, Minnesota a few more than that. Life Magazine ran a photograph of an economics class held in Minnesota's Northrup Auditorium where each of 5,000 seats was occupied by a student.

Upon entering the University, I scored well in several General Educational Development (GED) tests; these tests were given to veterans as a means of saving time, to see if people who had spent time in military service or elsewhere in the real world after high school really needed the sort of entry level courses required of more recent high school graduates. Those who did not needed only to complete the prerequisite courses required for the fields of study in which they hoped to major, and then enter into their majors. By the time I was out of the Navy and into college I still had no idea how I wanted to spend my life, but it seemed to make sense to major in Journalism and minor in History.

Completing the prerequisite courses, I was accepted into the University's School of Journalism. At the time, it ranked in the top tier of the world's Journalism schools, along with those at Columbia University, Northwestern University and the University of Missouri. Minnesota's graduates included such eminences as the legendary CBS correspondent-editorialist Eric Sevareid, the novelist Tom Heggen ("Mr. Roberts"), the humorist Max Shulman (many widely red magazine essays, best-selling books, movies, and TV shows).

I was quickly introduced to the basics of news reporting, the quick gathering of facts and accurate, objective reporting: First, focus on the five W's and the H – questions in the coverage of any news event that needed answers immediately: *What* had happened? *Who* was involved? *Where* had it happened? *When* had it happened? *How* had it happened? *Why* had it happened?

Students were instructed to acquire such information quickly; thoroughness was essential, but so was speed. Get the answers, organize your thinking, get to a typewriter and write the story as fast as coherence will allow, and – most importantly – *be objective*. Just tell the reader the answers to the five W's and the H. That's all. If you have an opinion keep it to yourself; don't impose it on the newspaper reader. He only wants the facts, not what you think about them. Insert your opinion into a news story and your editor will be entirely justified in advising you to seek employment elsewhere. Editorial writing, an essay in which you express y our opinion, *might* come later, if and when you mature as a competent observer and demonstrate a keen analytical instinct.

We learned by doing: One day as class began our instructor pointed out that ours was a huge campus, that all sorts of things that would be of interest to most students and teachers were going on all the time all over the place. We were to leave the classroom, go out separately, find stories worth the telling, do the necessary interviews, get back to the classroom, where we all had desks with typewriters, and get our stories written. We had 90 minutes. I don't remember all the different stories I came back with that quarter; most of them dealt with the school's athletes and athletic teams with, but the first was about a student with an extremely well educated dog, a Golden Retriever. On command, the dog would do fantastic gymnastic tricks on the mall, a gorgeous greensward stretching several blocks from the face of Northrup Auditorium, in the center of the campus, to Washington Avenue, a busy artery which divided the campus and, along with several other arteries, connected the Twin Cities. I found a sizable crowd of students watching and applauding as the dog would stand up on its hind legs and walk like a man, do somersaults, back flips, whatever its master asked for. I got the five W's and the H and got back to class and wrote the story in less than an hour. The instructor was highly approving. College life was good.

But then not so good. Instructors would order stories that I felt certain would bore the reader just as much as they bored me – meetings of the University's Board of Regents, meetings of the City Council, meetings of the city's Board of Education, union meetings, political speeches. They bored me to the extent that I had a hard time paying attention to what was being discussed at such events, which meant I had a hard time putting together coherent stories, which meant my stories came back to me with terrible grades and full of nasty but well deserved notations to the effect that no newspaper editor would tolerate such sloppy work. Thus was I made to understand that what was said and done at such meetings were important to a lot of people, and that I had better get interested and get it all properly reported, or find some other field of work.

I thought hard about that.

One instructor got so turned off on me when I was in this phase that he kept urging me to stop taking up space in the School of Journalism and get into some other field, Business, perhaps, or Botany; I seem to remember that "sanitation engineering" – janitorial work – was mentioned, too.

At the same time, I had a professor in Creative Writing who seemed convinced that I walked on water. One day, to my embarrassed astonishment, he insisted aloud to the whole class that they all would do well to "pay close attention to Mr. Hubbell's skillful use of the language." That made me very nervous, and aware of the glares and smirks of my classmates. It also made me feel wonderful. I thought that if only I could get him together with the Journalism instructor who so devoutly wished me gone that he might get him to agree that I was at least a mediocre person.

Stay on top of the news, we were constantly advised. Keep up with what is going on, in your town, your city, your state, your nation, your world. Often, there were surprise news quizzes on current events, and you had better have the answers to questions, for example, about the effort in the Middle East to found a state of Israel, and know who the key people were on all sides of the issue, and what their arguments were. You should know all that has been in the news about the Marshall Plan, the American effort to revive and save a shattered Europe. You should know what had been turned up in the so-called concentration camps of Germany. You should know what was happening at the war crimes trials, in Nuremburg. You should know how the World War II allies divided up Germany, and how the behavior of Josef Stalin, the leader of the Union of Soviet Socialist Republics (USSR), was discombobulating the Western Powers. You should know what is happening in Japan, under the leadership of General Douglas MacArthur. I was most interested in all of these important matters, and did well in the pop quizzes.

There was a course in Magazine Writing, in which we were required to go out and find an interesting subject somewhere, anywhere, write an interesting magazine piece and sell it to a magazine. We were *not* told that most college students were not going to be able to produce articles for which magazine editors would want to accord any space or pay any money, but rejection slips from authentic magazines could be submitted as proof of an authentic effort. I liked to play golf; in my grade school and high school years I had done a lot of caddying. I played now at a number of the public courses around the Twin cities. At one of them, I found a professional who had achieved great results from a well thought out effort to teach his members how to treat caddies. I wrote an article explaining how this had been accomplished and sent it to Golfdom, a magazine that dealt with the business side of the game. I received a $30 check in return., and my article was published. I was amazed; I reveled in seeing my name in a byline, and reading my work in a real magazine. My instructor seemed as pleased as I was, and held me up as a good example. Even the instructor who had wanted me gone congratulated me, and smiled at me.

If anyone else in the class ever sold a piece, I was not aware of it.

I thought that maybe someday I could get as much as $100 for a story.

There was a pleasant social side to life at the University. Many of my high school friends were members of the Delta Kappa Epsilon fraternity; they were "Dekes. And soon, I was a "Deke;" I gained a number of new, close friendships, several that would last a lifetime. There was plenty of partying, but college in those years immediately following World War II was an intensely serious business, Millions of veterans had returned from military service, many were married and had wives and children to support, but married or not most were anxious to make up for lost time. The competition for grades was fierce; anyone who wanted a degree in any field had to stay focused on academics.

I pulled myself together, stayed focused and earned my degree.

25
Andy to the Rescue

A s quickly as I had my college degree in hand, my father retired and my parents returned to New Jersey, whence we had come ten years earlier; they considered it their homeland. Having spent all of my high school and college years in Minnesota, I could see nothing for me back there. I was a dyed in the wool Minnesotan now, just as my brother, Woody, had been a confirmed Georgian when he had graduated from Emory. He had not been happy when he moved back to New Jersey. He had yearned for Atlanta, and his friendships there. I wouldn't make the same mistake Woody had made when he left Atlanta. For the time being, until I could somehow work my way into the wonderful world of magazine journalism, I would stay here, where all my friends were, and where I had acquired a job as a billing clerk.

One problem for this Minnesotan was that the billing clerk job did not pay enough to provide for living quarters that I thought appropriate to an alumnus of St. Thomas Academy and the University of Minnesota – or anyone else. Aware of my plight, Bill Andersen, whom everyone called Andy and who had become a close friend in high school, proposed that since he occupied only one of the two beds in his bedroom, I should take up the empty space in the other, and residence in the house he shared with his long widowed mother and a friend of hers. His mother was agreeable, and I was much relieved and happy to do so.

My memory is that I was a somewhat unruly guest whose behavior I, at a later age, would not have tolerated, and which sometimes raised Mrs. Andersen's ire. But I was young and, although very poorly paid, anxious to make the most of my newly achieved independence. I found it difficult to understand why it should upset her when, for example, I returned in the small hours from an evening of hijinks and, having forgotten my key to the house, had taken a ladder from the garage, stood it on the front walk so that I could climb up to the window of the bedroom I shared with Bill, awaken him to let me in and left the ladder on the standing on the front walk, something for her to contemplate as she left for work in the morning.

There were other such events. Bill was completing his college education that year, and while his attentions to his studies often precluded his accompanying me into the excitements of the nights, he did manage to participate in numerous joyous evenings. This did not please his mother, who sometimes seemed to imply that I was a corrupting influence.

But I have warm memories of Esther Andersen's innumerable kindnesses to me and her incredible patience during the year I spent in her home. And I am proud and happy still, 70-plus years since we first met, to be able to count my pal, Andy, as my pal, Andy.

26

Excitements in Gotham

In the autumn of 1957, when I had been two years with the Digest, I took Punkin on her first trip to New York, to see the great city she had never seen and to meet some Digest editors. We checked into the Park Sheraton Hotel, in a corner room on the sixth floor. It was mainly a short sightseeing trip for her, but we saw a lot more than we had counted on. For one thing, the young Queen Elizabeth was also on her first trip to the country, and she was visiting New York City. We were among the crowds that got a couple of glimpses of her – one of our glimpses of her included a glimpse of our own President, Dwight Eisenhower, who had come up from Washington to greet her.

On our first night in Gotham we dined and partied with our good friends, Eileen and Al Melia. Actually, they were best friends of my older brothers, and like them about ten years older than I. But Al had practically grown up in our house in Teaneck, and was like family.

He had graduated in the late 1930's from Fordham University's law school. Then, after a World War II stretch in the Navy, he served the City of New York as an assistant district attorney and now as a Deputy Police Commissioner. He was important enough to rate a limo and driver, and Punkin and I spent our first evening with them traveling to various interesting entertainment centers in the city, including the Tonight Show, then hosted by Jack Paar (and later by Johnny Carson, then Jay Leno and currently by Jimmy Fallon); and the Astor Hotel, where we listened to a large African-American fellow named Chubby Checkers sing a song called, "Rock round the Clock," which seemed to excite everyone who heard it.

The next morning I shaved, showered, dressed and told Punkin, who was still dressing, that I was going down to the lobby for a newspaper.

The lobby was crowded with news people; reporters and photographers were everywhere. I thought that some celebrity was coming in, hopefully someone like Ava Gardner. But the news was about a departure.

"Albert Anastasia got shot in the barbershop," a reporter told me.

This was the kind of thing that could have kept me interested in being a newspaper reporter – except that it wasn't the kind of story you could count on covering very day.

Anastasia had been well known as the "Lord High Executioner" of "Murder Incorporated"; in fact, he and another thug named Bugsy Siegel had invented the organization.

I took in as much of the scene as I could, as much as any other reporter on hand.

The barbershop was on the south side of the lobby, just inside a door to 55th Street. Outside, a few steps to the left of the door, was a stairway down to a subway stop. It had only been minutes since the murder had occurred, but the police already had the scene secured. I was able to get close enough to the barbershop to see a river of blood streaming out of it, into the hallway. Two handguns lay in the hallway, obviously had been tossed there by the assassins, who obviously had left through the door to 55th Street. A cop told me that according to the barber, two men had walked into the shop, waving him off to the side, then had stood directly behind Anastasia, who had reclined with a hot towel over his face, and fired several shots into the back of his head. The barber reported that Anastasia had been blasted out of he chair and fallen to the floor, as dead as he was ever going to be. The two assassins had then departed the barbershop, dropped their weapons in the hallway and departed through the door onto 55th Street.

Commissioner Melia showed up. "Nice place you pick to bring your bride," he said.

I had a brilliant question for him: "Who did it?"

"This was a million dollar hit," he said. "This was so important that each of the shooters probably was paid a million dollars, and as we speak they probably are on their ways to a country or countries that have no extradition treaties with the United States, and they will never return. But good riddance; and there will be more good riddance when we learn who ordered the hit. And sooner or later, we will learn who ordered it." (Decades later it would be learned that the hit had been ordered by Vito Genovese, leader of one of the city's five major crime families; he was unhappy over Anastasia's efforts to take over the Gambino outfit, one of the other families.)

I returned to our sixth floor digs and told Punkin what had happened.

"What an exciting town!" she exclaimed, excitedly.

Murder Incorporated was believed to have been involved in a thousand or more killings; some 300 were credited to Albert Anastasia himself. He had two brothers. One, "Tough Tony" Anastasia, ran the Brooklyn waterfront. The other, Father Gerardo Anastasia, was a Catholic priest in Brooklyn. I don't know whether or not he asked, but the Archdiocese of New York made it clear that there would be no Mass of Christian Burial nor interment in a Catholic Cemetery. Instead, there was a service in a Brooklyn funeral home, and an old-fashioned gangland-type cortege, complete with mountains of flowers, to a burial site in Greenpoint Cemetery, in Brooklyn. All the crime world's biggest chiefs attended.

We put the Anastasia murder behind us the very next evening. John Allen, a senior editor at the Digest who had become a good friend, and his vivacious wife, Elizabeth, whom everyone called Lidge, came down from their home in northern Westchester County to take us to the best seats in the house to see the biggest smash hit on Broadway, "Auntie Mame," starring Rosalind Russell. Lidge's father was the famous Dr. Norman Vincent Peale, author of a number of big best-sellers, including "The Power of Positive Thinking." First, we dined at Sardi's, a famous restaurant across the street from the theater. We preceded dinner with cocktails. John and I each had several martinis, and following what must have been a scrumptious dinner we had brandy. Following which we proceeded to our wonderful seats at the theater, in which seats John and I both fell asleep and missed the show. Punkin and Lidge said it was a wonderful show, and that we both snored.

There were many other trips east. Normally, I would fly into New York's LaGuardia Airport, rent a car and drive 45 miles up to Pleasantville. Not when Punkin came. Next time we were in the St. Moritz Hotel, on Central Park South. The desk called to say that, "Your limousine is waiting." It was about an hour's drive up to Katonah, a few miles north of Pleasantville, to a lovely cock-tail-dinner party at Edie and Hobe Lewis's place. The guest list included Executive Editor Kenneth Payne, Managing Editor Alfred "Fritz" Dashiell, Ralph Henderson – who invented Reader's Digest Condensed Books – Senior Editor William Hard, General Business Manager A.L. "Al" Cole and their wives. Lila and DeWitt Wallace were traveling and unable to be there, but it was a dazzling evening – not so much for Punkin as for me and all those others who had the pleasure of meeting her.

27

The Seven Dwarfs
of Manila Bay

"**D**o you mean to tell me," the lawyer asked, "that you let Dimi Tiomkin take an option on the motion picture rights for $500? Am I hearing you correctly?" He was looking at me with a face full of alarmed incredulity.

We were having lunch at the Brown Derby restaurant, in Hollywood. Tiompkin was a famous Hollywood composer. He had written the scores for a large number of celebrated movies, including High Noon, The High and the Mighty, The Old Man and the Sea, Giant, Friendly Persuasion, It's a Wonderful Life and many others; his shelves must be crowded with Oscars. He had called me one day in mid-1961 to ask if I would accept $500 for an option to buy the movie rights to a story I had written for The Reader's Digest. I said that would be fine with me, and it was; it was as unexpected as finding $500 in the street, and Tiomkin had been sending me a $500 check every year since, but had not made a movie. I had mentioned it to a friend in the publishing business in New York City, and had been advised that if my work was going to attract the attention of people in show business I had best arm myself with legal representation. Since I was on my way to the west coast on another story, my friend had picked up his telephone and arranged a luncheon meeting with this show business attorney.

"Yes," I said, hoping I didn't look like one of those dunces from Flyover Land, which, as I understand it, is how show business people refer to all the geography between New York City and Hollywood. Actors spend their entire lives becoming very wealthy by pretending to be other people. Flyover Land, on the other hand, is populated mainly with unsophisticated field hands who don't often pretend that they are other people, and who gulp, blush, kick at the ground and say "Golly, *sure!*" when sophisticated showbiz people in New York or Hollywood call them and talk about "options," or "deals," or "scripts," and offer them $500.

Listen, I have a high maintenance wife and a whole bunch of kids back in Flyover Land, and an extra $500 was okay with me.

"He sends me a $500 check every year," I pointed out to the Hollywood lawyer. "I enjoy that."

"You don't need a lawyer," the lawyer said. He seemed exasperated. "You need a *keeper*. Dimi Tiomkin is a major force in this town. The minute anyone in this town talks to you in those terms you *must* refer him to an attorney or an agent. The story you wrote was a great drama. It was good enough to fill eight pages in The Reader's Digest. An attorney or an agent would have pointed that out to him, that it had captivated the Digest's millions of readers, that millions of people would want to see a screen dramatization and that an option was worth much, much more than $500."

He had said that Dimitri Tiomkin is "a major force in this town," and he had called him, "Dimi." I felt like one of those Flyover Land dunces.

"Well," I said, meekly, "if he contacts me again, may I refer him to you?"

"Yes, of course. You *must*! And if he sends you another check, don't cash it. Send it to me, I'll contact him, and we'll engage in a sensible negotiation."

But I never heard from Tiomkin again, and I never got another $500 check from him; I missed it. I thought he must have decided to stick to music, and not become a movie producer. So I never talked to the lawyer again, which was okay with me because when I had talked to him I had felt like one of those dumb Flyover People, and wanted to pretend I was somebody else.

The story all this was about was entitled, "The Great Manila Bay Silver Operation." I had spent the summer of 1958 interviewing all the key people involved, and writing it, and it had appeared in the April, 1959, issue of the Digest.

The key people were U.S. Navy deep sea divers named Moses ("Moe") Solomon, Virgil L. "Jughead" Sauers, Wallace A. "Punchy" Barton, P.L. "Slim" Mann and George Chopchick..

Briefly, the story began in early 1942, when the Philippine government realized that the country was going to fall to the invading Japanese army, and that it must put its national treasury beyond the conqueror's reach. The serial numbers of hundreds of millions of dollars worth of paper currency were recorded, and the bills were burned. Millions of dollars worth of gold bullion and silver were shipped to San Francisco. But the Japanese were advancing rapidly, time was running short and 17 million silver pesos, each worth 50 cents, remained in bags inside wooden boxes in a steel vault on the island of Corregidor, in Manila Bay.

A contingent of U.S. Navy divers dumped the silver, 425 tons of it, in Caballo Bay, which was formed by Corregidor's curled tail. The water was deep and rough there, and it was thought that the Japanese, even if they knew about it, would be unlikely to try to retrieve it.

But the Japanese had excellent intelligence; they not only knew about the silver, they knew exactly where it was and who had dumped it. They decided to recover it and deliver it as a gift to the emperor. The American divers were returned from a prison camp at Cabanatuan, 90 miles distant, ensconced a barge fitted out like a plush hotel suite, with comfortable beds and furniture and all kinds of good food. They were told to consider themselves on professional assignment, that they would be treated with the respect due professionals and that no guards would bother them.

Among themselves, the divers agreed to deliver enough silver to the Japanese to keep them salivating, and to find ways to deliver as much as possible to Americans in prisons around Manila who could use it to bribe guards for food, medicines, whatever they needed.

They also agreed that sooner or later they would be caught and shot. But they were happy to be back in the war and in a position to thwart at least one of the enemy's schemes.

Through friendly Filipinos they funneled so much silver to Manila's Chinese moneychangers that the Japanese occupation currency collapsed. Soldiers were finding it hard to buy so much as a beer with yen; they needed silver pesos.

There were some close calls. Once, a suspicious, angry Japanese captain conducted a surprise inspection of the barge. He poked and prodded everywhere, upending mattresses, emptying cupboards and trying to free himself of "Moe" Solomon, who glued himself to the captain and presented a perfect picture of incredulous indignation, loudly and endlessly pointing out how tough it was to work in these rough waters, of the risks the divers were glad to take for their benevolent captors, of the large amounts of silver they had delivered. He dogged the captain's footsteps, stayed in front of him, described in detail how the boxes containing the silver had rotted, how they would fall apart when being lifted, how the bags of silver would fall to the sea bottom and how the divers spent more time than was safe scrambling about on the bottom and bringing up the bags that had nearly been lost.

At the same time, Solomon's shipmates were quietly lifting ten buckets of silver they had stolen and hidden in the barge's bilges and lowering them back to the bottom.

The captain found nothing.

By fall, the silver was all over Manila, and the Japanese were aware that their recovery effort was a laughingstock. There was a face-saving announcement that a recent typhoon had washed all the missing silver ashore that it had all been recovered and that the recovery project was over. The divers were sent to work as stevedores on Manila's docks. They spent the rest of the war loading Japanese cargo ships in ways likely to capsize them if they ran into rough seas.

I talked at length with all the divers who survived the war. None was wealthy. Only "Jughead" Sauers could show me a single silver peso he had kept as a souvenir. "We might have been the richest POWs ever," he said. "We were kind of like Snow White's seven dwarfs, carrying our buckets off to work every day and bringing them home full of silver at night. It was pretty good duty."

The Hollywood lawyer was right. It would have made a great movie, an option was worth much, much more than $500, and I was a Flyover Land dunderhead.

28

Nuclear Showdown

"*It shall be the policy of this nation to regard any nuclear missile launched from Cuba against any nation in the Western Hemisphere as an attack by the Soviet Union against the United States, requiring a full retaliatory response upon the Soviet Union.*"

Wow!

The speaker was John F. Kennedy, the 45-year-old President of the United States. The date was October 22, 1962. The address, a direct challenge to the Union of Soviet Socialist Republics (U.S.S.R.) was beamed to a worldwide audience. And the world held its breath, poised on the threshold of nuclear Armageddon.

The Soviets had been caught sneaking nuclear-armed ballistic missiles into Cuba, a mere 90 miles from Florida. They were well into the process of making an end run around the tacit policy of Mutual Assured Destruction (MAD). Since 1948, when the

U.S.S.R. had opened the Cold War with its blockade of free West Berlin, that policy had militated against either the United States or the Soviet Union, the world's only two nuclear powers, launching a disarming first-strike against the other. But now, from Cuba, the Soviets would be able to launch a no-warning strike that could, in a matter of a few minutes, literally, before we knew what had hit us, largely eliminate the American ability to strike back, incinerate many millions of Americans and lay radioactive waste to a great deal of the United States.

We had reached the nuclear brink. We were embarked on the most dangerous and terrifying international crisis in all of history.

Minutes after the President finished speaking my telephone in Minneapolis was ringing. It was Hobe Lewis. By noon the next day I was in the Digest's Washington bureau, meeting with him and others:

Fellow Digest Roving Editor Jim Daniel, whom I had not known before, had joined the magazine about a year earlier. He was nice looking, trim, with a graying crew cut and deceptively quiet-spoken. He once had been a city editor at the Washington Daily News, had done stints on the national reporting staff of Scripps-Howard, then with Time Magazine. He was well acquainted and knowledgeable in the political and diplomatic arenas, and would focus on them. I would focus on the military response.

Andy Jones had been a Marine fighter pilot in the Pacific during World War II and looked the part. Well set up, good humored, with a bright smile and enthusiastic, he retained a deep interest in military affairs. After the war he had worked as a reporter for the Newark (NJ) News. An avid outdoorsman, he then joined Field and Stream magazine as an editor before moving to the Digest

Gene Methvin, burly, outspoken and deeply suspicious of government, had grown up in a family newspaper business in Georgia. He had developed productive contacts everywhere in and around Washington. He was a bulldog of a reporter and was eager to chase down any information anyone thought was needed.

Jones and Methvin would help Daniel and I research in all areas.

Lewis was by now an Executive Editor, one of the magazine's top three editorial executives, but in reality was second only to DeWitt Wallace.

It was a grim, scary time. A Kremlin leadership that was crazy enough to do this might be crazy enough to do anything; someone on the ground, in Cuba, might misunderstand an order, or miscalculate. If nuclear shots were fired, our nation's capital would surely be one of the enemy's prime targets; so, surely, was New York City, the world's financial center. We all wondered if we would ever see our families again. Kennedy had thrown down the gauntlet, and no one knew what would happen.

We had a report that an exodus was underway from Capitol Hill, that many members of Congress and their staffs had already retreated to their Districts, and more were leaving. There was a report of a run on supermarkets and grocery stores throughout the Washington metropolitan area; customers were clearing shelves of canned goods, bottled water and other staples.

What to do?

If nuclear war erupted we all would soon be dead. If it did not, we were embarked, with every other major journalistic enterprise, on the story of the century. Through us, The Reader's Digest would have its say. A monthly magazine, we were not in competition with the daily media, newspapers, radio and television news operations or weekly newsmagazines. Our big advantage was that we had time thoroughly to research every aspect of the confrontation, the ability to provide our many millions of readers around the world with everything that was worth knowing about this earth-shaking turn of events.

On the other hand, Lewis wanted a book-length feature, a 20,000-to-30,000-word piece that would run in the back of the magazine, where book condensations usually ran, and he didn't want it a year from now. He wanted a comprehensive history researched and written in quick-time. Daniel and I would co-author.

There was much spirited discussion. It turned out that we all were of one mind about our government's conduct concerning Cuba. In his inaugural address on January 20, 1961, Kennedy had stirred America's pride with his assertion that we would, "pay any price, bear any burden meet any hardship, support any friend, oppose any foe in order to assure the survival and success of liberty."

In late 1959 a revolutionary named Fidel Castro had toppled the corrupt government of Dictator Fulgencio Batista. Batista's closest friends and supporters had included leaders of the American mafia. Even so, Cuba's people had at least been free, and Cuba, with its beaches, resorts and casinos, had had been a playground for many Americans, who left lots of money there. At first, Castro was widely assumed to be a friend of democracy, but he soon made it clear that he was no such thing, that he was an admirer and ally of the U.S.S.R., and set about transforming Cuba into a Soviet bastion, from which the Kremlin would be able to extend its influence into the Americas. Castro quickly demonstrated himself to be a murderous tyrant. He kept his prisons full and his firing squads very busy executing many who were even thought to have opposed him.

In the spring of 1960, the Eisenhower Administration, in its waning days, became aware of armed resistance within Cuba to Castro, and decided that it would be in the United States' interest to get rid of him. Among other things, the Central Intelligence Agency (CIA) recruited some 1400 anti-Castro Cuban exiles who had reached Florida who hoped to recover their homeland. The CIA provided them with an invasion plan, trained them, armed them, and was authorized to promise them all of the American air support they would need in their effort to retake their country. It was assumed that an invasion would inspire the armed resistance that already existed inside Cuba, and would ignite a popular uprising that would bring Castro down.

Kennedy succeeded Eisenhower as President, and, in his ringing inaugural address had given hope to the world's oppressed. On April 17, the CIA's anti-Castro invasion force was transported to the Bahia de Cochinos, the Bay of Pigs, on the south coast of Cuba, and there the United States abandoned it. The air support the force had been promised was not forthcoming, even though plenty of air support was available, some of it aboard a U.S. Navy aircraft carrier, just over the horizon. At the very last minute Kennedy decided that in deference to world opinion the United States could not appear to be involved. Many in the abandoned invasion force were slaughtered, and many captured.

Most of the world, including many Americans, considered the Administration's performance contemptible, a disgrace.

Administration spokesmen tried to assign blame to the military leadership, the Joint Chiefs of Staff, the CIA, everywhere but where it belonged, to a failure of courage in the Oval Office of the White House.

Most Americans thought that Kennedy had demonstrated during World War II that he did not lack for personal courage. But now he was the leader of the free world, and it was a new world of atomic weaponry; he had to be concerned with the safety of hundreds of millions of lives, with the very survival of his country. But he had lost the respect of much of the world by withholding vital support from the force he had sent in at the Bay of Pigs.

The background to this situation was that a little more than a year earlier, in June, 1961, Kennedy had met in Vienna for the first time with the Soviet Premier, Nikita Khrushchev, and knew that he had left him with the impression that he was a weakling who could easily be bullied and bluffed. In fact, Khruschev, convinced that Kennedy would not challenge him, had decided to demonstrate to the world that the Kremlin was calling all the shots, that the decadent Americans and their allies in the West were in terminal decline, and that the U.S.S.R. was certain to win the Cold War. He would hurry things along by installing a nuclear arsenal in Cuba. The Americans would surely object, but he could deal with the fearful Kennedy. He would demand an American withdrawal from West Berlin, which had long been a bone in the Soviet throat. Confronted with a nuclear threat from nearby Cuba, Kennedy would have no choice but to agree. When the Americans caved in and retreated from Berlin, their allies, the British and the French, would have no alternative but to follow suit. Khrushchev would continue to brandish the Soviet will to use its military might, keep pushing the Western Allies until they were out of West Germany, keep it up until eventually the U.S.S.R. controlled all of Europe.

The establishment of a nuclear missile capability in Cuba was a giant step in what Khrushchev planned to be the final chapter of the Cold War.

But Kennedy's response had been nothing if not tough. He had let the world know that the latest Soviet move would not stand. It surely had all of us who met in the Digest's Washington bureau psyched up, anxious to be supportive of him, anxious to show the the magazine's many millions of readers worldwide how tough, how strong America could be when she had to be. The Soviets were the world's bullies, and our young President had called Khrushchev out, had made us proud, of him and America.

We combed every published news story and analysis as quickly as it appeared. We fanned out; together and singly we interviewed everyone in the relevant agencies who would talk to us, the State Department, the Defense establishment, the Central Intelligence Agency and the White House, every member of Congress who had anything to do with intelligence, armed services and foreign policy. A picture emerged quickly:

When World War II ended, the victorious Allied Powers, the U.S., Britain, France and the Union of Soviet Socialist Republics (U.S.S.R.) had agreed to divide defeated Germany into four zones, each occupied and governed by one of them. The Soviets had been granted all of the eastern half of Europe, which included the eastern portion of Germany, which included Berlin; but they didn't get all of Berlin. They were allowed to occupy the eastern side of Germany's former capitol city; the United States, Britain and France each governed sectors of West Berlin.

Not satisfied with all of Eastern Europe, the Soviets wanted all of Berlin. In June, 1948, they had tried to force the Western Powers out. They blockaded all surface access, all roads, rail lines and waterways into West Berlin, and made the city's 2,000,000 people their hostages. They would starve them of food, fuel and other vital necessities, such as the coal and clothing they would need to survive Berlin's harsh winter, until the Western Powers gave in and departed. The Soviet Premier at the time, the murderous Josef Stalin, judged that the Americans, British and French all were war weary and softhearted, had no stomach for a military confrontation, would not challenge the blockade and would not want to be responsible for the deaths by starvation and freezing of hundreds of thousands of Berliners.

The Truman Administration responded with history's most incredible humanitarian feat, a year-long, round-the-clock airlift, nearly 300,000 flights, landing at West Berlin's Templehof and Tegel Airdromes every three minutes, delivering daily millions of tons of food, coal and clothing. The Soviets were made to look to the rest of the world like the brutes they were. They gave up and lifted the blockade in May, 1949.

By 1960 noisy, aggressive, nasty, baldheaded, colorful Nikita Khrushchev was Premier, and no less interested than Stalin had been in evicting the Western Powers from Berlin and Europe. By now, 12 years after the Berlin blockade, West Berlin's war wounds were largely healed. It had been rebuilt, and in the free market environment fostered by the Western powers, glittered like a showcase jewel, in stark contrast to the dark poverty the communists had imposed on the eastern side of the city and on all of Eastern Europe. The communists built a concrete wall dividing East Berlin from the rest of the city so that its residents could not escape to the good life that was so visible on the other side of the city. The wall was topped with barbed wire and machine gun towers so that no one could escape to the West, but many died trying.

West Berlin had remained a prime Soviet target, and after meeting with Kennedy in Vienna and determining him to be a pushover, Khrushchev saw no danger in a scheme he devised to take it.

By the autumn of 1962 rumors were rife in diplomatic circles that Khrushchev planned to come to the United States in November and require Kennedy to agree to withdraw from Berlin. He believed that when Kennedy found himself facing nuclear guns aimed at the United States from Cuba, the threat of a no-warning strike that would largely disarm and decimate the United States, he would see that he had no option but to give into Soviet demands and abandon Berlin.

Throughout the spring and summer of 1962 the American media, which at the time was reasonably objective and pro-American and certainly pro-Kennedy, delivered a constant stream of reports that the Soviets were stuffing Castro Cuba with arms, including fighter aircraft and short range guided missiles. Hundreds of Russian and Czechoslovakian military technicians were said to be in the country, and there were reports that more and more Soviet troops were reaching Cuba every day.

On August 31 Senator Kenneth Keating (R., NY) asserted that he had information verified by U.S. government officials that, "between August 8 and August 15 at the Cuban port of Mariel 10 to 12 large Soviet vessels unloaded 1200 troops wearing Soviet fatigue uniforms," and that large Soviet motor convoys were moving along Cuba's roads.

The Kennedy Administration did not want to hear such things, and denied having any evidence supporting Keating's report.

When Keating repeated his warning on NBC-TV, Kennedy's Press Secretary, Pierre Salinger, called the network to complain that Keating's statements were "untrue." He got the interviewer to bring on another senator, Clair Engle (D., CA), Chairman of the Democratic Campaign Committee to declare that Keating, "didn't get his facts right," that he, "was just as wrong as he could be."

But Keating persisted, claimed that six missile-launching sites were under construction in Cuba, "pads capable of hurling missiles into the heartland of the United States and as far as the Panama Canal Zone."

By October 12, Keating had delivered ten warnings on the floor and had reiterated his charge in more than a dozen other venues. He kept demanding action.

Throughout this season of dire warnings Kennedy Administration "Kremlinologists" and "experts" in the State Department kept reassuring the President and the public, pointing out that the Soviets never had stationed nuclear weapons outside of their homeland, not even in any of the Warsaw Pact countries (the Warsaw Pact included several eastern European countries that had been taken under control by the Soviets; it was the communist response to NATO). According to these "experts" it was more than doubtful that they ever would do so and that assertions and so-called evidence to the contrary was not to be taken seriously.

But the media remained full of reports from Cuban refugees of a great deal of late night activity, huge truckloads of long, cylindrical objects being hauled off of ships and taken away to undisclosed destinations. "Experts" explained that these likely were sections of sewer pipe; moreover, that they were being hauled by vehicles whose descriptions did not comport with the amount of horsepower required to move Soviet missiles.

But ominous evidence continued to accrue, and professional intelligence analysts in both the CIA and the Defense Department became increasingly uneasy. They were noting that in recent weeks the U.S.S.R. had cancelled many private charters; the big ships arriving in Cuba were all Soviet. And they wondered why nothing ever was carried above decks, where it could be seen? Why all the dark of night activity? The unloading of a great deal of military equipment; the middle-of-the-night motor convoys along the roads; the debarking of large troop contingencies; and why were so many troops needed? What was going on? What were the Soviets up to?

By early August John McCone, Kennedy's CIA Director, was warning the White House that the Kremlin might well install offensive missiles in Cuba. A few weeks later he talked of mounting danger.

The Administration continued to rely on the judgments it was getting from State Department "Kremlinolgists," but by August 29 was taking matters seriously enough to send a U-2 reconnaissance flight over Cuba. The U-2 was equipped with fantastic photographic capabilities. It returned with photography that revealed clusters of Soviet surface-to-air missiles (SAMs) in western Cuba. The Soviets or Castro Cuba would explain that obviously the purpose of the SAM sites was to defend Cuba against a U.S. aerial assault; that in view of the American effort at the Bay of Pigs, the Castro government had every right to fear such an assault.

Almost certainly professional analysts would have suggested that another and more likely purpose of the SAMs was to protect offensive weapons yet to be installed that were capable of reaching targets in the United States.

On September 11, the voluble Khrushchev, doubtless aware of the suspicions being fanned by Senator Keating and much of the American press, asserted that the missiles with which the U.S.S.R. could deliver its nuclear warheads were so powerful that there was no need to install them anywhere beyond the Soviet Union – "for instance," he said, "Cuba." He said that the weapons being sent to Cuba were "purely defensive," and warned that a U.S. attack on Soviet shipping or on Cuba would unleash nuclear war.

New York Times columnist James "Scotty" Reston, at the time the respected dean of Washington pundits, wondered if someday soon "the fair white city of Miami might disappear under a mushroom cloud".

These reports and musings were dismissed by Kennedy's "Kremlinologists." They kept the Administration calm and kept trying to calm the public, pointing out that responsible governments simply did not do things secretly with nuclear weapons, and that the Kremlin certainly knew that the United States would not tolerate a nuclear weapons buildup in the Caribbean. It was absurd to think that the Soviets would provide a two-bit madman like Castro with such weaponry. The argument seemed to make sense.

But Senator Keating kept issuing warnings, the media kept publishing them and issuing warnings of its own, and they were having an effect on the public's nerves. President Kennedy had recently been awarded a Pulitzer Prize for his book, "Profiles in Courage," a series of chapters about American political leaders who had had the courage to stand firm on important issues in the face of seemingly contrary evidence and overwhelming public opinion. When Kennedy arrived in New Haven one day that autumn to make a speech at Yale University he found himself confronted by a crowd of students holding placards calling for, "More Courage, Less Profile."

The "Kremlinolgists" insistence that it would be absurd to think that the Soviets would install nuclear weapons in Cuba proved to be absurd itself on Monday, October 15. Photo intelligence analysts at the National Photographic Interpretation Center in Washington found themselves staring at photography just delivered from two U-2 flights that had been made a day earlier across the length of Cuba. They revealed Soviet ballistic missile sites, complete with intermediate range missiles, launching pads and erector-launchers at six different sites – just as Senator Keating had warned. Launchers already stood on half the pads, and others were being moved into position. Large buildings now stood where none had stood a few months earlier, presumably sites where missiles could be stored and made ready to fire. There were huge motor pools, and a tent city for troops. More than half of the U.S. retaliatory force's bases and every major American city except Seattle were now within range of a no-warning nuclear attack.

As the U-2's were collecting this proof McGeorge Bundy, Kennedy's National Security Advisor, was on ABC-TV's Issues and Answers program answering host Edward P. Morgan's questions about what was happening in Cuba. Bundy said, "I don't myself think that there is any present – I *know* there is no present evidence, and I think there is no present likelihood that the Cubans and the Cuban government and the Soviet government would in combination attempt to install a major offensive capability...everything the Soviet Union has delivered to Cuba falls within the categories of aid which the U.S.S.R. has provided to such neutral states as Egypt or Indonesia, and I should not be surprised to see additional military assistance of the sort. That is not going to turn an island of six million people with five or six thousand Soviet technicians and specialists into a major threat to the United States, and I believe that most of the American people do not share the views of the few who have acted as if suddenly this kind of military support has created a mortal threat to us. It does not."

That evening the appropriate officials were notified that a mortal threat to the United States was about to go operational in Cuba.

First, Bundy: He was hosting a dinner party at his Georgetown home. He was shocked; what to do? He took the information to bed with him. Later, in his White House office, he admitted to Jim Daniel and me that earlier he had found the arguments of the "Kremlinologists" to be convincing. He now told us that if he had simply made some calls to any of several intelligence agencies in Washington he would have known better than to say what he had said on the Issues and Answers program.

I was curious as to Bundy's behavior when he received the terrifying intelligence. I pointed out that upon learning that the ship of state was in grave danger, he, the President's National Security advisor, had decided not to tell the President until the next morning. I wondered if it was his prerogative to make such a decision, to delay in delivering such information to the Chief Executive. When a government that clearly is an enemy of the United States is found to be placing ballistic missiles on an island a few miles from the American mainland, shouldn't that intelligence be transmitted immediately to the Commander-in-Chief, and all the decisions concerning the situation be made by him, and not by an appointed aide?

Bundy's explanation was that "there were dinner parties going on all over town that night" and that he feared that the President might, "get excited, start summoning people to the White House, calling meetings, sending intelligence signals to the Soviets that they had been found out and give them a chance to do something about it." He insisted that all that could be done that night was being done. He also told us that there now were more than 20,000 Soviet troops in Cuba, several times more than "five or six thousand," as he had told his TV viewers.

Bundy recalled that early on the morning of October 16 he had entered the President's bedroom and found Kennedy sitting on the edge of his bed, in pajamas and robe, reading the morning newspapers. He said, "Mr. President, there is now hard photographic evidence, which you will see a little later, that the Soviets have offensive missiles in Cuba."

The bad news didn't seem to create a lot of anxiety among America's governing leadership. When the State Department's Chief of Intelligence, Roger Hilsman, got confirmation that Soviet ballistic missiles were about to go operational in Cuba, he telephoned Secretary of State Dean Rusk, who was preparing to host a dinner for West German Foreign Minister Gerhard Schroeder. Rusk decided to call for a full briefing and discussion on the matter the next morning.

Edwin M. Martin, Assistant Secretary of State for Latin America, was speaking to a meeting of the Sigma Delta Chi Professional Journalism Society at the National Press Club, explaining that Cuba posed no military threat to the United States. An aide stood nearby to tell Martin, as he finished speaking, that could not have been more wrong about everything he had just told the media.

Kennedy huddled with his advisors, tried to divine Khrushchev's thinking. For months the Soviet leader had been telling visitors that, "the United States is too liberal to fight." He had listed the ample clear evidence of America's lack of spine: For years when the Americans had owned a clear-cut advantage with nuclear weapons, when they were the world's only real military superpower, they had done nothing to prevent Soviet expansion into vast areas of the world. They had done nothing to forestall the communist subjugation of all of Eastern Europe. They had sacrificed oceans of blood and treasure for a stalemate in Korea. Perhaps the most convincing display of America's lack of fortitude had occurred only a year earlier, at Cuba's Bay of Pigs, on the American doorstep.

We kept digging. We learned that U.S. Navy reconnaissance aircraft had discovered in September, weeks before the U-2 photography was collected, that the Soviets were delivering IL-28 strategic bombers to Cuba. The Administration had never disputed Soviet assurances that the military weaponry it was sending to Cuba was purely defensive in nature; we wondered how such offensive weapons systems as strategic bombers fit into a so-called "defensive posture".

A second U-2 flight was made on October 3, then no more until October 14. A White House spokesman explained the eleven-day hiatus: "Hurricane Ella delayed flights for a week, then a cloud cover blocked high level surveillance."

As a matter of journalistic routine we checked this out at the Weather Bureau and found it to be a lie. Weather was never a factor over Cuba during those eleven days.

Now, having ignored or misinterpreted the months-long flood of intelligence, the Administration had to act or not act. To act might well trigger nuclear war. To fail to act would be to cede military superiority and all that it made possible for the U.S.S.R.

At last, the Administration acted.

No leader in history ever has spoken from a position of such overwhelming strength as did President Kennedy on the October evening when he demanded that the missiles be removed. The moment he began lights and numbers were flashing on display screens at every key U.S. command post in the world. With a single exception all elements of the American military went to Defense Condition (DefCon) 3. There are five DefCons: DefCon 5 is the normal peacetime alert posture; DefCon 2 is the most stringent, which puts a unit a on a full war footing, from which it needs but one signal to go to DefCon 1, at which point it is at war. The single Command which did not go to DefCon 3 was the Strategic Air Command (SAC); it went to DefCon 2.

In mid-afternoon, several hours prior to the President's address, SAC launched its bomber force and pressed it flush against the Soviet radar system, made it clearly visible to the denizens of the Kremlin.[5]

Added to that, the U.S. Navy had blockaded Cuba; no Soviet ships were going to reach the island without first being boarded and inspected by the Americans. And added to that, a great deal of tactical airpower and sizable components of U.S. Army and Marine Corps infantry had been rushed into the land and sea neighborhoods around Cuba. There was no question that Kennedy meant business, that the United States was very rapidly preparing for nuclear war.

As he listened to Kennedy's assertion that the making of Cuba into a Soviet ballistic missile base was unacceptable, Nikita Khrushchev had to know that the United States was fully prepared to lay the explosive equivalent of 30 billion tons of TNT upon the Soviet Union.

With America's history since the end of World War II in mind, and along with Kennedy's performances at the Bay of Pigs and at their meeting in Vienna, Khrushchev must have wondered how he could have been so wrong. What factor had he overlooked?

Certainly neither he nor his advisers, if he had any, understood the workings of a democratic republic. Convinced he could bully his way to final victory in the Cold War, he had taken a step too far. The overlooked factor was in plain sight: It was the overwhelming pressure to act applied by the American people. Senator Keating's

---

[5] Its fleet of KC-135 refueling tankers would enable the bomber force to remain visible to the Soviets for 30 days and nights.

persistent warnings, echoed by competent, objective editorialists and commentators had resulted in an unceasing and continually growing tidal wave of telegrams, telephone calls and letters to the White House and to Congressional offices with an increasingly impatient demand: *Do something!* If the Administration ever had considered the presence of Soviet ballistic missiles on an island 90 miles from Florida to be acceptable, the American people had made it clear that they would not stand for it.

Still, events in the days following were harrowing: the Defense Department announced that 25 Russian ships continued on headings for Cuba.

Khrushchev kept blustering, persisting in the lie that the weapons being sent to Cuba were "purely defensive".

On Wednesday morning the Defense Department announced that 25 Soviet ships continued to head for Cuba.

The same afternoon it was announced that many had turned back or gone dead in the water.

On Thursday morning a Soviet oil tanker was boarded and found to be carrying nothing but oil. It was allowed through the blockade; Kennedy wanted a first seizure to involve a cargo of offensive weapons.

On Friday the White House announced that new reconnaissance showed the Russians to be rapidly proceeding with work on the missile sites; there was no indication that any were being dismantled. The President said that the missiles must be removed from Cuba, or that "further action will be justified." A member of Congress who was in a position to know surmised that a bombing of the sites "could not be far away".

But Attorney General Bobby Kennedy, the President's brother and a member of ExComm, the Executive committee that was managing the situation, said, "My brother is not going to be the Tojo of the 1960's."[6]

No one knew what to make of that.

That night, Khrushchev sent a rambling message to Kennedy; he seemed almost incoherent, but basically agreed that the weapons at issue were not defensive. He seemed to say that they would be removed if the U.S. would agree not to invade Cuba.

On Saturday morning Khrushchev, who must have been under terrific pressure from his political opponents in the Kremlin, became belligerent again, insisting that the missiles would be removed from Cuba only if Kennedy first removed American Jupiter missiles from Turkey. That same morning a Soviet surface-to-air missile fired from Cuba brought down an American U-2, and the pilot, Air Force Major Rudolf Anderson, Jr., was killed. For some hours, war seemed inevitable. This was the darkest moment of the week. In a memo I wrote mapping out our account of the events, I called it, "Black Saturday".

Kennedy ignored Khrushchev's proposal for a missile swap; first things first, he said: the missiles must be removed from Cuba. Then, the United States would end the blockade.

On Sunday morning Khrushchev messaged Kennedy that he had ordered that the missile sites be dismantled, and that "the arms you described as offensive" would be crated and returned to the Soviet Union.

In my memo mapping out the story, I called it, "Sunny Sunday."

---

[6] Hideki Tojo was prime minister of Japan when the December 7, 1941, attack on Pearl Harbor was launched.

So ended the crisis.

We got the book written. It was published the following March, to a lot of good reviews.

Soon, the Jupiter missiles were removed from Turkey.

Two years after his failed gambit, Khrushchev's political opposition in the Kremlin removed him from power.

About forty years later Khrushchev's son, Sergei, now an American citizen, produced an article for American Heritage magazine in which he revealed that throughout the crisis week his father remained highly agitated, near or in a state of panic. The tough American response had been a shocking surprise to him. What frightened him most was that there were about 25,000 Soviet troops on the island, and this force was equipped with tactical nuclear weapons, designed for use in land warfare. Khrushchev's anxiety, his son reported, was due to the fact that he had little faith in the communications systems that linked him with his military commanders in Cuba. He feared that if the United States invaded, the Soviets' on-scene commanders, facing overwhelming force, would use their battlefield nukes in defense, and that if they did so it would surely trigger the nuclear response upon the U.S.S.R. that Kennedy had promised. He needed desperately to reach his field commanders with orders to not, under any circumstances, use their battlefield nuclear weapons, and needed to be reassured by them that they would not do so, for he no longer doubted American resolve. He knew now that the Cold War was not going to end anytime soon.

29

Cuba – After Action Report

As quickly as Hobart Lewis had organized the Digest's missile crisis team he blundered. He had written a letter to Pierre Salinger, Kennedy's Press Secretary, advising him of the Digest's interest, asking for the Administration's cooperation and promising him that to ensure that we did not inadvertently compromise national security we would clear with him anything that we planned to publish. Now, prior to publication of the book, he had sent him a copy of the completed manuscript.

None of which should have happened. The Soviet attempt to install nuclear missiles in Cuba was a world-shaking, world-changing event that was going to be covered by every journalistic enterprise in the world. We were the world's most widely read publication, and we certainly were going to provide Digest readers with as close to a definitive account as we could produce. For one thing, the Administration should have been anxious for the world to know the truth. For another, the White House really had nothing whatever to say about who covered the story, and should surely want to cooperate with us, if for no other reason than that the Digest was an American company, well and widely known for its patriotic impulses.

Secondly, it made no sense to offer to clear anything we wrote with the President's Press Secretary, even for security purposes; he was not an arbiter of national security, and it was not up to him to decide whether or how much the government should cooperate with us. The U.S. government belonged to the people, and the American people had a right to expect the government to cooperate with those who were working to get information to them concerning national security, how well or how ineffectively they were being protected. We were going to examine the government's performance closely, talk to everyone who had anything worth telling us, and we were as determined as any of them to guard the country's secrets. Moreover, we knew that our sources, particularly those in the military and intelligence agencies, would not be telling or showing anyone, including us, things neither we nor the country's adversaries needed to know. Additionally, it had long been our practice when questions of national security arose to consult with our sources and the proper agency of government as to whether or not a given piece of information should be published. Whenever we were shown even a possibility that publication might be detrimental to the nation's security, we had not used it.

In any case, we had not produced the laudatory account that we had, at the start, assumed it would be, or that Pierre Salinger thought it should be. It was unlike most of the other newspaper and magazine accounts that had appeared, which generally had been praiseworthy of the Administration's performance.

Our account depicted in detail the flood of warnings over a period of months in the media and from the floor of the Senate and elsewhere, demanding to know what the Soviets were up to in Cuba, while the Administration continued to issue denials and words of comfort based on the judgments of its foreign policy "experts" and its so-called "Kremlinologists." The inattention, misinformation and bungling that had attended the Administration's behavior until it was almost too late led us to the judgment that it had been prepared to accept the presence of Soviet strategic power in Cuba, that it had finally felt compelled to act in response to irresistible public pressure that had been aroused by Senator Keating and numerous editorialists.

Salinger was furious. On a January Saturday he called Lewis and demanded his presence Sunday afternoon in the White House, advising him in ominous tones that, "The President wants to talk to you."

Lewis called each of us who were involved; he was nervous about a confrontation with the President, and needed support. By Sunday afternoon he was in the Oval Office, where Kennedy greeted him with a handshake and a smile, saying, "I keep trying to explain to Pierre that we can't expect everyone to like everything we do, but he gets all excited and…" immediately, he turned the conversation to the current status of mutual friends.

Meanwhile, the rest of us were finding Salinger to be apoplectic. We listened to a long, obscene rant; if there is an obscenity or profanity that he did not utter, a bad name that he did not call us, it was only because it had not yet been invented. One had the strong impression that he wanted the book withdrawn, a public disavowal and apology from the Digest and doubtless he wanted all of us to be fired. A high-ranking officer of the CIA was also in the room, quietly paging through the manuscript. Salinger shouted at him to, "Show them! Show them all the security breaches!" At length, the CIA officer laid the manuscript down, saying, "In all honesty, Pierre, I can't find any security breaches."

Which was because there were none.

Salinger did not know that the man from CIA had been one of our sources, and who on this as well as on other occasions had guarded us against security violations. Salinger kept fuming and sputtering. "Well, how about the wordage, the use of the word, 'DefCon,' how about *that*?"

People were trying not to smirk and giggle. Was he actually suggesting that the contraction of the words "Defense Condition" was a military secret?

At last, almost bursting with anger, Salinger announced loudly that, "You'll never get another goddam ounce of cooperation out of this Administration!"

When we finished the book we couldn't agree on a title. There were many suggestions, but none sounded great to all of us; we all wanted something really dramatic, something that would excite the imagination, make people want to read the book, understand what the Soviets and Castro had tried to do and why it had been so important to stop them. Finally, a student of ancient history on the editorial staff in Pleasantville called our attention to the strategic wisdom of an eighth century Chinese strategician named Tu Yu. Tu Yu had advised that the best chance of efficiently acquiring a target lay in deception, to "Make a noise in the east, and strike in the West." We agreed that the Soviets were taking a page from Tu Yu's strategic lessons, that the reason for the missiles in Cuba would come clear with a Soviet demand that we abandon West Berlin.

So how about "Strike in the West" for a title. We all agree that it's dramatic, attention getting, a winner. We love it. The people at Holt, Rinehart and Winston, the company that will publish the hard cover edition, love it, too; they think it will sell lots of books.

The book reached the stores in March, 1963. It received many positive reviews. U.S. News and World Report magazine devoted three pages to it, and it spent some time on the Washington Post's best-seller list. Holt did a good job of promoting and advertising it – "Bound to be 1963's hottest best seller!" its ads proclaimed. Jim Daniel and I appeared on numerous television and radio talk shows, and several news organizations published lengthy interviews with us..

But it didn't do as well as we had hoped, and I think I know why. DeWitt Wallace didn't like our title at all. He thought people would think that a book entitled "Strike in the West" was about a longshoremen's strike on the west coast. He scratched it from the condensation that appeared in the magazine and replaced it with his own title, "While America Slept." Millions of people read our work in the magazine and were impressed. We know that because it not only generated a huge mail response, it came in high on the magazine's reader poll. I believe that if we had used Wally's title on the book it would have been a much bigger best-seller.

One more reason why Wally got the big bucks.

30
The Hilsman Story

During the missile crisis Jim Daniel and I both met a number of times with Roger Hilsman, the State Department's Director of Research and Intelligence. Roger was very friendly and gregarious. He briefed us and answered our every question at detailed length. He showed us the reconnaissance photos of the missile sites, and explained what the various pieces of equipment around the sites were. After a couple of meetings with him I wrote a bare bones, approximately six-page outline of the story as we thought it had developed and planned to write it; we did not include any opinions because we had not yet formed any. I took it to Roger to make sure we had everything straight. He assured me that we had it right, and asked if he could keep a copy of the outline. I made the mistake of allowing him to do so.

Shortly, the Saturday Evening Post came out with a sensational article on the crisis by Stewart Alsop, then one of Washington's important pundits. What made it sensational was Alsop's quote of "a high level Administration official" that, "Adlai wanted a Munich". The official was not identified. The reference was to Adlai Stevenson, who had made the United States' case citing Soviet treachery at the United Nations. The clear meaning was that Stevenson had wanted the Kennedy Administration to back off, appease Khrushchev as British Prime Minister Neville Chamberlain had appeased Hitler at Munich in 1938, preserve peace in 1962 by accepting the fact of Soviet strategic power in Cuba.

In fact, Stevenson's performance at the U.N. had been strong, and to say that he "wanted a Munich," was a disgraceful slander.

But what really amazed Daniel and me about the Alsop article was that it was full of the exact phraseology I had used in the outline I had left with Roger Hilsman; it even named the final two days of the crisis what I – and no one else – had ever named them: "Black Saturday" and "Sunny Sunday."

I did not believe at the time and have never believed that Alsop had deliberately plagiarized; he was too good a reporter and writer to do such a thing, so I never called him on it and never discussed it with him. I do believe and have always believed that Roger Hilsman, who was untutored in the ways of journalism, probably handed a copy of my outline to him saying something like, "Here's a good account of the whole thing" – he had said so to me, in almost those exact words. My outline had no names on it, and Alsop had no way of knowing that it was the work of another journalist. He probably took it to be a State Department press handout, was in a hurry to meet a Saturday

Evening Post deadline, found the writing acceptable and incorporated it with his own.

After our book was published I did return to Hilsman's office to ask him about it, but before I could get a word in he launched upon an angry tirade over our less than enthusiastic view of the Administration's performance. It was nothing like Salinger's obscene rant, but he did characterize the book as a terrible misrepresentation of the way things had been handled. I sat quietly, listening, knowing that we had it right, knowing that he knew we had it right and assuming that as a high official of the Kennedy Administration, this irate critique was something he felt bound to deliver. When he finished he asked, "Do you have any dinner plans?"

Having none, I accepted his invitation to dinner at his home in Chevy Chase, along with his lovely wife, Eleanor, and Eleanor's lovely mother, whose name I don't remember. One reason I thought Eleanor's mother was lovely was that she asked me how our book was doing. I replied that, "Roger doesn't like it, but we're getting good reviews." Whereupon she glared at Roger and said something, and he seemed embarrassed. We didn't pursue the subject. We had a great dinner.

That evening Roger told me a great story, which appeared later in the Digest under the title, "The Secret Mission of Lieutenant Hilsman." Here it is in a nutshell:

At the outset of World War II Roger's father, an Army colonel, visited with Roger, then a Cadet at West Point. The senior Hilsman had orders to the Philippines, and his parting gift to Roger was a small metal case that held cigarette packs so that the cigarettes wouldn't be crushed. When the Japanese invaded the Philippines Roger's father disappeared.

Roger never believed that his missing father was dead; he felt certain that he was a prisoner of war somewhere in the Far East. Graduating from West Point, Roger fought with Merrill's Marauders in Southeast Asia, then transferred to a combat unit of the Office of Strategic Services (OSS), which later would morph into the Central Intelligence Agency, (CIA). Intelligence sources somehow located Roger's father in a prison camp near Mukden, Manchuria. Roger got himself assigned to a rescue team that parachuted into the camp in the last days of the war. There was a brief firefight, and the captors were subdued. Roger found his father quickly. Minutes after they were reunited it was discovered that a bullet that had been headed for the left side of Roger's chest had been deflected by the top of the metal cigarette case his father had given him when they were saying goodbye at West Point years earlier. It probably had saved his life.

I never got around to asking Roger if he had given my outline of our story on the Cuban Missile Crisis to Stewart Alsop. It didn't matter. Roger succeeded Averill Harriman as Assistant Secretary of State for Far Eastern Affairs, but left the government in 1964 to teach Government and International Affairs at Columbia University, where, as this is written, he remains a Professor Emeritus.

31

Operation Pedro Pan

One of the most satisfying stories I ever wrote was entitled, "Operation Pedro Pan." It appeared in the February, 1988, issue, and was about something wonderful that had happened nearly three decades earlier. It began on Christmas Eve, 1960, when the telephone rang in the Catholic Welfare Bureau of the Miami, Florida, diocese. Father Bryan Walsh, then 30 years old and alone in the office, answered and found himself talking to a State Department official, in Washington, D.C.

It was explained to Walsh that the American embassy in Havana had entry visa applications for 200 unaccompanied minors whose parents, members of Cuba's middle class, had reason to believe that their children were going to be sent to Russia for "reeducation" – part of the Castro government's process of fashioning a new generation of communists. The U.S. wanted to grant the visas, Walsh was told, but needed a reputable agency to look after the kids. Could the Miami diocese help? He needed an answer *now!*

"Sure," Walsh said, "get the kids out of there." As quickly as he hung up it occurred to him that he had no authority to speak for the diocese. He began to worry: Where would he put 200 kids? How would he feed them, educate them? And how would he explain himself to the bishop? Then, his Bishop, Coleman Carroll, called. He had just heard from the State Department. "Why only 200 kids?" he asked Walsh. "Tell them we'll take all they can send. And Bryan, I want you to handle the whole thing. Look after them."

On January 3, the U.S. severed diplomatic relations with the Castro government, but only 14 kids had arrived. The American embassy in Havana was closed, and could issue no more visas. Walsh hurried to Washington to meet with people in the State Department, and a special visa waiver was designed, a letter saying that the State Department had authorized entry into the United States for the bearer. Some 50,000 such waivers reached Cuba in the diplomatic pouches of several countries friendly to the United States. These were delivered to the Cuban underground, which got them to the parents who wanted their children out.

In the next two years some 14,000 children were delivered to Miami. The kids arrived homesick, heartbroken and frightened. Many had only the clothing they wore, and most had no knowledge of English. Typically, 12-year-old Armando Codina, who knew only two words, "hamburger" and "Coke", wondered, "What's to become of me?"

Walsh got half the kids settled with relatives and family friends in and around Miami. For others he set up extensive living facilities and recruited couples from the city's large Cuban population as house parents.

Walsh was soon managing a staff of 300, and contacting hundreds of federal and state agencies for help. Directors of Catholic Charities came from all over the country and left with busloads of kids and house parents.

Walsh kept close track of the kids who stayed in Miami, their health, morale, grades, behavior. He understood their fears and soothed them, told them, "You are here because of your parents' great love for you. You have come to a place where people care about you. There is nothing to worry about. Until your parents come for you, you will have a home with us."

He loved them enough to discipline them as he thought their fathers would when they needed it: once, when two boys declared they were fed up with school and refused to leave their room. Walsh had a friendly judge send police to collect the two and take them in a squad car to a juvenile detention center. There, they spent a day with hardened criminals their own age. Walsh picked them up that evening and had no problem extracting promises that there would be no more nonsense about avoiding school.

In October, 1965, Castro agreed to allow thousands of Cuban dissidents to emigrate to the United States – they were troublemakers, his jails were full and he wanted them out of the country. As part of the deal parents of the Pedro Pan children received first priority. South Florida was awash in tears of happiness as families were reunited. Some kids, whose parents had died or were political prisoners, stayed with Walsh for as long as ten years.

Over the years, Walsh officiated at hundreds of their weddings and baptized scores of their babies.

I wrote the story. I had talked to many of the kids, including Ralph Sanchez and Armando Codina, who, by the time I met them, had become wealthy businessmen; in fact, both had had much to do with the making of Miami into a world-class city – Codina was the lad who, when he arrived, knew only two words of English "hamburger" and "Coke". I had also talked with Moises Hernandez, who had become one of Miami's prominent physicians. Recently, I Googled Operation Pedro Pan find to out who else had distinguished themselves. I found an impressive list, which is by no means complete:

Eduardo Aguirre became U.S. Ambassador to Spain.

Hugo Llorens became U.S. Ambassador to Honduras.

Frank Angones became the first Cuban-born head of the Florida Bar.

Mel Martinez became a U.S. Senator, representing Florida.

Guillermo "Bill" Vidal became Mayor of Denver, Colorado.

Carlos Eire became a professor of the history of religion at Yale University.

Twenty seven of the Pedro Pan boys followed Monsignor Walsh's footsteps into the Catholic priesthood; five became pastors of large Miami parishes and one, Felipe de Jesus Estevez, became Bishop of the Diocese of St. Augustine ("Be nice to your altar boy," Walsh laughed, "he may grow up to become your bishop.")

Armando Codina asked me, "Where else in the world could a young kid go alone, with nothing, not even the language, and grow up and do the things I have been able to do? There is no other place."

Nor, he added, was there another man quite like Monsignor Bryan Walsh.

Monsignor Walsh was 71 years old when a heart attack took him, in 2001.

He, too, had distinguished himself.

32

Why We Need Cantankerous Bullies

On July 10, 1986, a New York Times obituary described the Navy's Admiral Hyman Rickover, who had died that morning, as having been "somewhat cantankerous." Said the Times, "He generated controversy on all sides. He attacked Naval bureaucracy, ignored red tape, lacerated those he considered stupid, bullied subordinates and assailed the country's educational system."

I never met Rickover, but several who knew him whom I did know would have agreed. The obituary reminded me of something an officer who had been a young aide to the admiral told me that still made me smile. One day Rickover, by then a very famous man, sent for then Rear Admiral John S. McCain, Jr., another Submariner, who at the time was the Navy's Chief of Information. McCain had never met the great man, and when he entered his office, Rickover looked up, pointed an accusing finger at him and growled, "McCain, no Submariner has been of any help to me in getting this nuclear submarine program up and going."

McCain stood, looking stunned at the greeting. Although junior in rank by three stars, McCain had not himself earned the broad stripe of an admiral by accepting unjustified intimidation from seniors, even seniors with so imposing a reputation as Rickover. He removed the stub of a cigar from his mouth and said, matter of factly, "Admiral, that's a goddam lie, and you know it."

Many years later, McCain was himself wearing four stars, was Commander in Chief Pacific (CinCPac), and I had talked with him about all sorts of things on many occasions. When I asked him about the incident, he smiled and said, "We got along just *fine* after that. He was a great man. He made great things happen."

One January morning in 1960, I was aboard one of those great things, a submarine named Skipjack. The undersea Navy had liked the article I had written five years earlier, "The Making of a Submariner," and had invited me to take a ride on Skipjack. This was the very first nuclear-powered boat[7] to be married to an albacore hull, so named for a tear drop-shaped tuna that moves and maneuvers very quickly in the depths of the sea.

Then, Rickover married the nuclear powerplant to the albacore hull. Former Navy Secretary Dan Kimball called it, "The most important development in the Navy's history."

Skipjack is a tactical weapon, an attack boat. It's mission is to find and destroy the enemy's surface combatants and shipping.

---

[7] Submarines are the only Navy ships called boats; all other combatant vessels are called ships

This is all new stuff, but some things don't change. We are at sea for perhaps an hour, and I am standing near the Skipper, who is standing on a slightly raised platform in the Control Room, near his periscope, which is not up. All is quiet.

"Take her down," he orders.

And I see and hear the same things happen that I first heard years ago, on submarine in the Mediterranean: A voice on the boat's loudspeaker system shouts, "Clear the bridge! Clear the bridge."

The two lookouts up on the bridge, come hurtling through a hatch, the second one stopping only to pull the hatch closed behind himself and lock it. Then, he flies down a ladder into the Control Area.

That harsh signal, like an old-fashioned automobile horn, blasts through the boat: AHOOGA…AHOOGA….

Then, another voice on the loudspeaker, urgently: *"Dive! Dive! Dive!"*

But a lot of things have changed: A Chief Petty Officer at a Ballast Control Panel seems to be playing it like a piano. He controls four high-pressure air systems, four hydraulic systems, he raises and lowers radar and radio antennae, he dives and surfaces the boat. In the old boats his job needed four men. Bright red circles on his panels mean valves and vents are open. Quickly, they become bright red horizontal lines, which means the valves and vents are closed. We can hear sea water rushing into the ballast tanks.

Now the Chief shouts, "Green board, pressure in the boat!"

The Skipper says, "One five Oh feet."

"One five Oh feet, aye, aye, Sir," the Planesman responds.

The Planesman sits at a forward bulkhead. He controls the stern planes, takes the boat to whatever depth is ordered. Beside him is another man who controls the rudder; these two young men each have invested more than a thousand hours on simulators, developing the delicate touch this system requires.

We slide easily into the deep. There is quiet, almost serenity. Skipjack is at home here. We are at 20 knots, a little more than 22 miles per hour. I try to remember what top speed submerged was in the old boats – five knots per hour, but not for long before they had to surface and recharge. Skipjack, I am told, could stay submerged for about two years, could travel at full power for 90,000 to 100,000 miles. "We could cruise longer than food or sanity could hold out," the Skipper tells me.

How long *could* sanity hold out? There were news reports that another nuclear sub stayed down for 60 days recently.

"Sixty days is a long time," the Skipper says, "but in order to even get into the Submarine Service a man has to prove that he is a stable person, not someone who might get upset at something like that. In wartime we probably could push it a lot farther than 60 days."

I wonder about a station in the middle of the boat that is entitled, "Missile Control Center." Answer: Skipjack could take control of missiles fired from other vessels and guide them to their targets.

The torpedo room is the largest in the Navy. The old boats carried 24 "fish," fired singly, from ten tubes, six in the bow, four in the stern; they maneuvered so slowly that they had to be able to shoot from both ends. Today, we carry twice as many "fish" as the old boats; Skipjack can fire a salvo of six, each a split-second behind the other and in a pattern certain to ensnare and destroy a target on the surface or beneath it. But if she should miss or take on multiple targets, she could dart away, deep and distant, out of detection range, reload in four minutes and race back for another shot.

I learn what a shoot feels like: "Slugs" of water are about to be fired out of the tubes, and the sound effects and sensations will be almost identical to those felt in a real shoot. I pull covers, like earmuffs, only much larger, over my ears. Then, *"Fire One!"* Air pressure rams a column of water through the Number One Tube. A loud hissing, as though a pressure cooker is about to explode, then a quick, sliding sound, then a deafening, metallic *Bamm!* The "torpedo" was on its way.

The sound still echoes, when, *"Fire Two!"* Hisss…*Bamm!*

Six times I feel the boat quiver, just slightly, in recoil.

It is almost as though I am standing next to an artillery battery. Though my ears have been covered I feel slightly dizzy. A Torpedoman grins. "You get used to it," he says."

The old boats sometimes went as deep as 400 feet to sweat out depth charge attacks; they dared not venture into the hull crushing pressures beyond that. I can hardly believe it when I hear the Skipper order a dive to a level that was classified, had to remain secret. Skipjack noses over steeply, races downward. I brace my feet, grab at the overhead, watched the fathometer unreel, 200 feet, 300 feet, 400 feet, then, unhesitatingly, plunging onward, far deeper than 400 feet. We go deeper in the ocean than I ever dreamed ships could travel. The dense, high quality steel in Skipjack's hull allows her to live comfortably in these great pressures.

Now, the Skipper issues a series of orders to demonstrate her agility. She darts to the left and up, then to the right and down; she climbs and dives, twists and turns, faster and sharper than has ever been possible for any other vessel. She can reverse direction within her own length. For an instant, the head grows heavy under the hint of a G force. Skipjack is like an undersea jet fighter!

"One five oh feet," the Skipper finally orders, and we nose sharply upward, thunder back toward the surface; the fathometer subtracts distance from the surface so fast it's hard to read the blur. It's exhilarating, being engaged with a limitless power. Then, we level off, in a long, smooth curve. Finally, we return to the surface.

The Skipper explains, "Enemy anti-submarine forces couldn't find us unless we attacked them. Then, they couldn't keep track of us because we can go too deep too fast; we have made depth charges practically obsolete; they fall too slowly, and we can run away from them. We can even run away from homing torpedoes."

My day aboard Skipjack has been most impressive. One can only hope for America's sake that the military-industrial complex continues to include such cantankerous bullies as Admiral Hyman Rickover, who will continue to make things like Skipjack happen.

33
Awesome!

I extended an invitation to Digest readers: "Let's Go Into Orbit."
Did I say that I liked doing the first person stuff? A while back
I had been deeper in the sea than I had ever been or expected
to be again. Now, here I am, a continent away from that experience,
dressed up like an astronaut and prepared to go higher than I have
ever been, into orbit, 100 miles out into space, for a trip around
the world.

The launch pad is at Edwards Air Force Base, in California's
Mojave Desert, about 70 miles north of Los Angeles. My spacesuit
has a built-in air conditioning plant and a pressure system which, I
am told, will take over and keep my blood from boiling if capsule
pressure should fail.

Sounds good. I hate it when my blood boils. I pray, silently,
"Let it not fail."

Why the dry mouth? "There's nothing to worry about," the Launch Chief laughs. "We wouldn't let you do this unless we knew we could get you back safely.

Famous last words?

Still, one can't help being concerned as a short elevator ride takes him up to the capsule. There, I grab both sides of the capsule's hatch, pull myself inside and settle into the seat; I am on my back, but in a sitting position. The Launch Chief's assistant is there to harness me in, hook me to my oxygen, communications and pressure systems. Then, he briefs me on how to read the instrument panel and handle the controls.

"You will be launched by a Titan II missile," he says, "a two-stage rocket with 500,000 pounds of thrust. There will be a lot of noise and vibration. During the first stage you will be getting five G's, five times your own weight, pressing straight down on you. When this stage burns out you will hear the thrust diminish, and you will hear the bolts that connect the first stage to the assembly exploding away so that this stage can fall free. The whole process will be repeated with the second stage. When the second stage falls away you will be injected into orbit at a velocity of 25,600 feet per second – about 17,500 miles per hour."

"Is that clear?" he asks. Then, a look of concern on his face, he asks "Is that air conditioning system working? You seem to be perspiring."

"I am hot with impatience to get out into space," I tell him, courageously.

He tells me about the controls. At the forward end of my right armrest my hand grips a three-axis hand-controller. Bend it to the right or left and the capsule will roll; pull back on it and it and the capsule will nose upward; push forward and it will nose over. Twist the handle to the right or left and the capsule will turn right or left on what is called the yaw axis. Atop the hand controller is a small red button. "Hold it down if you want to talk to Ground Control," he says, "release to hear Ground Control. Ground Control will be in touch at every moment."

I am dazzled, flummoxed by the crowd of dials and indicators on the instrument panel. "Ground Control will brief you on them as necessary," I am told. There is a big red light atop the panel with the word "Warning" beneath it. What's that all about? "If that light goes on Ground Control will tell you what do. Do it, *fast*! But you will be on automatic pilot throughout the launch. All you have to do is sit back, relax, enjoy it!"

Sure.

"Any questions? No? Hey, good luck!" He grabs the handle on the hatch, pulls it closed, locks it and I am alone. I am looking straight up, through a glass windscreen. I see blue sky. I am going far beyond that blue, into a region where there is no atmosphere to scatter the sun's rays, and everything is dark. I am wondering how I got into this out-of-this-world fix.

Calm down, I tell myself, These guys are accomplished scientists and pilots, they know what they are doing. Just don't forget to push down on that button to talk, release to hear. Now, I hear: "Ready? Here we go. Counting down: five...four...three...two...one...ignition..."

Far behind me I hear a rumbling cascade of noise. It grows steadily in volume. I can feel it coming up behind me, bruting its way into my cockpit, filling my world, I can almost see it, beating itself into the structure around me and into my body. It sinks itself, roaring, into my legs and stomach, my arms, ears and eyes. It is overwhelming. And the vibration is hammering me like a high-speed jackhammer.

A voice says, "Watch your velocity control indicator." It shows me that I am hurtling upward at 2500…4000…6000…8000…10,000…12,000 feet per second. An enormous weight has pinned my arms, legs torso and head fast in place; I can move my eyes, nothing else, and the weight keeps building, pressing me downward, into my seat. Ground Control says all is well. So relax. Keep watching the sky.

What a sight! The light blue sky turns to lavender, then to purple, then deep, deep purple, beautifully, until now is a darkening velvet. As I continue to sail away from the earth's atmosphere the velvet continues to darken and I am headed straight for a field of brilliant stars.

I have outrun the noise; the first stage of the Titan II is decaying. The capsule begins to nose over. The stars appear to be falling upward. The heavy weight upon me is lifting, slowly, then more quickly. But the launch is only half over.

Somewhere behind me I hear a series of metallic staccato *boings* as the explosive bolts go. The burned out first stage of the missile is falling away.

Now, a new surge of sound and vibration is coming up behind me. Again, enormous pressure is pushing me deep into the seat. It's stronger this time; the vibration is greater. The instrument

panel is a quivering blur. But now, almost suddenly, I am accli-
mated, streaking straight upward, into the high, black void. The
velocity indicator shows me at 16,000 feet per second and accel-
erating…18,000…22,000…and beginning to nose over onto the
level…G forces are letting up…the vibration is lessening, the noise
is diminishing…the second stage has burned out…25,600 feet per
second…I am now in orbit!

All is calm. I am at 17,500 miles per hour and cruising smoothly
around the world at an altitude of 100 miles. I lean forward for a
good look through the windscreen. I have to write this, that it's like
sitting in the middle of the night and looking out at the day. There
is the Atlantic Ocean, huge, glittering silver blue, and stretching
ahead to the curve of the world. The earth seems suspended in a
shallow, almost luminous silver-gold glow. Coastline creeps upward
against the eedge of the curvature There is the squarish jut of the
Iberian Peninsula. Twist the hand controller to the right, move on
the yaw axis, and there, ahead and below is Gibraltar – I remember
Gibraltar; on the deck of a submarine I climbed into a thing shaped
like a lifesaver and was lifted 60 feet onto a helicopter, then was
taken to an aircraft carrier not far away.

Ahead, I can see the top of Africa. I turn back to the left and
the Mediterranean coast angles northeasterly. Northward, through
broken cloud cover and far below I see what I will describe as the
soaring white waves of the Alps.

Now, below, the earth is turning pink, then orange-red, then
beyond the sunset, and all across Asia, night.

Then, less than half an hour past sunset, all those colors again
in a spectacular sunrise. Far, far below the vast Pacific heaves and

glitters. There are the lush Hawaiian Islands. I have nearly completed an orbit. Time to return to earth.

I am hearing another countdown:

"four…three…two…one…and my retrorockets fire – a loud, rushing sound then a muted *whoomp!* Now, the capsule is shuddering again, as though it will shake apart, and making a quick tumbling of a turn. I am pinned against the seat and can't tell up from down or sideways. The shuddering and shaking stop, and I am out of orbit and headed for home, plummeting down through the earth's atmosphere toward Edwards. Suddenly, there is an almost imperceptible tug, and a light on the instrument panel tells me that my small drogue chute has opened. It will brake the descent to the point where the main chute can open without tearing itself apart. Now there is the gentle jolt of the main chute. And I can see it, billowing high above the windscreen.

I brace for landing; it's sure to be jarring. It doesn't happen. Instead, the hatch slides open and the Launch Control officer is grinning at me. "How was it?" he wants to know.

It was so real that even though I knew from the outset that the capsule would not leave the ground I am almost surprised that it did not. My entire trip was made on an amazing new space flight simulator, the first of its kind and the most ingenious teaching aid ever made. With a few minor exceptions my flight was a true duplication of what a space pilot would actually see, hear and feel.

The exceptions: There were none of the dramatic, roiling, almost overwhelming clouds of exhaust that are always visible in a space vehicle's liftoff. The G forces I felt during launch were only imitations of the pressures inflicted during an actual launch; these forces can't be truly duplicated on any vehicle anchored to the earth. During the first- and second-stage firings the capsule, mounted between two steel towers so that it can rotate in any direction, is tilted backward until sensations of increasing G forces are created. And because the "flight" did not actually take me out of the earth's gravitational field, I never became weightless.

And all those sights and sounds that I saw and heard as I orbited the earth? They were all accomplished with a half ton of highly polished mirrors and lenses, synchronized with sound and motion systems and hooked to closed circuit television.

The simulator was as close as man could get to the real thing, incredibly realistic and convincing, a brand new technological marvel that would supply space pilots, for the first time, with complete mission training.

Awesome!

34

An H-Bomb Is Missing

"Step back for a moment through the eons," I wrote, "literally into the Stone Age. Peace and survival in our hostile world may depend on our being able to do it. Follow me."

It was January, 1966, and I was in Cheyenne Mountain, just south of Colorado Springs, in the fantastic new headquarters of the North American Air Defense Command (NORAD). I was literally inside the mountain, under 1500 tons of solid granite, there to take our readers on a tour of what was one of the most important military command posts on earth. From here a battle staff of U.S. and Canadian air defense specialists now kept a day and night watch on the world, monitoring a marvelous, bewildering complex of intelligence and communications systems, ready to detect and identify any attack launched against the North American continent.

During the Cold War, NORAD's primary mission was to sound the alarm in the event of attack, to notify instantly and simultaneously the U.S. President, Canada's Prime Minister, The U.S. Joint Chiefs of Staff, the U.S. Strategic Air Command (SAC) and the Civil Defense authorities of both countries.

The mission included an effective defense of the 10,500,000 square miles of the North American continent and its seaward approaches; NORAD would have to direct many hundreds of U.S. and Canadian interceptor aircraft and ground-to-air missiles against any incoming attack.

But ultimately the mission was deterrence; no rational enemy was likely to attack knowing that as quickly as he launched, a signal from this command post would unleash an obliterating U.S. counterstrike.

This was a good story to tell, a confidence builder for the Free World and especially Americans in the middle of a hot war in Vietnam and a Cold War standoff with the Soviets that constantly kept the whole planet on edge. And right in the middle of researching it, something terrible happened:

A SAC B-52 bomber carrying four hydrogen bombs collided with a KC-135 tanker aircraft that was refueling it. It happened over southeastern Spain. The bomber had been part of SAC's Alert Force, a percentage of the force that had remained constantly airborne, ready to strike assigned targets should the United States or any of its Allies come under nuclear attack. Seven American airmen had died in the collision, but four members of the bomber crew had escaped in parachutes and survived.

The broken bomber had also lost four hydrogen bombs. The world was told the same day that three had been recovered. Nothing was said about the fourth. No one in the U.S. or Spanish governments would comment. Days and then weeks passed and still there was no mention of the fourth bomb. The world noticed.

The continued silence of the two governments kept sharpening the world's interest. Soon, virtually every important news organization on the planet had reporters roaming the villages and the countryside of southeastern Spain, talking to the natives, filing stories about what people had seen and felt, speculating about where the bomb might be, about the possibility that it might never be found, about the possibility that it might reveal its location with a nuclear explosion, about all kinds of possible disasters if it were never found. But their stories said nothing concrete about the search effort because no American or Spanish diplomatic and military personnel would talk about it. One U.S. Air Force officer's famous reply to a newsman's question was, "If you are referring to what I think you may be referring to, I have no comment."

The reason for the news blackout was twofold: it would have been folly to advertise that secret parts of a nuclear weapon might be lying about; and hopefully the missing bomb would soon be found. Plus, the Spanish government was worried at the possible economic consequences to the region, which was an important part of Europe's vegetable garden; the village of Palomares and its environs supplied Europe with most of its tomatoes and a lot of its citrus fruit. And the seas off the nearby coastal village of Villaricos supplied a great deal of the continent's seafood. With the media focusing day after day on the fact that a missing nuclear weapon was somewhere in the region, would the rest of Europe, even the rest of Spain, continue to buy the area's fruits, vegetables and seafood? What would happen to Spain's most lucrative business, tourism, which had yielded $1.15 billion the previous year? Thus, when reporters began asking routine questions as to the types of nuclear weapons the bomber had been carrying, the Spanish government had insisted that the answer be, "No comment." The United States had honored Spain's wishes because Spain had been a strong ally, had granted it bases for its new, nuclear-powered and nuclear-armed submarines and overflight rights for SAC's bombers when others of our so-called European allies had denied us such cooperation.

Even though no one was talking I had to get to Spain; sooner or later the story was going to break, and we could tell it better than anyone else.

I completed research in NORAD's mountain, hurried home, got the story written and left for Madrid. I was greeted at the airport by Victor Olmos, the Editor of the Digest's Spanish edition, and Dennis McEvoy, who at the time also worked for the Digest in Spain in some capacity, which no one ever seemed clear on. I had not known either of them before, but both were nice fellows, anxious to help. Dennis was one of those personalities who engage quickly; he had read many, if not most, of my articles, he was vocally admiring of my work, and he won my admiration when he expressed his pleasure that "Pleasantville had the good sense to send a writer of stature to cover the most important story in the world."

True or not, it sounded good to me. I loved Dennis.

Dennis was a *bon vivant*, not merely a man about whatever town he happened to be in, but a man of the world. He knew, in fact, seemed to be intimate friends with, absolutely everyone who was worth knowing., and everyone loved him. Dennis bubbled with *joie de vivre*.

Victor Olmos, a Spaniard who was fluent in American English, was probably in his late 30's, smiling, agreeable, wanted to do whatever he could in support of what I wanted to do.

Dennis and Victor whisked me off to a hotel. They waited patiently while I, just off an overnight transatlantic flight, showered, shaved and dressed, then whisked me to the American Embassy, where Dennis had arranged a meeting with Ambassador Angier Biddle Duke, who greeted me as though he had waited all his life for the pleasure of this moment.

As quickly as the formal introductions were completed, Dennis began addressing the Ambassador as "Angie." We had cocktails, the Ambassador expressed his deep admiration for The Reader's Digest and "all of the good that it has done in this world." Then, he ushered us into an elegant dining room where I was introduced to all of his senior staff. The conversation as we lunched was informal and pleasant. The Ambassador commented favorably on the book Jim Daniel and I had written a few years earlier on the Cuban Missile Crisis. As the party wound down I was astonished at Duke's instruction to his staff to "please open your files to Mr. Hubbell."

What? The biggest story in the world for weeks had been not only that a hydrogen bomb was missing, but also that neither U.S. nor Spanish officials would even admit it. It turned out that concurrently with my arrival, a decision had been made at the highest levels, and probably at Duke's urging, that sooner or later the whole story would have to be told, that sooner was better, it was now later, time to tell the world that while three of the four H-bombs had been recovered, a fourth was still missing and that every conceivable effort was being made to find it. Meanwhile, the world should be assured that no lethal radioactivity had been loosed in the area of Spain where the accident had occurred, but that even so the whole region was being cleaned up, sanitized.

The communists had been enjoying a propaganda field day. Radio Espana Independiente (REI), a Spanish language Communist broadcast beamed from Prague, advised Spanish listeners that they were victims of a great catastrophe, that the American nuclear devices had painted their fields and fishing grounds with deadly radioactivity; it spoke of "deformed babies."

Fear reigned in southeastern Spain. People in Palomares and Villaricos burned their clothing and bathed incessantly. Some sent their children to live with relatives in distant villages. Many considered moving away for good, but worried that it was already too late. Local morale was low.

The Soviets kept harping on the dangers to peace posed by the stockpile of American nuclear weapons in Spain, knowing very well that there was no such stockpile. At a disarmament conference in Geneva, Soviet Delegate Semyon Tsarapkin accused the United States of having made "a nuclear volcano of Europe." Soviet foreign Minister Andre Gromyko had sent a memorandum to U.S. Ambassador Foy Kohler, in Moscow, calling for an immediate end to "the criminal U.S. military flights over foreign countries."

Along with all the communist propaganda, the actions and inaction of the U.S. and Spain had been complicit in destroying the morale in the affected area. In Palomares, U.S. Air Force Air Police and Spain's Guardia Civil, a tough state police force, cordoned off all the areas where debris had fallen, including the cultivated fields; farmers were not permitted to attend to their crops, which were ready for harvesting. And in Villaricos, fishermen were barred from their fishing grounds. No one explained to them why these measures were necessary; that in two of the weapons the conventional high explosives used to trigger a nuclear explosion had detonated on impact. Each weapon had split like an axed pumpkin. The nuclear cores had popped out and been vaporized by the conventional explosion.

It should have been pointed out immediately to the residents – and to the whole world – that there had been no splitting of atoms, no nuclear blast and no release of the lethal products that fall out of one. The materials that had scattered would emit alpha radiation; unlike the deadly gamma rays which spring from the nucleus of a split atom, the range of alpha rays is extremely short. They can't penetrate skin, or even tissue paper, and can easily be washed off of anything they land on, like vegetables, or skin. But U.S. atomic safety procedures were designed with an enormous margin for error. While the contamination on these lands would certainly do no damage, they were to be cleansed of all trace of it; no exposure was better than some exposure.

At the same time, all the villagers were checked out with instruments, asked for urine samples, told to bathe, to launder their clothing and try not to breath too much dust. Idle men gathered in their taverns and plaza, where the radios were full of communist propaganda.

Low local morale was intermixed with a reverent wonder: Two giant aircraft had exploded into many thousands of huge and tiny pieces of fiery metal which had rained down into and all around Villaricos and Palomares, and not a soul on the ground had been killed, or even injured. The villagers noted that it had happened on the feast day of St. Anton de Abad, the patron saint of Villaricos, and agreed that they had indeed been favored with a miracle.

The same safety procedures required that all those men examining the ground with sensing devices be dressed up in clothing that made them look like space travelers. The local population and the visiting media saw all this. But the governing information policy had not allowed for any explanation to anyone, so the villagers feared the worst, and some visiting media wrote horror stories.

Uninformed or misinformed editors the world over published dark hints that Palomares and Villaricos were awash in a sea of "lethal" alpha radiation, which is not lethal nor even harmful; and speculated that the fields in the region might have been ruined for generations to come. In Paris, it was wrongly reported that a thousand Palomares residents had been evacuated. In London, the Sunday Express headlined an article on Villaricos, "The Village of Fear." United Press International (UPI) found a "victim" of what it called the "deadly alpha radiation", a man who had knelt beside one of the recovered bombs. He arrived in Madrid demanding an examination. An infinitismal spot was found on a tiny area of skin and washed off. Dr. Jose Maria Navascuez, head if Spain's Bureau of Nuclear Energy advised that the man's bathing habits were questionable, that if he had bathed during the eight days since he had knelt by the bomb there could have been no reading.

It took about three weeks to define the contaminated area, a rough rectangle three quarters of a mile wide and two miles long. It contained 385 cultivated acres on 854 separate plots owned by 854 different people. Harmless though the alpha radiation was, this had become a major battle front in the Cold War. To eliminate the possibility of ill-intentioned people coming into the region, collecting samples of contaminated soil, no matter how harmless, and making propaganda capital with it, every grain of suspected soil had to be scraped from the countryside and taken to the atomic waste burial ground near Aiken, South Carolina. The crops also were taken, and the farmers were paid for them; the on scene military forces ate most of them.

A decision had also been made at some level to cooperate to the fullest extent with The Reader's Digest, perhaps because in addition to being the world's most widely read publication, it was well known to be not only objective in its reporting, but patriotic. When the anti-Vietnam War movement began to take on an anti-American coloration, founding Editor-in-Chief DeWitt Wallace had gone so far as to insert American flag decals into every American copy of his magazine, inviting readers to remove them and place them in the windows of their houses and automobiles, and millions of people had done so. Also, the Digest had proved itself to be extraordinarily meticulous about fact checking its articles.

In addition to his senior staff's files, Ambassador Duke had files of his own, and invited me to his apartment one evening to extract from his files whatever I thought might be of value to the telling of the story.

We sat with ties loosened, drinking beer and going through the files. He called me by my first name, and asked me to call him Angie. "Dennis does," he pointed out, "and there is no reason why you shouldn't, why we shouldn't be first-name friends."

I met Tad Szulc (pronounced Shultz) at a hotel bar in Madrid. He reported on foreign affairs for the New York Times. I was well acquainted with his work and, it turned out, he with mine. We hit it off. He was driving the next morning to the scene of the action on the southeastern coast, and I was glad to accept his offer of a ride. It was about a three-hour trip to the beach at Palomares, and we had an enjoyable time talking about different stories we had covered.

An 80-tent city had been erected on the beach at Palomares. One big tent served as the command post for Major General Delmar J. Wilson, commander of SAC's 16th Air Force, headquartered at Torrejon, a few miles east of Madrid. Almost as quickly as I reached the beach I heard my name being called; it was Lt. Col. Mike Connolly, whom I had first met years earlier at Stead Air Force Base, when he was a captain, and had seen to my insertion into a bomber aircrew to do the Survival story.

"I've been wondering when you'd show up," he said, as we shook hands. Mike was now handling on-scene press relations for SAC, and he agreed that press relations here had been virtually non-existent. "People say 'Good Morning' to me," he said, "and about all I've been authorized to respond with is, 'I'm not authorized to comment on that.'"

"Any chance of talking to General Wilson?" I asked, knowing he would say, "Of course not," but I had to ask, and I was preparing to say, "The Ambassador opened his files to me..."

"Absolutely," Mike said, "Come on."

We entered the command post tent. General Wilson was on his feet to greet me, and I received a thorough briefing. First, about the hair-raising worldwide speculation that the missing bomb might signal its location by exploding: This could not happen. So foolproof were the safeguards built into the handling and use of America's nuclear weapons that they cannot be detonated except deliberately. To explode, the nuclear materials in an H-bomb first must be tightly compressed. This is achieved by a measured quantity of high explosive surrounding the nuclear core. The high explosive must implode – explode inwardly – so as to apply perfectly uniform force around the entire periphery of the core. Should the explosive detonate even slightly unevenly – as the result, for example, of fire or the shock of impact – there can be no release of nuclear energy because there would be no uniform squeezing of the nuclear mass. In such a situation the shock wave from the explosive would simply seek to escape out of the weapon. There could be a small explosion that might break the casing, but there could be no nuclear explosion.

Furthermore, a U.S. nuclear blast cannot be accomplished unless several highly trained men, all certified to be mentally and physically fit by competent, painstaking medical authority, agree that a "go-to-war code" originating with the President has been received. The code is programmed to come in voice, not through any device subject to misinterpretation or failure.

Only when a bomber is irrevocably committed to war would the men, each working controls from widely separated places in the aircraft, begin the arming, fusing and firing procedures, which must be followed by the numbers and to the letter, could there be a nuclear explosion.

The safety of America's unarmed nuclear weapons had been thoroughly tested. In a rigorous, years-long program at various sites such weapons were subjected to experiments which simulated the shock of being dropped from great altitudes, blown up with high explosives, burned, dragged at high speed over rough surfaces, smashed against concrete walls. The United States had tried hard, but had never been able to achieve an accidental nuclear blast.

Each H-bomb in SAC's inventory was unique, custom-tailored to its own mission. Each had a thermonuclear yield designed to deal with a specific target. Each had timing and sensing devices which reacted to, for example, the increasing density of the atmosphere as it fell over its target area. Each had its own arming, fusing and firing devices and techniques. Thus, from cosmic top secret files at the Atomic Energy Commission and the Defense Atomic Support Agency, men assembled serial numbers and matched them with the names of those who had designed them and supervised their fabrication.

General Wilson told me, "We're pretty sure the missing bomb is in the sea." He said that several fishermen from nearby Villaricos had been trawling five to seven miles off the coast when the aircraft had collided and broken up. A number of parachutes had carried into the sea, which that day was being driven by 30- to 40-knot west-to-east winds. Three of the 'chutes had carried airmen who had escaped the broken aircraft; they were quickly rescued by three different fishing boats. The master of the fourth boat, Francisco Simo Orts, had watched a 'chute carrying not a man but a rigid, silvery cylinder. He had no idea what it was, but assumed that since it was in a parachute it must be important. He went after it when it splashed down, but it had sunk. Mentally, he drew lines to the site from mountain peaks to his north and crossed them with lines from mountain peaks to his west. The subsurface at this point had been thoroughly searched, but nothing had been found.

Soviet trawlers loaded with all kinds of detection gear had taken stations just over the horizon. A cordon of American destroyers had interposed itself between the Soviet ships and the search area. The missing bomb was full of secrets that the United States did not want to share with the Soviets.

General Wilson and his staff spent a couple of hours briefing me, and answering my questions. Then, with an interpreter, I began walking the villages and the surrounding countryside, talking with witnesses to the tragedy. Julio Ponce Navarro, short, wiry, middle aged, had been irrigating a lemon grove by his house, at the western end of Palomares. He described a thunderous explosion in the sky and had looked up to see the bomber, directly behind and just below the tanker, begin to break up and then disappear into a huge, suddenly burgeoning cloud of black smoke and fire. The tanker aircraft seemed to rock ahead for a moment, then it, too, began disintegrating, and some 200 tons of fiery debris scattered across the morning sky and began falling toward the horror-struck observers below.

Julio stood transfixed. Strong winds were sweeping great balls of fire down the sky, *and one of them was coming straight at him*!

He ran, looking frantically for his wife, Maria, found her watering geraniums on the south side of the house. She had heard the enormous explosion, but the house had blocked her view so that she could not see what was happening. Julio shouted, "There is fire coming down. Come on!" He grabbed her by the hand and they ran away from the house. Julio looked back. The huge fireball seemed certain to land on his roof, but passed low over it and crashed into a narrow dirt road, just beyond.

A thick pillar of smoke swirled up from the wreckage. Julio and Maria could see that three men were strapped to it. They ran to them, saw that two were obviously dead, but the third was struggling to move, groaning. They wanted to free him from the flaming rig – it was part of the tanker aircraft's cockpit – but the fire was too intense. They scooped up handsful of dirt and tried to smother the flames with them. After a few minutes, Julio motioned Maria to stop; the man had died. Maria and Julio each made the sign of the cross and bowed their heads in prayer.

Antonio Sabiote Garcia had been working his field in a wide valley near the northern edge of Palomares. He had heard the explosion and seen the collision, then had seen an enormous scythe of flame come hurtling down toward him. As he ran he heard a terrible crash behind him, then a wave of heat washed over him and past him. Looking back, he saw the flaming wing and four engines of the bomber.

At the eastern end of Palomares an object on a parachute smashed against a stone retaining wall in a tomato terrace 75 yards from the house of Eduardo Navarro Portillo. There was a jarring explosion. Part of the wall and hundreds of tomatoes were damaged, and every window in Navarro's house was blown out. Navarro and some friends ran to the terrace, found the object burning, threw dirt on it and kicked at it, and soon the fire was out. They had no idea they were kicking a hydrogen bomb.

Rear Admiral William S. Guest, Deputy Commander of the Navy's forces in Southern Europe, came from his headquarters in Naples to organize a search of the sea east of Palomares. It was a formidable task; nothing like it had ever been done before. The Mediterranean reached depths here of thousands of feet, and the bottom was not flat; it was a range of high mountains and steep hills, a replication of the rugged landscapes to west and northwest of the coast.

The search involved America's most experienced and talented undersea operators: Navy Lieutenant Commander J.B. Mooney, who only months earlier had piloted the Trieste, the Navy's deep-diving bathyscape to a depth of 8400 feet off the New England coast and found the remains of the U.S.S. Thresher, a submarine that had been lost three years earlier with 129 officers and men.

Lieutenant Commander DeWitt Moody, a deep sea diver who was schooled in nuclear weaponry, headed a team of 130 divers and Frogmen gathered from the Atlantic and Mediterranean fleets.

From the Philadelphia Navy Shipyard came the Mizar, a research ship fitted with a sled it could pull along the bottom containing an underwater camera powerful enough to see through the black depths and relay pictures to the top.

Reynolds Aluminum, Inc., sent its own research submarine, the Aluminaut, 75 tons, 51 feet long and designed to operate at depths of 15,000 feet.

The Oceanographic Institute at Woods Hole, Massachusetts, sent its deep submersible, the Alvin, which had worked at 7500 feet.

From the far Pacific the Navy sent an ungainly structure that looked like it had been invented by a seriously disturbed naval architect. It was called CURV, an acronym for Cable controlled Underwater Research Vehicle. It stood six feet high, was five feet wide and thirteen feet long. It had two ballast tanks on each side of the frame, and motors to drive it up, down and sideways. It was fitted out with television cameras and the latest in sonar equipment, a still camera with a strobe light and a recovery clamp which its operators, who were using it to recover test-fired torpedoes, thought might fit around a hydrogen bomb.

In addition to its own technological wizardry, the Navy brought in such world class expertise as Jon Lindbergh, the deep sea specialist son of the late Colonel Charles A. Lindbergh, the first man to fly non-stop across the Atlantic Ocean.

Even with all this going for him, Admiral Guest found himself lying awake nights as the search dragged on and on, and developing a fearsome analogy: It was like going into steep, dark hills inland on a moonless night with a pencil flashlight, covering one eye and searching with the other through a long, hollow tube.

It took 79 days to find the bomb – it teetered on a ledge in 2500 feet of water, just above a 9000-foot chasm. CURV wrapped it in its arms and brought it up.

It was one of the great technological achievements of the age. I wrote the story at the length it deserved, and it appeared as a book-length feature in the Digest.

35
How to Take a Vacation

After the inside-the-mountain story in Colorado and then traipsing around southeastern Spain for several weeks and then spending more weeks at home putting it all together for the Digest, I needed some free time. I had just delivered the H-Bomb piece in Pleasantville and a well-meaning editor was wondering if I would like to look into the possibility of a story in the Antarctic. I said, "Right now, I am only interested in going home and spending some time with my kids, and then I am going to take my wife on a vacation to Hawaii, which she richly deserves."

"How long will you stay in Hawaii?" Hobe Lewis asked.

"Two weeks, at least," I said. "Maybe more."

"Good," he said. "Take all the time you need. You and Punkin need to relax. You've earned it."

Life was getting better all the time. Then, it improved.

Hobe had long yearned for a color story on what had happened at Pearl Harbor when the Japanese attacked, on December 7, 1941, but no one, myself included, knew how such a piece could be framed. It stood out in history; it was a well-known story that had been done many times in many ways, in newpapers, magazines, books and movies, and was a quarter of a century old. How to present anew it in a way that would capture the reader's attention?

The day after we arrived in Honolulu we visited the Arizona Memorial. The great battleship, submerged in its watery grave next to Ford Island, where Japanese bombs had sent it, still held the bodies of more than a thousand of its officers and men. The memory of what had happened here still moved the souls of Americans who visited. What I saw moved me. An elderly lady came aboard, placed a small bouquet of flowers below a large plaque inscribed with the names of all those who lay below. She was prayerful for a few moments, then left, dabbing her eyes. An older gentleman came aboard; he had been one of the crew, had been ashore, on liberty, the night before, and had not made it back in time to die with his shipmates.

It seemed a good idea to remind people, Americans especially, of what had happened here. I wrote a mood piece that appeared as the center spread of the December, 1967, issue. A gorgeous color photograph of the Memorial was spread across two pages.

I was in Washington in the midwinter of 1967-68 when I was notified that the judges of Sigma Delta Chi, the Professional Journalism Society, had found my book-length feature, "The Case of the Missing H-Bomb," to be the best magazine reporting of

1966. This was the apex of the world of magazine journalism. I especially appreciated the judges' citation: "His painstaking search for the facts and his skillful use of prose helped to defuse a nuclear age accident that could have resulted in severe political repercussions for the United States." I was advised that the award would be among those presented (the others would be for newspaper, radio and television reporting) at black tie dinner in the St. Francis Hotel, in San Francisco, on a Saturday evening in May.

At the dinner I was seated next to another award winner, Pat Oliphant, the great editorial cartoonist. A waiter interrupted our conversation to ask Oliphant if there were something wrong with his dinner, since he was not eating. "Nothing wrong at all," he said, "it's just that Hubbell is using the fork."

He was supplied with the necessary cutlery.

Many years later, long after The Reader's Digest as it had been originally conceived and developed and, as we who had labored for it in its best years had known it, had passed into history, I received an honor I prize even more: The magazine's last great Editor in Chief, Edward T. Thompson, asked a group of his very senior colleagues (including me) to help him put together a list of "The Reader's Digest's Greatest Hits," to nominate from the more than 30,000 articles that had appeared in its pages over an 88-year span. Rated Number Two was, "The Case of the Missing H-Bomb."[8]

---

[8] Number one was "...And Sudden Death," by J.C. Furnas. A second-by-second account of what happens to the human body during an automobile collision, it appeared in the August, 1935, issue. More than 100 million reprints were ordered. It was credited with saving vast numbers of lives.

36

The Navy That
Never Happened

In case I haven't said so, I liked doing the first person stuff.

From the dark deep of the Atlantic Ocean to the dark of deep space to – where now?

Panama City, Florida, that's where, to the Navy's Coastal Systems Laboratory. And what to do there?

I'm aboard a big, ungainly looking vessel. A lump of a cabin sits center rear on the deck. I have spent a lot of time on destroyers, which are called, "greyhounds of the sea." This thing looks like an overfed mutt.

But if destroyers are "greyhounds of the sea," I am told, this mutt is lightning. It's called the SES-100B, which means, "Surface Effects Ship, 100 tons." It was built by a division of Bell Aerospace Textron, which I had thought designed and manufactured only really good-looking airplanes.

In the cabin, the Control Area looks complicated, like the cockpit of an airliner. The Skipper and his second in command strap themselves into big leather chairs in front of a console full of throttles. There are big steering wheels in front of them, and a dashboard full of dial faces.

I strap myself into a third leather chair and listen as the Skipper explains that we have three gas turbine engines, each of which can deliver 4500 horsepower. These engines drive two propellers astern that are nothing like traditional ship's screws; these are made of light titanium, and each has six blades, each with a slight angle scalloped into them near their trailing edges. When these blades whirl they remain completely enveloped in a water vapor which prevents bubbles from collapsing against them.

In case you didn't know it, collapsing bubbles can ruin a high speed titanium blade.

We swing around in the bayou and rumble out into the Gulf. A portable tracking station will record our mission. Two chase boats stand by to rush to us in case of emergency. Let there be no emergency!

The cabin is full of people doing various things. One is monitoring an oscilloscope that measures vibration levels in ten gear boxes. Another is operating a data acquisition system that is supplying 350-plus readings, including wave height sensors and the temperatures of each engine at its inlet and exhaust points. A super maintenance man and troubleshooter stands by, ready to deal with any problem that can't be managed from a control panel.

This is exciting. Naval engineers have long dreamed of super high-speed ships, ships that could in quick time reach distant areas where U.S. interests were involved, but it couldn't happen until aeronautics yielded high-powered propulsion systems and lightweight structural metals.

By 1961 it was beginning to happen. The Navy was testing an almost hull-less ship with partially submerged sidewalls and hinged seals. The four sides surrounded the apparently insubstantial substance that gives the Surface Effect Ship, the one we are aboard now, its remarkable capabilities – air. Nearly a decade has been spent proving things out, first on paper, then on scale models, then on small test craft, and now on two experimental 100-tonners, the SES 100B, the one we are aboard; and the SES 100A,

They don't resemble each other. The A was built by the Aerojet General Corporation, and looks like a speedboat; she's much better looking than her sister. The A's engines drive water propulsors that pick up seawater and ram it through steerable nozzles, which is to say that the ship is steered by its nozzles.

The Navy's hope was to install as many good ideas as were available aboard sister ships, then put the best of them together in a larger, more advanced model. The A has more new ideas aboard her, but she's stationed up north, in Chesapeake Bay, where winter weather and waters too often get in the way of things. Meanwhile, the B, down here in sunny Florida, holds all the records, which is why we are here.

It's a brilliant day, bright sunshine and blue skies. The Skipper eases his throttles forward and we surge ahead, smoothly; it's as though we are sailing on air, which we are. Behind us, our propellers are flinging huge white rooster tails of sea at the sky. We nose upward, just slightly. It's as though we are ascending a long, shallow hill.

Below decks the engines are driving fans that are sucking air through vents at 6000 cubic feet per second. The air is taken into the huge central cavity of the ship, the empty area below that is surrounded by the rigid sidewalls and the fore and aft seals. An enormous air bubble is forming beneath us. Suddenly, the bubble is captured and we are – literally – flying!

At rest, the ship's sidewalls dip six feet down into the water. Now, no more than nine inches touch water. Yet, we are stable – we can turn on a dime, stop within our own length, with no sideslipping, jump from dead in the water to 80 knots – 92.2 miles per hour – within six minutes and, while we hear a lot of high-pitched jet engine noise on the surface, we make little noise in the sea. We would make a poor target for a submarine; it couldn't fire torpedoes close enough to the surface to hit any part of us, and even if he could we could probably outrun any torpedo."

I am pressed against the back of my chair as the ship steps out –

30-plus knots was flank speed for our faster destroyer types, but we're just getting started…40 knots…50…55…60…we cruise down the bay and out into the Gulf. Here, a breeze laces the surface with a mild chop. I unharness myself, rise, walk about. With little hull in the water, there is no problem. But how would it be in heavy seas? It had been hoped that men would be able to walk about and do their jobs at 30 knots in six foot seas; that's about the best destroyers can do in smooth seas. But it's been found that men can function effectively on the100B at 50 knots in six-foot seas – that's nearly 60 miles per hour.

The Skipper waves me into his seat, lets me know that I have the ship. I ease the wheel to starboard and we make a wide, very careful turn to the right, then, more boldy, a turn to port. There is no lag time in response to commands. this bullet of a ship responds instantly. On a conventional ship a change-of-course command must be given to a helmsman, change of speed telegraphed to an engine room. An SES Skipper needs only to manipulate his throttles and wheel; it's like a speedboat, but much faster.

I race about the Gulf. Through earphones I hear calm exchanges of information: someone reports a rising vibration level in one engine. The Skipper makes a minuscule speed adjustment, and the vibration level falls. The Data Acquisition System operator says we are getting slightly uneven rooster tails, and our propellers are adjusted. No one says anything to me; I'm racing about and turning about and doing fine.

Reluctantly, I give the ship back to the Skipper, who embarks on the day's important business. He orders chase boats to make certain a large area is clear because, "we'll be coming at approximately 75 knots."

The ship does not labor at all; in fact, it's almost though she is holding back, and the Skipper decides to let her out a little. "Speed 78," someone says. No problem with stability, and we stay on course for our entire eight-mile run and cruise for a bit at our target speed – 86.36 miles per hour.

A few minutes later we make another run and top out at 95.6 miles per hour!

I am most impressed.

After a couple of hours we rumble home.

That really happened, a long time ago; I didn't make it up. I wrote an article about it entitled, "Here Comes the 100-mile-an-hour Navy" that the Digest's famous research department checked out, found to be true and accurate and which appeared in the magazine. The article envisioned a fleet that included anti-submarine forces that could search several times more ocean area for submarines than the latest anti-submarine warfare task groups could, and carrier battle groups that could rush airpower into crisis zones in quick time – say, 60 hours from Norfolk to the Middle East, or 70 hours from San Diego to the coast of Korea.

It seemed to be a great idea, and it certainly looked to me like it would have worked well on behalf of The Great Republic. But the 100-mile-per-hour Navy never showed up.

37
Robert McNamara

Nine years had passed since I had profiled Robert McNamara for the Digest. The article, "For the Defense, Robert McNamara," was, frankly, representative of the awestruck opinion the media and, thus, the general public, held of him at the time. I had long since changed my view. Here's the story:

One day in 1960, shortly after the election of President John F. Kennedy Hobart Lewis, called to suggest that McNamara, whom Kennedy had just appointed Secretary of Defense, would make an excellent profile for the magazine, "a piece that would introduce our readers to this man, explain who he is, where he came from, what he's all about. I understand he's a wonderful guy."

McNamara had a lot of admirers. Apparently, the Ford Motor Company had been hemmorhaging money and McNamara had led a group of young geniuses, called "McNamara's Band," who had instituted financial analysis, financial planning and administrative control that had stanched the bleeding and begun to turn things around. Now, at 43, he was the first non-member of the Ford family ever to ascend to the company's presidency. The media was heaping encomiums upon him as the savior of a major American manufacturer. He had been in his new job less than six weeks when Kennedy tapped him for the job at Defense. Surely this talented manager would whip the Department into shape, and everyone knew that had to be done. After all, no less an icon than President Dwight D. Eisenhower, who, as Supreme Commander of the Allied Forces that had brought down Hitler, had, in his farewell address as President, warned us of the danger posed by an "overweening military-industrial complex."

There was not the slightest doubt in my mind that Hobe wanted an article that demonstrated that McNamara was just the guy to de-complex the military-industrial complex.

My first call was to the public relations department of the Ford Motor Company, in Dearborn, Michigan. I wanted an interview with Ford CEO Henry Ford II, who only six weeks earlier had appointed McNamara to head the family enterprise. I wanted to know exactly what it was about McNamara that had so impressed him, and how did he feel about his leaving after so short a time – after Ford himself had spent a year reorganizing his executive suite in order to fit McNamara in at the top. I needed him to define the special qualities about McNamara that should stand the Defense Department and the country in good stead. What were McNamara's strongest attributes? How could it be demonstrated that he is an inspiring leader? Did he look forward to McNamara returning to the company in some capacity after public service? If so, in what capacity? If not, why not?

To my amazement, I found myself a few days later having lunch with Henry Ford II in his private dining room atop the Ford headquarters building in Dearborn, Michigan. I would continue to be amazed at how quickly the doors of important people opened when the name of The Reader's Digest was invoked.

Ford was welcoming, gracious, talkative, informative. He told me of several of the efficiencies McNamara had seen to, and how valuable they had proved to the company. "Automobile manufacturing has always been a business of hunches," he explained, "and it's hard to guess right consistently. But it's hard to find Bob guessing wrong. His decisions invariably are based on careful personal research and sound analysis. They are strong. They are final. I'm sure he'll do an outstanding job as Defense Secretary."

I left the luncheon puzzled. Clearly, Ford had enormous respect for McNamara as a manager and executive, but I had the impression that he was not enthusiastic about the prospect of his eventual return. When I asked, he simply observed that, "Life moves on. We all do what we think we have to do. Bob decided that he has to be Defense Secretary."

It was much easier to see and have lunch with Henry Ford II than to see McNamara. I cooled my heels in the Pentagon for a couple of days while he was busy doing whatever people do when they are becoming Defense Secretary.

When he became available I found him to be of average height, trim, his dark hair was slicked back and he wore rimless glasses and a dark blue suit. He seemed pleasant enough. He told me that his parents had migrated from County Cork, Ireland, and that he grown up in Piedmont, a small California city completely surrounded by Oakland. In the 1920's it became known as "The City of Millionaires," because it was home to more millionaires per square mile than any other city in the country.

He had just arrived at his new job and was not yet well enough versed in military affairs to talk much about them. From his wife, Margaret, I learned a lot more about him. For example, that he had been a prodigy. When he was two years old his mother had begun reading to him for an hour each day, that his astonished first grade teacher discovered that he could read at the eighth grade level and that he had a most retentive mind. Straight A's had come easily to him all the way through college. By the end of his second year at the University of California he was an elite student, Phi Beta Kappa, majoring in Economics and Philosophy. He was also blessed with energetic initiative, and had decided that there was no reason why his father should shoulder the entire financial burden of his college education, so had spent the summers of his college years roaming the Pacific as an able seaman aboard tankers and cargo ships.

Upon graduating from California, he completed work on a Masters Degree in Business Administration at Harvard University, compiling one of the outstanding academic records in the school's history.

Margaret told me that from the day he first walked he had loved to hike and climb, and had spent much time doing so in California's hills and mountains, and had scaled many of the Sierra Nevadas and Grand Tetons, as well as the Matterhorn, and he could not remember ever not being able to ski.

I liked all these things about him. I was as impressed as everyone else. I produced an article showing that he was just the man to do the tough job that had to be done in the Defense Department.

What made it so tough was that the Army, Navy and Air Force had been "unified" in 1947 into a single integrated Department of Defense, but each service had been left with its own identity and sovereignty over its special field. In the 14 years since, the Department had seethed with bitter dissension that had forestalled anything resembling a smooth-working unification. In the annual brawl over how best to distribute military appropriations the three services displayed, often quite snidely, widely divergent views as to how most effectively to keep a volatile world at peace and America safe through military strength.

Fast forward to 1964: Lyndon Johnson is President, McNamara is still Defense Secretary, and I am increasingly aware that many senior officers in all the Services have at least one thing in common: they dislike the Secretary and loathe his ideas – dislike him because he demonstrates a lack of respect for them professionally, and his ideas because they judge them to be foolhardy and dangerous.

On August 4, 1964, the Johnson Administration made a decision to plunge the United States into the Vietnam War. Here's exactly how the plunge was taken, as told to me by the man to whom it fell to actually take the country off the high board, then Navy Commander James Bond Stockdale:

Stockdale was a squadron commander aboard the aircraft carrier U.S.S. Ticonderoga, on station in the Gulf of Tonkin. He was asleep in his bunk, having spent most of three hours the previous evening leading flights from Ticonderoga and its sister carrier, the U.S.S. Constellation, in a frantic, fruitless, low-level search of waters well-lit with flares, looking for North Vietnamese targets – allegedly, a covey of torpedo boats that were attacking two American destroyers, the Maddox and the Turner Joy, that were patrolling in the gulf. "There was nothing there, no torpedo boats," he reported, "only two American destroyers and lot of black ocean and American firepower. It was all a Chinese fire drill."

Then why the almost hysterical messages that had been emanating from the destroyers? How could this be?

Stockdale recalled that as he had climbed into the cockpit of his FA-18 Crusader jet that night he had noted that the entire region seemed to be smothering under a blanket of clinging, high humidity heat, that heat lightning was flashing wildly in the skies to the north and west, that the atmosphere was charged. He theorized that the two destroyers' radars and sonars and their operators had been spooked by the weather atmospherics.

So after a couple of hours of leading squadrons from two carriers in a search that found nothing, he had returned to Ticonderoga and hit the sack, relieved that it had been nothing more than an electronic snafu; he had sent messages to that effect to all interested parties. He was shaken awake early the next morning by a young officer who told him that Washington had ordered that air strikes were to be flown that day into North Vietnam, that he was to lead the strike that would take out the torpedo boat base and oil storage facilities at the city of Vinh, and that his target was Washington's Number One priority.

He was flabbergasted. He was being told that the country was going to war, and that he was the tip of the spear.

"Why the strikes?" he asked.

"Reprisal, Sir."

"Reprisal for what?"

"For last night's attacks on the destroyers, Sir."

He couldn't make sense of what he was hearing. Having had what he later would describe to me as "the best seat in the world" for what would be called "The Gulf of Tonkin Incident", he wondered for a long moment how to contact the President, to warn him that there had been no torpedo boat attacks, no such "incident." As the search had continued he had become aware that the Commodore in charge of the two destroyers, Commander John Herrick, had clearly lost confidence in the messages he was hearing, that an attack was underway. Hadn't the word reached Washington? It *must* have!

Then, second thoughts: Obviously, the decision for war had come from "way up on top." No one was going to put a lowly squadron commander in touch with the President, to explain things to him, to urge him to countermand himself. There had to be more to it than he knew, more to it than last night's non-attacks. The feeling that war could erupt at any time had been prevalent for weeks. Indeed, last Sunday three North Vietnamese torpedo boats had attacked Maddox and Turner Joy, and Stockdale and two of his pilots had driven them off. It had been a minor dustup; no one had thought much about it.

The "Gulf of Tonkin Incident" of August 4, 1964, an "Incident" that never happened, was the pretext for taking the United States to war.

On that first morning of the war, Jim Stockdale ordered that his squadron be armed with the kind of weaponry that would enable it to take out the assigned targets.

That was the last time Stockdale or any other air commander he knew ever would be permitted to decide how his aircraft would be armed when going into combat. Thereafter, he told me, every such decision was made by civilians in the Pentagon, who soon became known, derisively, as "The Whiz Kids." They were not military professionals, but civilians, economists, accountants, political scientists.

What President Johnson and his Defense chief, Bob McNamara, knew, or thought they knew, was that this was not the kind of war that could be handed over to the military professionals. In their view, all the Military knew how to do was to break things and kill people. In these times American power had to be handled more responsibly, had to be utilized in a way that would not offend world opinion, that would assure the communist leadership in Hanoi that the United States did not intend its destruction nor the destruction of its country, that would not risk intervention by communist China, as China had intervened in the Korean War. America's only purpose was to persuade the North Vietnamese leadership that it could not succeed in its attempt to take South Vietnam, and that a continuation of such an effort would cost them far more than it was worth. This kind of war called for a strategy of squeezing the enemy of his assets until the price became more than he could pay, a strategy of "gradualism."

"The Administration had the naïve idea that delicate peacemaking signals could be transmitted by military action," said Stockdale.

"Civilians in the Pentagon chose all the targets, decided what weapons would be delivered upon them, even dictated the courses and altitudes that were to be flown. We were foolishly risking airplanes and pilots' lives on meaningless targets, on specified flight plans with specified ordnance loads that frequently were dangerous or incorrect or both."

It got worse: Reconnaissance aircraft kept bringing in "very clear photos of the docks at Haiphong, North Vietnam's major port, just after a Soviet merchant ships were unloaded. The Soviets were North Vietnam's chief supplier of weapons and ammunition. The photography was of large piles of guns, ammunition and many SAMs (Soviet Surface to Air Missiles) that would be coming up to meet our pilots soon. We were required to give communist merchant ships free access to the Haiphong docks, then watch them wave to us as they passed us by on their way home, sometimes while we were holding a memorial service for a pilot who had been killed by one of the missiles they had delivered. We were wasting lives on targets that weren't worth hitting while we had to fly right by targets that we were not permitted to hit that were crucial to our enemy's ability to make war."

The Johnson-McNamara "strategy of gradualism" was surely among the worst war fighting ideas anyone ever had. It was the reason the Vietnam war lasted nearly a decade. It cost the lives of some 58,000 young Americans, many thousands more were maimed, hundreds suffered many years in an unimaginably vile captivity, countless billions of dollars were squandered and America was divided as it had not been divided since the Civil War.

Among the important lessons the American people should take from the Vietnam experience are that we should never commit to war unless there is no reasonable alternative, and unless we are prepared to do all that is reasonably possible to end it as quickly as possible. Also, that a brilliantly successful business career does not necessarily foretell success in the management of military affairs – in fact, in this case it's clear that the ego that flowered out of an amazing success in business led to catastrophe in war. For the conduct of any war we deem necessary, we must rely mainly on the military professionals, for it is they who know more about how to make war than anyone else, who know its horrors and who thus hate it the most and are committed to ending it with dispatch.

And it taught me to refrain from writing enthusiastic portraits of political appointees at least until they have proved themselves to be competent public officials.

38
The Most Fun

I startled myself and a lot of other people, including the editors of the Digest. From the beginning I had been free to do much as I pleased, and had focused on military affairs, current affairs, inspirational pieces, profiles of interesting people, subjects that would be of general interest.

All of a sudden, I began writing stuff that made people laugh.

It began one day when my wife brought home what appeared to be a washtub. It was oversized, oblong, quite old and very dirty. "Isn't it *ador*able?" she squealed, and it wasn't a question, but a statement of fact that demanded agreement.

"I'm *sure* it is," I said. "What is it disguised as, a filthy old tub?"

There was a nasty stillness, then a vicious personal attack. "You're very sarcastic." she said. That's bad, when she says something like that, without italicizing any of the words to emphasize them. "You would have gone out and spent a lot of money on a new one," she charged, "and they don't have half the character this one does."

"I'll bet they don't," I responded, foolishly. "I do not recall ever expressing a desire for a new filthy old tub, but I'm glad you didn't buy one when this one was available for only…"

"Two dollars," she snarled, then, for emphasis, "*Two dollars*!"

"After all," I continued, crazily, "this one can do the same thing as a new one, can't it? By the way, what do these things do?"

"Let's not discuss it any further, please," she said, picking the thing up and disappearing with it into the basement. And we didn't' discuss it or anything else for about 48 hours.

Then, I came upon the filthy old tub again, but I didn't recognize it. It stood beside the fireplace, looking like it belonged there, looking like that had always been its purpose and I could not imagine ever again not having this delightful object beside my fireplace. It gleamed a deep, brilliant copper. Somehow, a top had been attached and covered with a tweed cushion, maroon touched with shades of old gold. It was a masterpiece!

"Where did this marvelous object come from?" I cried.

"Some junkyard," she said, in an arms-folded tone. "Some people thought it was a filthy old tub."

This happened a lot in the early years or our marriage. The notion of shopping for household furnishings in retail stores bored her to death. She was enthusiastic about estate sales, where the heirs of the recently deceased sought to disencumber themselves of his earthly possessions.

That's how she furnished our house, from the attractive carpets on the downstairs floors that looked brand new, which I learned were some sort of fantastic wool and would last a century or so, to the spectacular Waterford Crystal chandelier that hung from the dining room ceiling – listen, once there was a big old wagon wheel that had been rusting for a long time in somebody's barn. Triumphantly, she told me she had "stolen" the thing for five dollars.

"Lie down," I said. "You're all mixed up. "Five dollar bills are not going out of style, wagon wheels are."

Shortly, the wagon wheel reappeared as the greatest looking coffee table of all time. She had cut it in half, fashioned the cut down spokes of one half into the legs of the other half, applied very busy hours and elbows to the applications of paint remover, oils and stains. A crystal plate had been cut to fit precisely inside the rim. The wheel hub was no longer a wheel hub, but a container for a bourgeoning fountain of ivy.

"Well." I bleated, brightly. "Well, well, *well!* That is *stunning*, HONEY?"

"Thank you, Dear," she said. But I knew what she really meant, she meant, "You said it, stupid," and without a capital S on the stupid, either.

"I was dead wrong to quarrel with your creative instincts," I continued, manfully.

She smiled, lovingly. "I accept your apology," she said. But I knew she meant, "I hope you're beginning to wise up, Knucklebrain."

"It won't happen again," I assured her.

Now, she really got vicious. She said, "I know, Dear." But I knew what she really meant: "I'd like to whack that cement head of yours with a pickaxe."

It was spooky, the way she got all that across in such an agreeable way; a casual observer would never guess what she was really saying.

"I feel like a perfect ass," I confessed.

"Nobody's perfect," she assured me.

It went on like that. I have in my study a handsome, comfortable chair that surely was headed for a landfill when my wife rescued and rehabilitated it for me. In a bedroom stands a once delapidated armoire that she squandered twenty hard-earned dollars on and restored, and for which a neighbor who owns a furniture store offered me $1500.

I wrote about all this in detail, took the piece to Pleasantville and laid it on Hobart Lewis's desk. Next thing I knew a famous illustrator, Constantin Alajalov, whose work had appeared on numerous magazine covers, was commissioned to do an illustration to run with it under the title, "The Things My Wife Drags Home!" It depicted a young man, much handsomer than I, his face a picture of astonished dismay, standing behind a very pretty woman, her hands clasped beneath her chin, smiling happily at her newest acquisition, perhaps the ugliest coat rack, boot rack, clock ever conceived. It was even decorated with some animal's horns.

The issue of the Digest containing the article was current when one Saturday my wife rode her bicycle to an estate sale, dithering over a mirror she thought she might want; how would she get it home? "I'll have to call my husband," she said.

The lady running the sale thought she was worried about what her husband would think of it. She said, "Listen, if you like it buy it, never mind what the your husband thinks. Let me show you something. She brought out a copy of the Digest and showed her my article. When my wife explained that it was about her, she became a celebrity.

Finishing a round of golf that Saturday, I called home to ask if she wanted me to pick anything up. Yes, she said, and asked me to pick up the mirror and gave me the address of the estate sale. When I arrived, the lady in charge summoned her half dozen helpers, pointed at me and explained, "This is the guy!"

I couldn't tell whether I was a celebrity or an object of scorn. I escaped.

Alajalov presented me with the original of the illustration he did for the piece. It hangs on the wall of my study.

Funny relaxed me, and I did a lot more of it, all of it about my family; a family with nine kids is a family with a full slate of laughs. I could always tell that I had a good one going; I found myself laughing as I wrote.

In a piece entitled, "All I Ask is a Tall Ship," I showed the reader how to handle a sailboat that I had never planned to own after an adventurous daughter tricked me into buying it. I found that I loved sailing, but I couldn't find time to take lessons, and as a result was angrily accused, with good reason, of reckless sailboating by less adventurous "skippers" on the lake. But the story made Digest readers laugh.

You can't help but laugh about it – eventually – when a fifth grade son awakens you at 3:30 a.m. on a Sunday and tells you it's time to go to hockey practice, and it turns out that he's *serious!*

And when the kids are old enough to take care of themselves while you and your wife go on vacation and you give them your vacation phone number in case of emergency – and emergencies do occur – like, the dog is lost; or, a hockey puck broke the bathroom window and it's cold in here; or how do you cook chicken wings? Or, "Joey's a skunk", etc.

The Digest published 15 of my humor pieces. They were the most fun I ever had with a typewriter and sheets of paper. They were fun for readers, too. They said so in lots of letters they sent me. Some insisted that I should have a humor piece in every issue. But I only had nine kids, not enough for a story in every issue.

Guess how much mail I got when I wrote all those other articles that I was sure would help save the world.

Up with funny!

39
The Editorial

G etting back to the saving of the world: Never in its history had The Reader's Digest run an editorial, an opinion
directed to its readers. In a conference call Hobe Lewis,
David Reed and I agreed that it probably was time to run one.

We would meet the next day in the Washington office and "put
our heads together." I don't remember which of us said that, the
part about "putting our heads together."

When we met, Reed immediately excused himself from the
"putting-our-heads-together" conversation, pointing out that he
had an important State Department interview scheduled in an
hour, but would return as quickly as possible.

Lewis turned to me, explaining that he, also, had an important
meeting somewhere, but would be back as quickly as possible, and
that meanwhile it was up to me.

"*Churchill!*" Hobe said as he was leaving the office, "Make it sound like Churchill."

"I don't think I'm that good," I said.

"Yes," he said, "you are. You're a great ghost writer. You've ghost written wonderful pieces for personalities, congressmen, mayors, cabinet officers. You got what they wanted to say into The Reader's Digest. They couldn't have done it without you. Just pretend you are ghosting a piece for Winston Churchill."

I said, "The late journalistic icon, Edward R. Murrow, pointed out that Churchill 'mobilized the English language and sent it to war.' Indeed, Churchill's vocal leadership proved to be one of the most effective weapons in the Allies' arsenal. I am inclined to doubt that I am in Churchill's league."

"Your modesty becomes you," Hobe said, "I didn't even know it was there. But just think of the way he inspired the British people, the whole Free World, when it looked as though the Germans were going to invade England. How he rallied them, shook the fist of his spirit, saying, 'We will fight them on the beaches, the landing grounds, in the fields, in the streets.' He said, 'we shall never surrender!' He said, 'Never give up. Never, never, *never!*'"

"Since you put it that way," I said, "I shall *never* give up. I'll give it a try."

"You can *do* it!" He headed for the door, then turned back.

"*Lincoln!*" he said. "Try to get some of the kind of profound stuff into it that Abraham Lincoln might have said."

I was beginning to feel pretty good about myself.

What had led to this meeting was a column by Joseph Alsop, Stewart Alsop's brother, and like his brother an esteemed columnist.

He had just returned from his eighteenth visit to Vietnam. He knew the country, the people and the war as well as it was possible to know them. This time, he had visited many hamlets in every district, from the Demilitarized Zone (DMZ) in the north to the southernmost point of Ca Mau. He had talked to every leader, to many villagers who had joined the People's Self Defense Force, to rice farmers everywhere. He conclusively demonstrated that despite the shocking negativity of the American media, the days of the communist effort to enslave South Vietnam were numbered – "unless President Nixon is finally driven to throw in the sponge."

The last line in Alsop's column worried us. If any journalist was a Washington "insider" it was him, and we thought it probably was a clue to the thinking that was going on in the Nixon White House. We wanted the war ended as quickly as anyone did. What we three agreed we did not want was an American betrayal of an ally to whom we had given a solemn pledge, an abandonment of a cause in which our country purported to believe in to the extent that many thousands of our young people had been sacrificed; wouldn't a withdrawal be a betrayal of them? And wouldn't a withdrawal convey to the world that it would be unwise to count on the United States as an ally? We believed that most Americans shared these views, and opposed the views of the many editorialists, academics, politicians and celebrities who led and supported the anti-war movement and whom communists described, accurately, we believed, as "useful idiots."

An observer who had standing with the public had to make the counter argument. The Reader's Digest had such standing, and the world's largest print audience. We agreed that the Digest should express its views to this audience in an editorial.

By the time Lewis and Reed returned I had an editorial written. Both agreed it was excellent. Lewis was almost ecstatic. He returned to Pleasantville with it and rewrote the whole thing; it now sounded a lot more like Hobart Lewis than Winston Churchill, Abraham Lincoln or John G. Hubbell, but it said all the right things, and I thought it was good – not as strong as what Churchill-Lincoln-Hubbell had written, but strong enough.

It led off the December, 1969, issue under the title, "Patience! – An Editorial." Originally, it had been billed as from, "The Editors of The Reader's Digest," but this had ignited an uproar; there were editors on the staff who were practically rabid in their disagreement with our views, and refused to be associated with them. In fact, three had resigned when the editorial was scheduled. It had simply explained again why we were in Vietnam, reminded Americans how much they had invested in blood and treasure in this effort to protect an ally from enslavement and in halting the spread of communism, pointed out that a summary withdrawal would send a dispiriting message to our allies around the world and called attention to the uncivilized behavior of the anti-war movement that had created so much division at home in time of war.

It could not have appeared in the magazine unless Wally had agreed with it. I wondered how he had reacted to the resignations. I was told, "He said that it probably was a good idea to shake the tree every so often."

40

How I Saved Drew Pearson

One day in the late 1960's, when the country was simmering with dissension over the Vietnam War, I was in Washington researching I don't recall what, but it had to do with military affairs and it occurred to me that I could quickly get all the information I needed from the Chairman of the House Armed Services Committee. At the time, this was L. Mendel Rivers, a South Carolina Democrat. I called his office for an appointment, and was advised that the Chairman was busy most of the day, but suggested that he could meet with me at 5 p.m., if that was agreeable.

I arrived on time and the Chairman greeted me warmly, getting up from behind his desk to shake hands and to express a favorable opinion of my work and of The Reader's Digest in general, which he called, "a great American institution."

He quickly turned the meeting into a social event. "Can I fix you something?" he asked, walking to a sideboard and adding that, "The sun is sinking, day is done, and I was just about to have a little bourbon and branch water."

I agreed to join him, and we had a couple of drinks while he answered the questions I had come to ask. It was a very pleasant meeting. It took perhaps 45 minutes to acquire the information I needed, and to visit in general terms over the state of the nation's defenses. I left with the impression of a nice, most hospitable southern gentleman.

The following mid-morning I was typing my notes in an office in the Washington bureau when the office manager and my good friend, Virginia Lawton, stuck her head in to tell me that Congressman Rivers was on line two.

"Mr. Rivers?" I said into the phone.

"Hubbell," the Congressman shouted, "did you see what that son of a bitch Drew Pearson said about me in his column this morning?"

"No, Sir," I replied, "I did not." I had not yet looked at that day's Washington Post.

Drew Pearson had a syndicated column entitled "Washington Merry Go Round." He was famous for advising his readers of outrageous behavior on the part of policy makers and other prominent people with whom he disagreed, whether or not he knew his allegations to be true. His columns made juicy reading and triggered dark suspicions of those whom he found offensive, He was published in hundreds of the nation's newspapers

The Chairman ranted, "He said I drink too much! Do *you* think I drink too much?"

"Well, Sir, we had a couple of drinks when I visited with you yesterday, but it was the cocktail hour, and I thought it was… very pleasant…just right."

"Y'know," he said, those boys come up to visit with me from South Carolina, that's a dusty trip and they're thirsty when they get here, and they got to wet the whistle a bit, and what's wrong with that?" He yelled, "I'd like to shoot that bastard!"

I thought about this for a moment, then said, "Mr. Rivers, I would like to make suggestion to you."

"I would be most pleased to hear any suggestion from you," he drawled.

"My suggestion is that you do not call any other media people and tell them that Drew Pearson is a son of a bitch and a bastard; most of them know that, but they will make headlines with it if it comes from you. They will make the most of any chance to make you look bad because you are a strong supporter of the Vietnam War. They think that anyone who supports the war, including me, and I'm one of them, should be sent into exile or committed to a lunatic asylum. They will portray you as a foul-mouthed incompetent who should not be chairing one of the most important committees in Congress. There will be demands that you be censured and that you resign. And don't tell anyone that you would like to shoot Drew Pearson; it just sounds bad, and if somebody does shoot the "son of a bitch" some people will try to pin it on you."

He giggled. He calmed down. He said, "You think I should just keep quiet? Other journalists are going to be asking me about this."

"Tell them that you won't dignify Pearson's slander with a response. Pearson says terrible things about lots of people. Why worry about what he says? If you respond, it will become an issue. If you don't, it will soon go away."

"That makes sense to me. All right, Hubbell, I'll take your advice, and thank you."

And that is how I saved "that bastard" Drew Pearson from being shot by The Hon. Rivers.

41

He Dared to Stand Alone

L ove him or hate him, and notwithstanding the fact that he was – so far – the only U.S. President who had to resign from office for criminal misbehavior, Richard Nixon certainly was what his rival, John F. Kennedy, would have called a "Profile in Courage."

On May 6, 1970. I am seated in the Oval Office of the White House, facing the President across his desk. Seated in another chair nearby is the President's National Security Advisor, Dr. Henry Kissinger. A few nights earlier, on April 30, the President triggered what has the look of a national insurrection. With the United States bitterly and often violently at odds with itself over its participation in the Vietnam war, he went on television to tell the country and the world that he had ordered U.S. forces in Vietnam to enter into Cambodia, Vietnam's next door neighbor, and destroy more than a dozen communist bases the North Vietnamese had established along 600 miles of the country's easternmost border, flush against South Vietnam. For five years North Vietnamese forces had been able regularly to launch attacks from these bases into South Vietnam against American and South Vietnamese forces, knowing that under the rules by which the U.S. governed its forces in this war they were prohibited from pursuing the attackers back into Cambodia – Washington feared that someone might accuse us of "invading" another country.

In return for the sanctuary bases Hanoi had pledged not to meddle in Cambodian politics; in any case Cambodia lacked the military muscle to do anything about it.

Nixon knew that his decision would provoke savage criticism. He had reminded his audience of the several steps the U.S. had taken to end hostilities: it had stopped the bombing of North Vietnam; reduced all of its air operations; announced the withdrawal of a quarter of a million troops, and announced that it would withdraw all of its troops if North Vietnam would do likewise. The communists had ignored every concession, every offer, had instead conducted massive military aggressions in Laos and Cambodia

The rules banning effective counterattack were absurd, and had cost many American and South Vietnamese lives.

In mid-April, 1970, the President learned that the enemy was rapidly consolidating his Cambodian positions into a single, well-fortified supply and staging area. A network of roads was being developed that would enable strong communist forces to move quickly and laterally and with much improved logistic support and to attack from any point along a 600-mile front. The enemy was also in the process of guaranteeing himself water entry into the southern half of South Vietnam. Indeed, the communists were now in the process of moving some 30,000 troops into the Cambodian sanctuary. Additionally, Hanoi had ordered a declining kill rate against the Americans to be raised to at least 100 per week.

Nixon found this to be intolerable.

He insisted to the world that the move against the sanctuaries was not an expansion of the war, that our forces would leave Cambodia in a few days, as quickly as the enemy's ability to make war from Cambodia was destroyed.

I was elated! I hoped that now, at long last, we would destroy the enemy's ability to make war from North Vietnam.

For years we had been slogging along ineffectively under a stupid war fighting policy called *gradualism*, terribly costly in terms of both blood and treasure, a country virtually at war with itself and suffering the world's contempt.

Predictably and immediately following Nixon's address, politicians, pundits, professors, opinion makers of every stripe one after another were condemning the action, insisting that with what was called an unwarranted invasion of another country. Nixon had taken America into a whole new war. We would become bogged down in Cambodia just as we were in Vietnam. American casualties would skyrocket. Failure was inevitable. The country was disgraced. No less than former Defense Secretary Clark Clifford, who should have known better, authored a shameful and utterly nonsensical condemnation which Life Magazine saw fit to publish. Nixon was damned as a bloodthirsty war monger, an imperialist, a maniac who was far exceeding the powers of the Presidency.

Some in Congress proposed steps that would limit those powers. Throughout the country the behavior of anti-war protesters became so unruly that governors felt compelled to call out the National Guard. At Kent State University, in Ohio, nervous Guardsmen fired at a crowd of students, killing four of them. At Jackson State College, in Mississippi, police fire killed two students and wounded another dozen.

America lay in the maw of a deep, grieving anguish.

I reached Washington the day after the speech, a Wednesday. By the weekend I had conducted exhaustive interviews, examining every pro and con of the President's decision with every major participant in the decision-making process, including the Secretary of Defense, the Deputy Secretary, the Chairman of the Joint Chiefs of Staff, the Director of Central Intelligence and others. Then, on the following Monday morning, I spent 55 minutes in the Oval Office, interviewing President Nixon and his National Security Advisor, Dr. Henry Kissinger. When I left the White House that morning, I had to make my way through an enormous anti-war crowd who were jeering, and chanting, "All we ask is, give peace a chance."

Which was exactly what Nixon had done. I was certain, I *knew* that those who were insisting that his action would fail, who were promoting anger and despair, were wrong. It would all turn out just as Nixon said it would; it wasn't rocket science, it was – finally! – an infusion of common sense.

By Monday afternoon I had the article completed. It appeared in the July issue of the Digest, which reached the magazine's audience by mid-June, *only a few weeks after* the Cambodian incursion had accomplished its purpose: Not only had the communists' sanctuary bases in Cambodia been smashed, but more than 1,500 tons of their weapons and ammunition been captured, instruments of war that otherwise might have maimed and killed more than 150,000 American troops and their allies. And as quickly as it was done all the American forces were withdrawn from Cambodia, just as the President had said they would be.

I had never felt better about any article I had written.

A few years later Nixon would resign the Presidency under a cloud. But in the spring of 1970 he stood alone, he gutted it out against assurances of ignominy and defeat from one of the strongest assemblages of hateful and wrongful dissent in American history.

42

Bad Judgment and Disgust

No sooner had I completed the article on the Cambodian incursion than Life Magazine published an anti-incursion, anti-war and what seemed to me to be an anti-American piece by Clark Clifford, a Washington lawyer who had succeeded Robert McNamara as Defense Secretary. Then, I was astounded to learn that DeWitt Wallace himself had selected the Clifford article for inclusion in the August issue of the Digest.

I immediately wrote a memo to Hobart Lewis, hoping he would show it to DeWitt Wallace, which he did. Here it is, with Wally's and Hobe's handwritten comments.

[handwritten annotations in margins, including: "Wally — you know all of this, but points marked on P. 1 + 3 are worth a glance." and "May 28, 1970" and initials]

Dear Hobe:

Now that I have had my say re: Nixon and Cambodia, I feel absolutely obliged to try to interfere with others having their say, which is to say that I understand the Clark Clifford *Life* piece is scheduled for August.

A couple of thoughts occur: 1) Perhaps it is a good idea to let the opposition speak out in order to show how foolish it is. If so, I doubt that we could do better than the Clifford piece, which is not a good argument at all, but merely an anti-Nixon rant, and a pretty reckless one at that. But also if so, might not too many pay too serious heed to one who is a former Defense Secretary? 2) Isn't there some danger that RD is placing itself in an ambivalent position? In July, we are strongly supporting the President's Cambodian move; in August, we rather fervently are to denounce it.

In any case, I have studied the Clifford piece at careful length, and have some thoughts which may be worth considering:

Clifford begins by equating Nixon's Cambodian decision with Kennedy's Bay of Pigs. There is not the remotest resemblance. By every authentic record -- and no matter what Kennedy's apologists want to call it -- the failure at the Bay of Pigs was a failure of Presidential courage.

Nixon's decision to move against the communists' Cambodian sanctuaries can hardly be described as a failure of courage.

But, says Clifford, Nixon's action "is an infinitely greater mistake...far graver damage has been done to our nation, both at home and abroad."

It's true that divisions at home are deeper now, but with every passing hour the Cambodian operation becomes a more and more outstanding military success, and within a few months obvious success should serve to heal a lot of the division. Moreover, these divisions are not just over the war -- it's a convenient peg for radical leftists and others, all of whom for their own reasons are determined to create domestic division. When the furor over the Cambodian move dies away, it will be something else.

Damage abroad? I suggest that America earns higher marks around the world for at long last demonstrating the will to move sensibly against a communist military threat than she does when she just sits back and lets it happen. Surely she earns far higher marks than she did when she armed, trained, encouraged and transported an allied force to the shores of Cuba, there abandoned it and permitted the communists to secure on our doorstep a base for aggression and subversion in our own hemisphere.

Clifford claims Nixon is repeating the mistakes of the past five years. Not so. Nixon has been implementing and protecting a plan for American disengagement. Johnson had no such plan. Nixon has made the enemy understand he will not tolerate sanctuaries from which his forces can threaten American lives. Kennedy and Johnson gave the con-

-2-

munists carte blance to infiltrate men and materiel into South Vietnam
from the Laotian border and then from Cambodia. Nixon is not repeating
mistakes, he is rectifying them.

Clifford points out that the enemy's war materiel is produced
not in North Vietnam, but in the Soviet Union and in Communist China.
Nixon knows this, tried to reason with the Russians and was rebuffed.
But Clifford ignores this effort, and ignores the fact that the Kremlin
and Peking cannot afford not to support a communist war. Instead, Cliffor
makes new reference to one of the great mistakes of the Johnson administration: "We attempted to impede the flow of weapons into South Vietnam
by a bombing campaign in the North. In my opinion, the results did not
warrant the enormous cost to us."

We covered this pretty well with the article by Admiral Sharp,
wherein Sharp described the tight restraints imposed on American airpower, how so many vital targets were left unscathed, how our aircraft
were not allowed to attack materiel until it got onto the jungle trails
into South Vietnam, how they were never permitted to attack the great
stockpiles in Hanoi and Haiphong. Sharp clearly explained the folly
and failure of the Johnson-McNamara policy of gradualism. But Clifford
does not explain this, does not tell the reader why the air campaign
against the North was not worth the cost.

Clifford says, "A program for orderly disengagement will
create the conditions in which productive negotiations become possible."
This is precisely what Nixon is trying to accomplish -- an orderly disengagement of American forces, and productive negotiations. But, says
Clifford, "Nixon, while he proclaims his dedication to a political settlement, by his actions still seeks to gain the military victory that cannot
be won." This strikes me as sheer, empty anti-Nixonism -- if Clifford
really believes this, he hasn't been listening.

Clifford insists the Cambodian move was "reckless" and "foolhardy," says the decision was made "precipitately" and failed to take
into account the possible reaction of Communist China and imperiled the
success of the SALT talks. He calls the Vietnamization plan "a formula
for perpetual war."

These things simply are not true. These arguments are destroyed in advance in the July article, and also by Stewart Alsop in his
column in the current Newsweek.

Clifford says, "It seems clear the Administration believes it
has proposed in Paris a genuine basis for compromise. In my opinion,
however, these proposals are not realistic, nor will they lead to any
progress." But he neglects to explain to the reader that in Paris our
government has made every concession and offer that has yet been made
and repeatedly has asserted its willingness to negotiate everything
except the right of the people of South Vietnam freely to choose their
own government, and that the only response from the communists has been
the continual demand for immediate and total withdrawal of all American
forces and the destruction of the Saigon government.

Clifford does not tell us what he thinks would be a realistic
basis for compromise -- unless it is his fantastic 1-2-3 plan which fails
to take into account the communist history of treachery and which seems
a formula for surrender and disaster. He lightly glosses over the

3

possibility of a communist bloodbath -- no reference whatever to the bloodbath at Hue, where some 3000 innocents were murdered -- hundreds of them buried alive -- during the 1968 Tet offensive.

Clifford tells us that the "North Vietnamese negotiators have indicated their willingness to talk seriously if the United States declares the total and unconditional withdrawal of its troops from South Vietnam." One recalls that the communist negotiators indicated such willingness to talk seriously if only the United States would stop the bombing of North Vietnam -- and they and their noisy allies in this country got Lyndon Johnson to stop the bombing. That's when they began indicating their willingness to talk seriously provided we first agreed to get out and give them everything they want. And it might also be noted that after we stopped the bombing, they continued blindly to lob rockets into the population centers of South Vietnam.

Clifford claims for his plan that, "This approach could serve to get negotiations started again..." The clear implication is that the United States did something to cause negotiations to stop. I am unaware that negotiations ever really got started. We have made concessions and lots of offers trying to get them started, but there's never been any response.

Clifford ends by telling us, "The enormous upswing in anti-war sentiment, following the Cambodian transgression, must be maintained and strengthened." It distresses me to permit anyone to advocate in our pages the sort of thing we have seen going on in this country.

My final objection to the use of the piece is that by the time the August issue is out, the jury might well be in with a favorable verdict on the Cambodian operation. At that late date, might we not look a little odd in giving over pages to a condemnation of the decision?

Those are my unsolicited, unexpurgated thoughts on the Clifford piece, offered in the belief that RD pays me for what goes on in my head regarding such matters, as well as for what comes out of my typewriter.

All best to you,

Hubbell

The handwriting on the upper right side of page 1 is Hobart Lewis. He writes: "Wally, you know all of this, but points marked on p. 1 and 3 are worth a glance.

/s/ Hobe

Atop the memo, Wally responds: "Hobe, I must confess that I read this memo for the first time four days after deciding to kill the Clifford piece.

/s/ Wally

Then, Wally adds: "The decision to use the article was bad judgment on my part."

Then, on the left margin of the memo, Wally writes in obvious disgust that, "Three Digest editors wrote me expressing their delight that the Clifford piece was being used."

So while my memo was not the deciding factor, Wally's reaction to it indicates that we thought alike, and that he was not happy with the thinking of some of his in-house editors.

43
Surprised at Surprise

Many years after the death of DeWitt Wallace Ed Thompson, who by now was retired, convened a luncheon reunion that included some editors and a writer. I was the writer; the editors were Thompson and Hobart Lewis, both of whom had been Editor-in-Chief, Andy Jones and Walter Hunt, who had long been in charge of the books and book-length features that appeared in the back of the magazine. We reminisced, and many of the memories were about Wally. I was surprised that I surprised everyone with one of my own experiences with the founding father.

I had submitted a story that had especially impressed Wally. I had long been disgusted at the anti-war movement, which had been made possible by the Administration's ineffectual war fighting policy. Political leaders, editorialists, pundits, academics and celebrities throughout the world and throughout America continued to rail against the United States' "unjust" and "immoral" war. In huge demonstrations in cities across the country American protesters were marching in the streets, waving the Viet Cong flag, chanting things like, "Hey, hey, LBJ. How many kids did you kill today?"

Celebrities like movie star Jane Fonda traveled to Hanoi, the enemy's capitol city, to encourage the enemy who was shooting at and killing the young Americans who had been sent to save South Vietnam from a communist takeover. The media published a famous picture of Fonda as she posed, wearing one of the enemy's helmets, at an anti-aircraft missile emplacement, while hundreds of American pilots who had been shot down by such missiles were suffering who knew what in Hanoi's prisons.

There were many visits that must have comforted the enemy from such as a famous American author, Mary McCarthy; a number of others who called themselves "Women's Strike for Peace;" and a University of California biochemist, Dr. John R. Neilands, who was permitted to talk with American prisoners of war and who, when asked by them why he was there, explained, "No son of a bitch like Dean Rusk can tell me where I can go and where I can't go. I am free to go anywhere any time." Dean Rusk was the U.S. Secretary of State at the time.

I thought – I still think –there was an element of treason in this behavior.

Young Americans continued to die in Vietnam, and other young Americans were ruining their lives by dodging the draft, by escaping the country, often to Canada, because they were understandably anxious to avoid being sacrificed in a deliberate effort *not* to win a war, but simply to somehow convince an expansionist communist government in Hanoi that the United States would not allow it to subjugate its neighbor.

Then, Marine General Lewis Walt, who had been one of the top commanders in Vietnam, lit my fuse. He recalled standing in a village and talking with a village chief and his wife, who both were distraught; their seven-year-old son had been missing for four days. They feared that the Vietcong (VC) had kidnapped him, and imagined that horrific things might have happened to him. Just then, the boy emerged from nearby jungle and ran across a rice paddy toward the village. He was crying. His mother ran to him and swept him up in her arms. Both of his hands had been cut off, and a sign hung around his neck warning his parents that if they or any others in the village dared to vote in an upcoming election something worse would happen to each of their other children.

"The little boy was seven years old," Walt said, his voice quavering with anger. "How could anyone *do* that?

He found there were many unspeakable things the VC could do: He described the "revolutionary purity" of VC in two other villages. In one case, a 15-year-old girl who had supplied information to his Marines was taken into the jungle and tortured for hours, then beheaded. As a warning to others in the village her head was placed atop a pole in front of her home. Her torturer-murderers were *her brother* and two of his VC comrades.

In the other case, when a VC learned that his wife and their two young children had cooperated with U.S. Marines, he himself had cut out their tongues.

The day before Walt's arrival at a district headquarters the VC overran it. They executed all of the defending soldiers, then their wives and children. A number of kids two and three years old were herded into the middle of the street, their throats were cut, they were beheaded, disemboweled and their remains were hung on fences with signs warning that this would be the fate of any who resisted the forces of glorious Ho Chi Minh.

I heard of more and more of stomach-turning VC atrocities. Had they been verified? Had records been kept? I combed files in the Pentagon and the State Department. The horrors General Walt reported were confirmed, and had been matched and overmatched hundreds of times.

Some VC stopped a school bus, climbed aboard and told the children to stop attending their school. Their parents kept putting them on the bus and sending them to school. A week later the VC boarded the bus again, selected a six-year-old girl, chopped off each of her fingers and warned the others that this would happen to each of them if they continued to attend the school. The school closed.

And so on, and on, and on. These were not isolated instances. Vicious, horrifying terrorism was the Vietnam communists' way of warfare. It was a story that had to be written. I thought the Digest's millions of readers ought to be able to consider it when confronted with the anti-war movement's rants and lies. I knew some Digest editors were very anti-war; I myself had never been certain that it made sense for the U.S. to commit itself to this war, but once we had done so I thought we should have done all possible to end it as quickly as possible. This wasn't done, and among the terrible results was the VC's reign of terror. I did wonder how the piece would be received in Pleasantville.

I didn't have to wonder long. I was on the third green of the Minneapolis Golf Club, which is as far as one can get from the clubhouse, when an emissary from the clubhouse arrived in a golf cart to say that Mr. DeWitt Wallace was on the phone and wanted to talk to me, and that he had been urged to come and get me, that it was very important.

"Did he leave word where to call him?" I asked the emissary. "Is he in his office?"

"I don't know where he is," I was told. "All I know is that he's on the phone, waiting to talk with you."

"You mean he's actually *still* on the phone, right *now*, waiting for me?"

"Yes. That's what he said. He said he would hold."

"Better hurry," I said. I couldn't imagine what this was about. The Founder/Editor-in-Chief had never called me before. The golf cart couldn't go any faster. It was a seven or eight minute ride.

"Wally?," I said, breathing heavily, having run about the last 100 yards to the phone.

"John," he said, "this is a great piece you have written, about communist atrocities in Vietnam. It's a compelling response to this so-called anti-war movement.

"Thank you very much. It wasn't much fun to write, to think that human beings are capable of such savagery."

"Yes, it must have been difficult, but you've done a great job of gripping the reader's attention and making him understand what is going on over there. I want the reader to know that the article has authoritative support. I want to insert two boxes in the body of the piece: I want a box from General Westmoreland,

and another from General Walt. I will see to it that they both receive copies of the story today. I want you to call them and tell them the article will reach them this afternoon, and ask them if they will be good enough to read it right away and give us a few lines attesting to its truth, that it shows what kind of monsters these communists are."

I said. "I'm sure they both will welcome the chance to comment."

"Tell them that we feel that this article is an effective response to the anti-war movement. Give them my number and tell them they can call me or call my office and dictate their comments, or write them out and send them directly to me."

Westmoreland had been in command of U.S. forces in Vietnam since 1964. He recently had returned to Washington to become the Army's Chief of Staff. I knew that Wally had met him and thought highly of him. And early in the Vietnam War I had written a favorable profile of him that had appeared in the Digest. I anticipated his enthusiastic cooperation. I believe he would have been glad to provide it if I had been able to reach him.

Instead, I was put in touch with some colonel, one of Westmoreland's aides or maybe his chief of staff – whatever else he was, he was a condescending bureaucrat. He had the article in hand. "Well," he said, "this article seems to be pretty political. It says that Ho Chi Minh should be brought before the bar of justice. I don't think the General ought to get involved with an article that makes a statement like that."

I could hardly believe what I had heard. I said, "You don't think that General Westmoreland would agree that Ho Chi Minh ought to be called to account for the atrocities the article describes? He's been leading a war against Ho Chi Minh for four years, he is certainly aware of the kinds of atrocities Ho's forces have been committing. And you don't think he will want to associate himself with an article that describes them and condemns them?"

"No, I don't think he'll want to be involved in a political argument."

"The article is a report on communist *atrocities*. Has the General seen the piece?

"No. He's the Chief of Staff. He's very busy. He hasn't got time for every…"

"Colonel," I interrupted, "We *know* the General, we really think he would want to *see* this article, and that he would want to comment…"

"He's in an important meeting now," the colonel interrupted, "he's the Chief of Staff, he's got meetings scheduled for the rest of the day, he hasn't got time…"

"All right, Colonel," I said, angrily, "we're busy, too. We'll leave it to the Marines." I hung up and called General Walt.

He was now Assistant Commandant of the Marine Corps, and was also very busy. I was put right through to him. He had just finished reading my article, "The Blood Red Hands of Ho Chi Minh" – Wally's title – and was, to say the least, enthusiastic. He provided a statement confirming the article that covered a quarter of a page in the magazine.

When I told Wally what had happened when I tried to contact Westmoreland. He said it didn't matter, that Walt's comments filled the bill nicely, and again told me that I had done a great job."

My four luncheon companions were amazed; they knew none of this. And none of them, including the two who had followed Wally as Editor-in-Chief, had ever known him to engage personally in the production of an article.

44

L'Amour

By 1980 I was aware of Louis L'Amour's books; they were all over the place, on display everywhere, in bookstores, drug store magazine racks, grocery store checkout counters, everywhere. I had never read one because I assumed the name to be the *nom de plume* of someone who wrote kissy face romance novels involving cowboys; not my kind of stuff. I had never even bothered to look at one. Then one day as I left the house on my way to Pleasantville and anxious to have something to read on the plane, I grabbed a paperback entitled, "The Empty Land." Reaching my seat on the airplane, I found to my dismay that the book was one of those sappy L'Amour stories. I was not happy, but started reading anyway

How dumb can you get? This wasn't some kissy face romance. This was a gripping, entertaining piece of history. I was engrossed. L'Amour had fashioned a dramatic page-turner of a novel around the opening of the American West. By the time we landed at New York's LaGuardia Airport I had read the whole book.

As quickly as I deplaned I found a phone booth, called the publisher, Bantam Books, and was connected with a gentleman named Stuart Applebaum. I introduced myself and said, "I need to talk with Louis L'Amour."

It turned out that L'Amour was really his name, and he had never written a kissy face romance novel.

A few days later I was in California, visiting with L'Amour in his study in Beverly Hills, and learning all about him. He was a big, rugged looking man, a little more than six feet tall, and probably a little more than 200 pounds. His face was square, weathered, friendly and his deep-set eyes were searching, "the kind of eyes," I wrote, "that listen as well as look." And he had lived an amazing life.

He was born in Jamestown, North Dakota, maybe 70 years earlier – he wouldn't say when, because he considered age "no measure of a man; what counts," he said, "is what he has experienced, learned, accomplished."

By that standard, Louis counted for a lot: He had been a merchant seaman, a lumberjack, a miner, had worked in a circus, had won 55 of 59 bouts as a professional boxer and had been an Army sniper in Europe during World War II. And by the time I met him he was one of the most widely read authors in history; his 77 novels had sold more than 100 million copies in 19 languages. Twenty three of his books had been made into major motion pictures.

He pointed out that none of his titles ever had appeared on a best-seller list. I thought that was odd. So did he, but he supposed that the people who composed such lists didn't read books like his, thought of them as "cowboy stories" that weren't worth their time.

I didn't tell him what I had thought.

Louis' father, Louis Charles L'Amour, had been a farmer, and when an agricultural depression hit in the 1920's he took his family from Jamestown to what he hoped would be greener pastures in Oklahoma. Louis dropped out of school at 15 to help out, but he never stopped educating himself. He spent every spare moment in libraries, steeping himself in Tolstoy, de Mauppasant, Robert Louis Stevenson, Victor Hugo, Dostoyevsky. And he worked.

One of the best jobs he ever had, he told me, was skinning all the dead cattle on a rancher's spread. "There were 925 of them," he said, "and a lot of them had been dead for a while. The aroma was such that, "Nobody else would come near the place, but the rancher paid me $3 per day, and had stories to tell: Kidnapped by Apaches when he was seven years old, he had been raised as one of them. He had ridden with the great chiefs, Nana and Geronimo. I had him all to myself for three months, and he supplied me with material for three books I wrote years later, 'Shalako', 'The Skyliners', and 'Hondo'."

"Hondo" sold more than three million copies, has been rated the best western novel ever written; it is used in many college writing classes and was made into a smash hit movie starring John Wayne.

Louis was one of the most fascinating people I ever met, and I spent several days getting to know him and extracting his life story from him. He rose early and wrote all morning. I would get to his house about noon, and we would go the Beverly Hills Hotel for lunch; he liked to go there every day and watch the movie stars. He said he didn't know any of them. I said, "You must have known John Wayne."

"Never met him," he said, then boasted, "but I was standing as close to him as I am to you."

L'Amour was shy. Had he made his presence known, I'm sure the movie people would have flocked to him; one thing they always needed was a good, imaginative writer.

After lunch we would return to his study, where I would continue to mine his memory.

At the time, Louis was writing a novel on Silver City, Nevada, and he had approached his subject just as he had all of his others: He had researched exhaustively, had walked, climbed, jeeped through and helicoptered over the countrysides where he planned to set his story. He had read the reminiscences of old timers, often had traveled far to visit with any who were still alive. He had combed libraries and bookstores and had attended estate sales, looking for genealogical histories, old diaries, family journals. Once, high on a mountain, he found an abandoned cabin whose occupants 70 years earlier had used newspapers to insulate it against frigid winds. He spent several days carefully removing the insulation, took it home and gleaned valuable material for his stories.

For the current project he had copies of every topographical map, a relief map and a mine chart that existed on the area in and around Silver City. "My descriptions must be right," he explained.

"When I tell my reader about a well in the desert, he knows it's there, and that the water is good to drink."

One day I rode in his limousine with him to a book-signing session in a store in Escondido, not far from San Diego. All the way down he fretted that no one would come, and how embarrassing that would be.

"You must have had lots of book signing sessions," I said. "Were there many when no one came?"

"No," he said, "but you never know."

"Were there *any*?"

"No, none that I remember."

When we reached the parking lot in Escondido, shortly after noon, a line stretched from the free-standing bookstore all the way around it and out into the lot; we had trouble finding a place to park. Louis was kept busy signing copies of his books until after 6 p.m.

I read all of Louis' books, couldn't get enough of them, learned a great deal of American history in them. Examples: the white man had been a lot less savage in imposing his own civilization on the West than most Indian nations had been in supplanting one another. What happened to the American Indian was simply that he was supplanted by another civilization, just as the various Indian civilizations had supplanted one another. The Iroquois in New York drove the Cherokee south to Georgia and raided as far west as the Black Hills. The Sioux remained in Minnesota and Wisconsin until the early 1600's, when they acquired horses. Then, they became a conquering nation, at one time controlled more territory than Charlemagne ever did.

I learned that many so called "rustlers" in the old west were cowboys who simply wanted to be independent, work for themselves. After the Civil War there was a great demand for beef, ranchers were offering their $30 per month cowhands an extra $2 for each stray longhorn they could brand for them. When the cowboys began forming herds of their own, as they had every right to do, the big ranchers labeled them outlaws and put prices on their heads.

The people who opened the West were tough, rarely intimidated by bad men who came to town. Most never hesitated to face up to gangsters who raided their towns. Typically, businessmen and farmers in Northfield, Minnesota, shot to pieces the Jesse James-Cole Younger gang when it tried a bank robbery there.

In every one of Louis' books I found myself marveling at his story-telling skill. We became good friends. He came to Minneapolis, where he had a meeting scheduled with a major bookseller. My whole family met him, and he had an autographed copy of one of his books for each of the kids. They started Louis L'Amour book clubs in their schools.

The publisher told me that shipping policy with any new L'Amour book was unique, that he was the only author to whom it applied: Shipments to booksellers always included large numbers of several of his other titles, because there was always such a demand for them.

One evening a few months after my story about him appeared in the Digest he called. He was on a nationwide book promotion tour. He wanted to know if I had noticed that his latest book was on a lot of best-seller lists.

"Louis," I said, "the people who compose those lists must have learned how to read, just as I did when I picked up 'The Empty Land.'"

45

"Check Your Hubbell"

After many frustrating attempts to talk peace with North Vietnam's leadership, President Richard M. Nixon decided to end the Vietnam War. On the evening of December 18th, 1972, the United States began pounding sledge-hammer blows into North Vietnam's war-making capacity. The Navy mined the harbor at Haiphong, shutting off the influx of war materiel from the Soviet Union; and the Strategic Air command (SAC) began destroying all of the military sites in and around Hanoi, North Vietnam's capitol, and the port of Haiphong.

What became known as "The Christmas Bombing" continued by the hour for eleven consecutive days and nights. During the daylight hours Air Force and Navy fighter bombers took over and kept up the pressure. Then, when darkness fell, the B-52s returned, every night and every hour on the hour.

Few Presidents have been despised by the elites in their own country as was Richard Nixon. He was hated by the political opposition, the media, academe, and the entertainment industry. Now, the hatred was super magnified, more intense, if possible, than it had been when he had destroyed the communist sanctuary bases in Cambodia. Day after day newspaper headlines and editorial pages, television and radio newscasts reviled his bombing campaign as "barbaric," a "slaughter," portrayed it as an "indelible stain on the American conscience." It was alleged that the population centers of North Vietnam were being "carpet bombed," laid to waste, just as the great German industrial centers had been obliterated during World War II, and there was much editorial hand-wringing over the massive numbers of deaths being inflicted.

None of this was true.

Post attack investigation revealed that North Vietnam's cities were not "carpet bombed," as had been claimed; if that had been the case there would have been nothing left of them; and their populations, numbering in the millions, would have been decimated, reduced by hundreds of thousands. The cities of Hanoi and Haiphong were not destroyed. Hanoi reported 1,308 deaths from the bombing, and most of those at the military sites to which the air strikes had been restricted: airfields, power plants, anti-aircraft artillery and missile sites, communications centers, rail yards, bridges, military storage depots, maintenance depots and port facilities. It probably was history's most surgically precise bombing campaign.

The 11-day campaign ended on December 29th, when Hanoi agreed to talk peace. The war ended.

If similar American determination had been displayed a decade earlier there would have been no war; neither nation would have lost so much in blood and treasure, and the United States would not have become so bitterly divided.

A mesmerized America watched on television the dramatic homecoming of the prisoners of war. Most were smiling, and spoke with what seemed an old fashioned enthusiasm for America. Some were on crutches and a few needed wheelchairs, but generally they looked so good that there was some suspicion that their long confinement had not been unduly harsh; was it possible that their captors had treated them well? In news interviews, such notions were quickly dispelled; the returnees left no doubt that their long exile had been a horror.

In the Washington Office Ken Gilmore and I wondered what had it been like? American military men were taught that the prisoner of war camp is an extension of the battlefield, and that if captured they are to continue the fight, to keep as many as possible of the enemy tied down as long as possible. Thus, in this longest of American wars many of these returnees had remained in combat longer than any other Americans in our history. What had been the nature of their battle? What of their captors' strategy and tactics, and how had the POWs countered them? How had they acquitted themselves? How had they endured?

"This needs a book," Gilmore said, "a big one. People will want the answers to these questions."

I agreed. I was sitting across from him, at his desk. I was in Washington on another matter.

"Would you be interested?"

"Yes," I said, "I would."

He picked up the phone and called Hobe Lewis, in Pleasantville. Lewis was enthusiastic. "Who should do it?" he asked.

"Hubbell wants to do it and has all the credentials," Gilmore said. I was sitting right across his desk from him. "He knows the Military, and they know him and trust him."

Then, Ken and I were in the Pentagon office of the Chairman of the Joint Chiefs of Staff, Admiral Thomas H. Moorer, outlining our proposal to him, a narrative history of the whole decade-long experience. We would need exhaustive interviews with scores of returnees. We wanted to construct in detail a narrative history of the POW experience. Moorer was enthusiastic; he had been a force in making the nation POW-conscious, and agreed that the whole story should be told to the American people and the world. He put us in the hands of his aide, Navy Captain John H. Mackercher. Jack was an old friend whom I had come to know well during many a journalistic adventure; he was a superstar at arranging background briefings and access to vital informational materials and finding locations and telephone numbers.

Alone in my hotel room that night, I felt overwhelmed. Several hundred men had come home after many years in captivity. I was to tell their story. How to organize it? How to weave together the strands of hundreds of lives over such a long period of time? How to focus the experience, make sense of it, do it justice, make it as interesting and dramatic as it surely must be? This promised to be an epic. Was I the one to write such an epic? Maybe not. Maybe I should back off, tell Hobe Lewis to summon someone who was experienced in writing epics; someone like James Michener. He had done a lot of work for the Digest, but rarely bothered with anything that wasn't epic.

No, I thought, when I awoke next morning. I can do this as well as anyone, maybe *better* than anyone else; I've spent a lot of time working with military people. I know them. Come on, let's get up and get at it!

Plenty of competent help was made available: two excellent journalists to do a lot of the leg work and interviewing. One was my longtime good buddy, Senior Editor Andrew Jones, with whom I had worked many stories, including the 1963 book on the Cuban missile crisis. And in Washington, Ken Gilmore cut loose Ken Tomlinson, an energetic young reporter who had joined the Washington staff five years earlier. Jones and Tomlinson would be with me as long as I needed them. And my editor, in Pleasantville, would be Senior Editor Edward T. Thompson, another old friend who most of us thought to be the very best in the business. In three years DeWitt Wallace would name Ed the magazine's Editor-in-Chief.

Tomlinson was from Lynchburg, Virginia. When he graduated from Randolph-Macon College, near Richmond, in 1965, he did exactly what I was determined *not* to do when I graduated from the University of Minnesota, 16 years earlier: he took a job as a newspaper reporter, with the Richmond Times-Dispatch. But he had in mind the same aim I did; he yearned for the world of big time magazine journalism. He was good reporter, and by 1968 had sold himself to Ken Gilmore and joined his staff in the Washington office. He was 24 years old, the same age I had been when I sold my first article to the Digest in 1951.

Tomlinson was of average height, burly, had a full head of black hair and wore a full black beard, the purpose of which I suspected was to conceal his youth. He was very much the southern gentleman; he oozed charm and wit, and it was impossible not to like him. He was also a convinced political conservative, and was active in the Conservative Movement.

Our first step was to find those to whom the others had looked for leadership in the POW camps, drain them in detail of their memories of captivity, take their advice as to whom next to interview next, then take their advice as to whom next to see, and so on. The returnees had returned to homes that were scattered from coast-to-coast and border-to-border. Andy, Ken and I went in different directions and kept talking with returnees, tape recording them until we knew that we had the whole story.

We interviewed more than a hundred of the returnees. The interviews ranged in length from an hour or so to more than 20 hours. It worked. The returnees were eager to tell the details of their captivity. There came a time when they were telling us that we knew more about what had happened to them than they did themselves.

It took me two and a half years to wrestle this floodtide of information into readable condition and deliver it to Ed Thompson. We entitled it, "P.O.W. A Definitive History of the American Prisoner of War Experience in Vietnam., 1964-1973." At 600 pages, the finished product was nothing like your average Reader's Digest article or condensation, but a condensation did appear as a back-of-the-magazine book-length feature.

We all were satisfied that we had achieved the deep perspective the Vietnam P.O.W. experience deserved. More importantly, the POWs themselves generally agreed that we had done justice to their performance. In fact, one of them, Medal of Honor winner Air Force Colonel George E. "Bud" Day, an attorney, said the book, "is to our experience as Blackstone is to the law." Another told me that when returnees meet and disagree about something that happened in a North Vietnamese prison, someone always says, "Go check your Hubbell!"

That's good enough for me.

46

Stockdale

Jim Stockdale was nervous, upset. He paced back and forth before Punkin and me as we sat in our living room. We watched him, expectantly. He had explained that he had agreed to deliver a speech to the Economics Club of Chicago. He had been working on it for days, and was not happy with it, and wanted us to hear it and tell him what we thought, how he could improve it, make it worth the listening. He started, then stopped, then restarted, then stopped again.

"This is *terrible!*" he said. He was very upset, seemed almost desperate. "This audience is going to include a lot of the most important people in the country. What am I going to do?"

The scene was preposterous: Stockdale was famous for his courage, demonstrably one of the most courageous people on the planet. He had been famous for quite a while by the time we met him; he had received a lot of media attention for having led the August 4,

1964, air raids that had plunged the United States into the Vietnam War – he had explained earlier that it was not an assignment nor a memory in which he took pride.

Stockdale had been shot down and captured in North Vietnam in September, 1965, and had spent nearly eight years in a brutal captivity that had included a great deal of physical torture and many years in solitary confinement. Even so, he had found ways to survive and communicate, and had remained throughout one of the primary leaders. By the time I met him I had completed extensive interviews with many other returnees and knew him to be revered by them. I had made several attempts to meet with him, but had been unable to fit myself into his schedule until one day he called from his home in Coronado, California, and said, "I have to give a speech in Chicago next Friday, and I thought that if it's convenient for you I could go to Chicago by way of Minneapolis."

"Please come and stay with us," I said.

We spent a couple of days and nights together dealing with the story of his captivity, and then turned to the speech he had written and was scheduled to deliver in Chicago, which seemed to frighten him more than the Vietnamese ever had.

He asked Punkin and me to listen and tell him what we thought. After he had made a number of abortive, embarrassed attempts, I said, "Jim, let's go into my study, where I can sit at my typewriter, and help you get this thing in shape."

He told me what he wanted to say. I organized it and wrote it, using language I thought sounded like him (with dashes of Winston Churchill, Abraham Lincoln and John G Hubbell thrown in). Soon, we were back in the living room and he delivered the speech to Punkin and me, and it was terrific. We were all delighted; he was very happy. I put him on a plane to Chicago on a Friday morning. He called that evening to say that the speech had gone over better than he had hoped, and to thank us for our help.

Jim's Chicago hosts had deemed the speech worthy enough to publish in booklet form, and see to its wide distribution. A few weeks later Ed Thompson, who was editing the book, sent one of the booklets to me, explaining that Ken Gilmore had obtained a copy and thought that I might find "some of the information and Stockdale's thoughts helpful."

Ed and I had some fun with that.

Stockdale was awarded the Medal of Honor for his heroic leadership as a prisoner of war.

Jim and I stayed in touch. We visited back and forth with our families. We remained close friends until the end of his life. He ascended to the rank of Vice Admiral, and completed his Naval career as President of the Naval War College, in Newport, Rhode Island. He then became President of The Citadel, in Charleston, South Carolina, and finally accepted a Senior Research Fellowship at the Hoover Institution on War, Revolution and Peace, on the campus of Stanford University, in Palo Alto, California. At the Hoover, he produced several books and articles on Ethics, Foreign Affairs and the Greek Classics.

He died at his home in Coronado on July 5, 2005, a victim of complications from Alzheimer's Disease. He was 81 years old. He lies in the cemetery at the U. S. Naval Academy, but he remains a towering figure in the Navy's institutional memory. A new guided missile destroyer bears his name, as does the headquarters of the

Pacific Fleet's Survival, Evasion, Resistance and Escape (SERE) School at the North Island, California, Naval Air Station; and a statue of him stands before the entrance to Luce Hall, at the Naval Academy, the location of the Vice Admiral James B. Stockdale Center for Ethical Leadership.

It was more than a pleasure to have known him, and it is more than an honor to be able to say that he was a friend.

47
He Soared With the Eagles

Y ou have to love a Washington bureaucrat who affixes to his office door, only a few step's from his boss's office, a poster that reads, in big, black letters, "It is difficult to soar with the eagles when you have to work with turkeys."

Of course, Michael D. Benge was no Washington bureaucrat, and there was no prospect that he ever would become one. He was an agroforester, an employee of the Agency for International Development (AID), "a blunt, down-on-the-ground, dirty finger-nails activist", I wrote, "dedicated to the development of the under-developed areas of the world". The reason he was sitting in an office in Washington, where he did not want to be sitting, was that only recently he had returned, along with several hundred American military men, from five harrowing years as a prisoner of war in North Vietnam, and his AID superiors thought he needed to take it easy for a year or so. Mike would have none of it.

When I met him, he said, "I think the luster on my hero badge won't be worn off before I get my pink slip."

A civilian, Mike had been advising Montagnards in Vietnam's Central Highlands on efficient farming procedures when he was captured by the North Vietnamese Army. He had been chained to two missionaries, Betty Ann Olsen and Henry Blood. The three had been marched 200 miles through jungles and mountains, and given little to eat or drink. Malnourished they survived mainly on sheer willpower. They fought off jungle leeches and infection, and became exhausted, sick with dysentery, fungus infections and jungle ulcers.

After a few months, Henry Blood contracted Pneumonia and died, and Mike and Betty Ann buried him.

Mike developed cerebral malaria and only survived because Betty Ann Olsen kept forcing him to eat and drink rice soup and water. Their captors kept them chained together and moving. Covered with sores, they had pyorrhea from beri beri, their teeth came loose and their gums became infected. Eventually, Betty Ann weakened to the point where she could no longer walk. The North Vietnamese kept kicking her and dragging her. When Mike tried to defend her he was beaten with rifle butts. When she died, Mike buried her.

Mike made up his mind that he would not die, would not allow these despicable people to kill him. His hair turned snow white, he was covered with jungle ulcers and weighed perhaps 70 pounds Other POWs who saw him judged him to be about 70; he was 33.

Whenever the chance presented itself, he treated his ravaged body by lying in streams and letting small fish nibble away the dead tissue.

He was taken to Hanoi, where he never minced words when interrogated. His captors found him to be, "rude, bellicose and odious". He spent 27 months in solitary confinement, in a windowless room painted black. His companionship was limited to large rats that visited on the infrequent occasions that he was fed.

Mike had been back in Washington about five months when, unable to persuade his superiors to let him return to Vietnam, he returned at his own expense. He went back to the Central Highlands to see how his Montagnard friends were progressing with the programs he had begun before being captured. He stayed six months, then returned to Washington with detailed proposals for a dozen new programs.

Mike was an Agricultural Engineering graduate of Oregon State University, and had had long been worried that the world was losing about 12 million acres of forest annually to "slash and burn" farming. Forests were being uprooted, brush was being burned off, fields were planted where trees had once stood. Within a few years the fields had lost vitality, were abandoned and overtaken by tenacious growths whose root systems inhibited anything else from growing. Those who had destroyed the forests and farmed the land had moved on to take down more forests.

Mike ruminated, thought he might have seen the key to the problem in Vietnam, a plant called leucaena leucocephela (pronounced looseena lukosefela). He thought it could be a major weapon in the battle for food and against deforestation. Its roots went deep, and reacted with bacteria to form nodules on their surfaces. The nodules gathered nitrogen, the critical element in fertilizer, and fed it to the leaves. Harvested and worked into the ground, the leaves reinvigorated the earth. Livestock fattened on the nutritious leaves, seedpods, even twigs.

He talked with many agroscientists about leucaena. One, James L. Brewster at the University of Hawaii, told him of a strain of giant leucaena tree he had discovered in Central America. It grew very rapidly and produced large quantities of forage material for animals. Mike found the trees in southern Mexico, and found them to be as Brewster had indicated.

Two years after his return from prison in Vietnam he was posted to the Philippines, where millions of acres had been lost to "slash and burn" farming. He put together a leucaena technical manual entitled, "Banyani," which in the Philippines means, "Hero", or "Savior". The U.S. Information Agency published it and sent 3,000 copies to embassies and agriculturalists around the world. By the mid-1980's dozens of third world countries were engaged in leucaena trials, and many had launched major reforestation programs with the tree. An American, Aart van Wingerden, who was trying to help farmers in Haiti, reported, "In four years we had trees that were 34 inches around!"

In June, 1986, Sweden's King Carl XVI Gustaf bestowed upon three men Sweden's equivalent of the Nobel Prize: Awards that Help to Solve the World's Social and Economic Problems. The recipients were James L. Brewbaker, who discovered the giant leucaena tree and told Mike about it; Australia's E. Mark Hutton, who developed a leucaena strain for feeding animals; and Michael D. Benge, who was the plant's Johnny Appleseed to the world.

Mike's hero badge had a new luster. At last, he was soaring with the eagles.

Civilian though he was, he was one of the great P.O.W. heroes who returned from captivity in Vietnam.

48
Peggy

My sister, Margaret Catherine Hubbell, whom we always called Peggy, was born in the Bronx, like me, but in 1922, five years ahead of me. My first and continuing memory of her was of dark, curly hair and a big smile.

In her very early childhood, before I was born, she was a victim of poliomyelitis, then called infantile paralysis. Every few years it visited the world in epidemics, until the Sabine and Salk vaccines virtually eradicated it, and a great many of those whom it caught were killed or left physically crippled.

It didn't kill or maim Peggy in any visible way. But it did dreadful damage to her nervous system. She periodically suffered devastating *gran mal* seizures; they were terrible. I can't remember how often, when a seizure would occur, nearby family members had to reach into her mouth to ensure that she did not swallow her tongue and strangle herself, while others rubbed her wrists vigorously, which seemed to help bring her out of it.

In those days there were none of the pharmaceuticals that later became very effective in the prevention of epileptic seizures. She was kept on a menu of barbiturates, which seemed to drain her of mental and physical energy; she spent a lot of her life just sitting and reading, or taking naps.

Even so, she was a much better than average student. But when a seizure occurred it seemed to erase from her brain much of what she had most recently studied and learned, and she had to spend a lot of time retracing her educational steps. But she kept on working at it and earned good grades all the way through college, and earned a degree from the University of Minnesota.

Following college, in the mid-1940s, she took a course at a business school and became competent with shorthand and typing. A few times she acquired secretarial jobs, but was not able to keep them; in the workaday world of that era there simply wasn't the time or inclination to deal with employees with her kind of problem.

So she stayed home with her parents all of her life, while her three brothers all were able to go out into the world and live exciting lives, one as a writer for a major magazine, the other two as highly successful Naval officers. She was very proud of all of us; she let us know it. But it could not have been easy. We'll never know how any of the rest of us might have handled what became her life after the polio struck in early childhood.

Our mother died in 1955. That left a big hole in all of our lives – a real cavern in Peggy's.

Our father died in 1966, and now she was alone.

Except for relatively short visits periodically to each of our homes, she stayed alone until she died, in 1969, at age 47, victimized by a seizure, and no one there to help.

49
Arriving In Style

During the Vietnam War years I traveled several times across the Pacific, and always checked in at CincPac Headquarters, at Camp H.M. Smith,[9] near Honolulu. Each time I would meet again with CinCPac, the Commander-in-Chief Pacific, first Admiral U.S. Grant Sharp, then with his successor, Admiral John Sydney McCain Jr. I had first met MCain some years earlier, during the Cuban Missile Crisis, when he was the Navy's Chief of Information. At that time, the Kennedy Administration's orders were to give the media nothing that pertained to what was going on in Cuba until a decision was made as to what was going to happen. Everything was top secret. It was a tough situation for all the information officers, who wanted the media to like them so that they could get reporters to write the stories they wanted written.

---

[9] The headquarters was named after one of the great Marine Corps leaders of World War II, General Holland McIntyeire Smith, whose troops used his initials to nickname him "Howlin' Mad."

But McCain had continually invited members of the media, me included, into his office, where he delivered never a word about events concerning Cuba, only long lectures on the endless positives of the United States Navy. His captive listeners had always left in a state of impatient frustration, but he insisted, when I reminded him of it years later, that "You all were well educated."

Since then, he had acquired four stars, served in London as Commander-in-Chief U.S. Naval Forces Europe (CinCUSNavEur), and now was boss of all U.S. military forces from the west coast of the Americas to the middle of the Indian Ocean, including those engaged in the Vietnam War.

His son, Lt. Cdr. John S. McCain III, a hero of the fire that had gutted a major carrier, the U.S.S. Forrestal on July 27, 1967, had been shot down and captured in North Vietnam on October 10, 1967, and now was imprisoned in Hanoi. Admiral McCain never mentioned the fact of his son's captivity to me, nor, to my knowledge, to anyone other than his wife, Roberta.

I learned much later that notwithstanding the fact that his son was imprisoned in Hanoi, Admiral McCain had been a foremost proponent of ending the war by taking it north, to Hanoi and Haiphong and destroying the enemy's war-making capacity.

I had traveled Admiral McCain's "beat" with him, from Panmunjom to Nakom Phanom. I had written a Digest piece about him and the way he dealt with his job – it intrigued me that his aircraft contained a bewildering array of communications devices which put him in touch with every major American command post in the world, including the White House – and, no kidding, that his plane was piloted by an Air Force Captain named Harold

Liberty and that the last three numbers identifying his aircraft were 007, just like the code number of author Ian Fleming's fictional Agent James Bond. No one had arranged this; it just happened.

In the fall of 1968 I had invited McCain to Digest headquarters, in Pleasantville, where he had laid before DeWitt Wallace, Hobart Lewis and the Digest's entire Editorial staff irrefutable evidence that in Vietnam, the enemy was beaten, that the United States had won a convincing military victory and that there was absolutely no way the tables could be turned.[10] Wallace and Lewis were sold, and sent me to Hawaii to get McCain to repeat his argument to the Digest's reader's. I sat with him in his office and asked a series of blunt questions, tape recording his fulsome answers.

The article, "In Vietnam, The Enemy is Beaten," ran in the February, 1969, issue, accompanied by a favorable review from Hanson Baldwin, Military Editor for the New York Times.

So I had a lot of experience with McCain. He became more than a source; he and Roberta, became my good friends. Both had urged that I stay with them whenever I was in Hawaii. Meanwhile, he never hesitated to call me at home, in Minneapolis, from his

---

[10] It was true. Although the media portrayed the early 1968 Tet offensive as a catastrophic defeat for U.S. and South Vietnamese forces, the truth was exactly the opposite: a devastating defeat had been inflicted on Ho Chi Minh's forces; the entire leadership of the Vietcong had been wiped out, and the North Vietnamese Army had lost nearly 80,000 troops. But media accounts were not well researched. The Johnson Administration remained wedded to its policy of gradualism. In 1975, two years after President Nixon forced Hanoi to sue for peace, an impatient U.S. Congress abruptly ended promised American financial aid to South Vietnam, and Hanoi, which had spent the time rebuilding its Army, was virtually unopposed in a new effort to take over the South.

home, at Pearl Harbor, even in the small hours of the morning, to ruminate and seek my opinions on matters within his purview.

Once, early on a Saturday afternoon, I had just checked into the Illikai Hotel, on Waikiki Beach, I was there to research a story about an Air Force pilot named James W. Young, who lived in Mililani Town, in the middle of the island of Oahu. I thought readers would thrill to Young's story:

As a young fighter pilot during the Korean War he had survived seemingly insuperable injuries, including frightful burns, during a crash landing. He was hospitalized for 40 months, during which he had undergone 58 surgeries. By enormous strength of will he had recovered, had rebuilt his body and his career to the extent that he had flown more than two hundred combat missions during the Vietnam War and had achieved flag rank; he was now a brigadier general. When I called him to say that his story in the Digest would be an inspiration to other seriously damaged people, he had agreed to cooperate, but said that any interviews would have to be conducted in a golf cart on a golf course during the course of a round of golf. He said that he spent every possible moment of his free time playing golf, and would allow nothing to interfere. A golf lover myself, I quickly agreed to this condition. I packed my clubs and a pocket-sized tape recorder and flew to Hawaii. I was not scheduled to meet with the General until Sunday, for a golf game, so I picked up the phone to check in with Jack McCain.

"Goddamit, John," he said, "what are you doing in that hotel? You know we have plenty of room in our quarters, and that Roberta and I want you to stay with us whenever you're in the area. Check out of that place and I'll have a car pick you up in an hour."

He accepted my explanation that I was on a story that required me to be in a hotel, where I could work and entertain, but said, "We're having a cocktail reception for Lon Nol on the back lawn at 1800, and I want you to join us for that. I'll send car anyway."

Lon Nol was Prime Minister of Cambodia. I knew from news reports that he was in Hawaii for some medical problem.

I stood in the hotel entryway, reading a newspaper while I awaited the car. It was late, by thirty or more minutes. I didn't know what to think; maybe McCain had decided the Cambodian politician didn't want to meet a media guy, maybe he had left a message. I was about to go in and ask the hotel operator when the car arrived. The Marine driver got out and apologized, seemed almost to be in tears. He tried to explain something about confusion at the motor pool. I told him it was okay, but let's hurry, we're late. We broke the local speed limit, but when we got on the base at Pearl Harbor he slowed to fifteen miles an hour. I thought I could walk faster. "Gotta hurry!" I insisted, "we're late."

"Sir," the driver said, "they are *really* tough about the speed limit here…"

"Don't worry about it," I said, "let's go!"

We went. And almost instantly a siren went off behind us.

"Oh, *God!*" the driver moaned.

I jumped out of the car to meet the oncoming traffic cop. He looked like a casting director's version of an arrogant small town sheriff. He was overweight, chewing on a toothpick, wore a forest ranger-type hat, aviator-type sunglasses, a couple of holsters filled with pistols and his big belly hung over a bandolier of bullets.

I pleaded with him: "Give me the ticket, not the driver. I'm way overdue at the McCain residence, and I kept yelling at the driver to pay no attention to the speed limit. It's my fault, not his, so give me..."

The cop removed the toothpick. He said, "You going to the CinCPac reception?"

"Yes," I nodded.

"Follow me," he said, climbing back into his car. He pulled in front of us, kept his lights flashing and took off, turning on his siren! The siren was very loud. Oh, *lord, I thought, they can hear it in San Francisco!* I was mortified. A few sailors on the street stopped and stared at us. How to escape this crazy situation? I tried to disappear down into my seat.

A circular drive led up to the commodious front entrance to the residence. Several Marines, an Honor Guard, all in dress blues lined both sides of the walk from the driveway to the front stairs. My driver jumped out of the car and opened my door. As I stepped out the Marines brought their rifles to present arms, which is a salute. They are saluting me because it is clear from all the noise and color that has accompanied my arrival, that I am a person of very considerable importance. I wanted to get back in the car and sneak away, very quietly. CinCPac and his lady appeared at the top of the stairs, anxious to see what is causing the commotion. The Admiral smiled down at me, removed the stub of a cigar from his face and said, "Goddamit, John, you *do* like to arrive in style, doncha?"

On the back lawn I was introduced to Lon Nol. He was in his late 60's. He was cordial, mannerly, pleasant, struck me as a nice person. He gazed upon me with undisguised curiosity, and who could blame him, considering the manner of my arrival? He had earlier been Commander in Chief of the Cambodian army, then Defense Minister and was now, for the second time, Prime Minister. He was as anti-communist as a Southeast Asian politician could afford to be, so he was okay with me. We made careful small talk, because neither of us was prepared to discuss matters of state with the other. It was a nice party.

I was much happier the next day, when I reached Mililani Town and played golf with Jim Young. He was a good player, and had a wonderfully inspiring story to tell. It appeared in the Digest under the title, "The Man Who Would Not Die."

50
Re: Father Ritter

Father Bruce Ritter was a Franciscan priest. He died at age 72 on October 7, 1999. His ashes lie beneath a statue of St. Anthony in a yard behind a farmhouse he owned in Otsego, New York, 60 miles west of Albany. In the late stages of his life he was reviled by many as a sexual predator and a thief, although he denied each and every one of several allegations, and four thoroughgoing investigations yielded not a scintilla of evidence to support any of them. He is long forgotten now, but I remember him well and got to know him well enough to believe that he was a martyr to his cause, and is today a saint, enjoying all the rights, privileges and glory of a citizen of heaven.

Something I read in a newspaper about him had impelled me to find him. I needed to talk with him, maybe because Punkin and I had so many kids of our own; I worried about kids. Father Ritter worried about kids. I wanted to tell the world what he was doing. I found him on West 41st Street in New York City, close to Times Square in a building he had rented from the, state for a dollar a year. He called it Covenant House, after the biblical covenant between God and man. He had filled it with homeless children he had had found wandering the streets, searching for ways to survive. He estimated that at any given moment there were 16,000 to 20,000 of them on the streets of New York. His worry was that he would need a couple of places the size of the Empire State Building to house all of them. But he could only do what he could do. He would care for as many as possible, feed them, clothe them, educate them, equip them with the mental and moral tools and the self respect they would need to live successful lives.

I wanted to know why this was so, how it had happened – how *he* had happened?

He told me of his epiphany: he had been lecturing a class in Theology at Manhattan College, in the Bronx, assuring his students that they did not do enough for "the unfortunate." A young man raised his hand and asked, "What about you, Father, do you practice what you preach?"

"It was as though a bucket of cold water had been dumped on me," he said. "I was shocked at my own smugness. Who was *I*, to be telling other people what they ought to be doing? I began thinking about what *I* ought to be doing."

And then he did it: resigned his tenured professorship, moved from Manhattan College and moved from the campus into a tenement apartment on the city's crime-ridden lower East Side. He was determined to find and minister to any who needed his help, the poor, the homeless, the drug-addicted. He was jump-started a few nights after moving in. Two girls and four boys, ages 14 to 17, knocked on his door, pleading for shelter. They had been living in an abandoned building nearby, and had left to escape some junkies who wanted to pimp them, sell their bodies to people looking for young sex. He brought them in and let them curl up on the floor of his apartment. Next morning he interviewed each of them at length, learned their stories, went out and bought food for them, stopped in a nearby church to pray for them and for help in helping them. He contacted every welfare agency in the city and got no help, nothing but excuses: "The kids were too old," I was told, "or too young, or too sick, or not sick enough, or the agency could not be reimbursed, and so on."

Frustrated and angry, he decided too look after them himself. He drove a cab, and every day said masses and preached in churches around the city. He told parishioners about the kids, that they had been decent young human beings, that they had not been hookers or hustlers when they had arrived in the city, but typically decent young human beings who were being denied even a halfway chance at a decent life. Most had run away from or had been kicked out of homes where they had been emotionally and physically abused for long periods of time. Their parents or guardians had hated them, and they had learned to hate back. They had come to the big city in hopes of somehow finding a way to make it on their own. In most cases they had not been educated or taught any skills. No one had been willing to spend any money on anything like that.

So what they had found were pimps who were glad to supply them with the necessities of life. All they had to do in return was provide their bodies for people who paid the pimps handsomely for their sexual services. And kids who tried to escape paid a price. He told me of a 12-year-old girl who had been arrested six times for prostitution. She had come to him, begging for help, but had been too frightened of her pimp to stay, to accept the help that Covenant House offered. Shortly, she was found dead in an alley, and in saloons around the neighborhood a pimp was joking and laughing about "a bitch" he had thrown out a window.

Another brutally battered girl showed up on a bitter December night explaining that her pimp had almost killed her for withholding a little of her earnings for herself. She wondered how she could get him to forgive her. Ritter was unable to convince her that she didn't need her pimp's forgiveness, that she should stay at Covenant House. But she was too frightened to stay. Soon, parts of her dismembered body were found in colorfully wrapped Christmas packages around the city.

He kept preaching, telling people in the church pews and reporters what was happening in the streets. He explained how a pimp thinks: "You have a troublesome kid on your hands? You OD him. Who cares? It's just some stupid little whore or some dumb kid who OD'd, and that's the end of it."

He began to attract substantial financial support, and volunteer helpers, including a lot young people. They went out on the streets, looking for kids who needed someone to find them. The population of Covenant House burgeoned, so the incoming financial support was never enough, and Ritter had to keep on begging.

It was a heartbreaking business. It kept Bruce full of anguish. He prayed a lot. He remembered a pregnant 16-year old girl who had pneumonia and gonorrhea. While he was talking to her and worrying about her, a 13-year-old boy called to tell him in a quavering voice that he had been making pornographic films for three years and wanted out, but he was sure that he would be caught and killed if he ran. Before Bruce could get his location, the frightened youngster had hung up.

The street, he explained, exerted an evil magic; virtually all of the kids who came in were hungry or needed clothing or both, but about 70 percent were scared out of their wits and/or had been hooked on drugs, alcohol and sex, and returned to the streets. Unable to convince them to stay, he made sure they knew there would always be a clean bed, clothing and hope for the future for them at Covenant House, and that its cafeteria would be open for a meal or three meals a day.

There were some spectacular successes: a 17-year-old young man who had suffered a great deal of physical and psychological abuse in a long series of foster homes, where the only interest in him had been the money the city paid for his keep. He could not read or write and had no job skills, and had finally run away and sold himself in a thousand beds and a thousand cars. He did not like what he knew of life, and wondered if Ritter could explain to him why he should not jump off a bridge. Bruce knew he was contending for the boy's life. He talked him into staying, helped him discover an interest in cooking. By the time I showed up, the boy had a job as a cook in a good restaurant, and was enthusiastic about his job, life and Father Ritter.

Seventeen girls who grabbed Ritter's lifeline were students in colleges around the country.

Bruce was practicing, successfully, what he once had preached.

When my story about him, "Father Ritter's Covenant," appeared in the Digest, it inspired a great reaction. A well known financier, Louis Wolfson, paid to have it reprinted on an entire page of The Wall Street Journal. Which helped with fund-raising.

Then, trouble: Nine years later a man name Kevin Kite claimed to have had a sexual relationship with Ritter, and that Ritter had used as much as $25,000 of Covenant House's funds to finance the relationship.

Ritter denied it. He was shocked. He had helped Kite obtain a scholarship to Manhattan College, and was incredulous at the public lie, knew it could be ruinous. He denied it. Then, Kite's father explained in a New York Times article that his son was "a chronic liar and thief with a personality disorder, and a history of hurting those who try to help him."

Then, one John Melican claimed in the Village Voice newspaper to have had a 13-year affair with Ritter. He told the same thing to the New York Times.

Ritter denied it.

Then, Darryl Bassile, 31, told the Times that he had had an affair with Ritter.

Ritter denied it.

Then, a 33-year-old felon named Paul Johnson reported a six-year-long affair with Ritter.

Ritter denied it.

Then, a number of young men who had worked at Covenant House reported that Ritter had made sexual overtures to them.

Ritter denied it.

Lots of smoke. Any fire? Any evidence? Four full blown investigations found none, not a shred.

Suspicions: Few if any of Ritter's accusers could be characterized as upstanding citizens. What moved them to make such serious complaints, none of which could be found to contain an iota of substance? Was it possible that the sex dealers whose business Ritter was trying to ruin had paid them to do what they did? To rid the neighborhood of their worst enemy and, if possible, his effective tool, Covenant House?

Of course it was possible, even likely.

By this time news reports concerning the Catholic Church's sexual abuse scandals were in full flower. Investigators who had run down these cases estimated that one-third to half of them were bogus. Which by no means ameliorates the fact that half to two-thirds of them were true. But it does say that in many cases it was all about money, that many priests were wrongly accused and many liars extorted large financial settlements from the Church.

Engaged as he was in rescuing homeless young people from the streets and having been lionized for it, Father Ritter presented an especially rich target. The allegations against him all were widely publicized. His reputation and that of Covenant House were savaged. It could hardly fail to affect the donations, which were Covenenant House's lifeblood. Ritter resigned, explaining that in view of "the controversy that has surrounded me" his departure was in the best interests of the institution he had founded and "thousands of street kids."

In the climate that prevailed at the time, that still prevails, he was made to look guilty. He refused his Franciscan Superior's order to move into a friary and take counseling, insisting that to seek counseling would be to admit guilt, and that he was guilty of none of the crimes that had been alleged.

Bruce then made the painful decision to resign from his beloved order, but retained his priestly faculties. He aligned himself with a diocese in India so that he could keep working as a priest. He lived alone and quietly on the farm near Otsego. Friends helped with financial support, and he received stipends for saying mass at churches in the area. His closest neighbors became his close friends, and said that he was at peace with himself.

But his legacy, Covenant House, lives on. In fact Covenant Houses continue to rescue desperate youngsters from the mean streets of 21 of the largest cities in the Americas.

51

Evenings With the Joneses

As Hobe Lewis had kept advancing to the top of the editorial pyramid and his duties had increased, he had divined, accurately, that Andy Jones and I were kindred spirits, and we had been working well together for a long time

Andy had come to the Digest as an editor, reading and condensing articles that had been purchased, but he reveled in every chance to leave the office and participate in projects. He did lot of important legwork for Jim Daniel and me when we co-authored our 1963 book on the Cuban missile crisis and again for me when I was in Spain researching "The Case of the Missing H-Bomb." He also spent months interviewing a long list of returned Vietnam POWs for me when I wrote the book, "P.O.W." And he did a lot of research legwork for at least two of James A. Michener's epics. Additionally, he was a crucial and imaginative player in many of the practical jokes David Reed constructed.

A graduate of Princeton University, Andy had been a Marine fighter pilot during World War II. At the start of the Korean War some of his fighter pilot buddies from Boston who had remained in the Reserve came by on their way to the new conflict and invited him to join them. By that time, though, he had lovely Janny and they had three wonderful kids, a son, Seaver, and two daughters, Brookie and Audrey, so going off to war again was not an option. He talked about it a lot, though. I think that if he could have had it both ways, he would have fought the war as a Marine fighter pilot by day, and gone home to be the husband and father by night.

Janny and Andy lived in a barn they had bought and renovated, made into a comfortable home atop a hill just outside of Bedford Village, perhaps ten miles from the Digest. I had countless dinners there with them, and was often their house guest. Many were the nights when Andy and I stayed up much too long, having imbibed more than we should have, and carefully and loudly explaining to one another our brilliant solutions to most of the world's ills. Only occasionally did Janny, having prepared dinner and then favored us with her company until she was nearly unconscious, arise from her bed, where she had been sleep-deprived for long periods by Andy's and my noisy arguments and orations, to insist that we "get to bed, and save the world tomorrow."

I spent many interesting evenings at the house, but one night it got complicated: It was mid-winter, and for some reason, I had bunked in at the Guest House, a luxurious manse on the Digest's campus, then motored in a rental car over to the Jones'. Much later, in fact in the very small hours, I crawled back into my rental car, unaware that while we had been saving the world, Father Winter had overlain the road down the long drive from the Jones' house to the county road with an icy veneer. Instead of responding to my effort to turn left at the bottom of the drive and on to the county road, my rental continued across the road and onto a fairway of the Bedford Hills Country Club.

After several unsuccessful efforts to back up onto the road – the wheels kept spinning themselves into ever deeper depressions – I trudged back up the drive, perhaps a third of a mile through deepening snow and stomped into the house shouting for Andy. He emerged from his bedroom in pajamas, and I explained that a rental company had supplied me with an automobile that had been unable to turn left at the bottom of his drive.

"What the hell kind of a car is that?" he asked..

"Doesn't turn well."

"Where is it?"

"On the golf course. Across the road."

"Well, we better get it out of there before the golfers show up."

"It's February. The golfers won't show up for a couple of months yet."

"That's right, you play golf, don't you?"

"Yeah."

"So you'd know about these things."

"Yeah."

"I wonder why they would rent you a car like that?"

"I'm gonna talk to them about it."

Andy pulled on a robe and a pair of overshoes.

"It's pretty cold out," he said. "I think we should have a drink."

"I'll pass. I'm driving."

"That's right. But I'm not."

He fixed himself a drink and we trudged down the drive and onto the golf course. Much more snow had fallen. Andy put his drink down in the snow, climbed into the driver's seat, turned on the ignition, shifted into reverse. I went to the front of the car and pushed. The wheels spun. He shifted into Drive, and I pushed from the rear. Nothing happened. We tried several times, and the wheels spun deeper into the snow and the golf course, but nothing else happened. Andy turned off the ignition and got out of the car.

"Where's my drink?" he said.

I walked to where I thought he had put it down. I couldn't find it..

"It's gone," I said, helpfully.

He became agitated. "Where is it?" he said, impatiently. "Where the hell's my drink?"

"It's gone," I repeated, then made a constructive suggestion: "Maybe we should go back to the house and get another one."

"Yeah. Let's go."

We trudged back to the house. Andy fixed drinks. I remembered that I belonged to the American Automobile Association. I made a phone call and was told that somebody would come and help me. We relaxed with our drinks. Soon, a tow truck arrived and yanked the rental car out of the golf course and onto the road. I coaxed it back to the Guest House, very slowly and carefully, so as not to attract the attention of any traffic officials, arriving in time for a short nap before being served breakfast by the Guest House manager-butler-valet.

The guest house manager-butler-valet was a very tightly wound German who had arrived sometime after the end of World War II. He ran a very tight house; everything was always absolutely perfect.

He tsk-tskd me when I struggled down to the dining room in the morning and asked for a beer before breakfast. "Oooh, Mista Hoppel," he said, most disapprovingly, "beeah in da mawnning!" He shook his head and went "tsk tsk." I knew from several experiences with numerous editors that a beer would help wash away the hangover. I knew that Andy was having a beer over in Bedford Village. I demanded a beer. The manager brought me a beer, and stood by, tsk tsking, as I applied it. Soon, everything was fine.

Damage to the car, if there was any, was not even minimal; none was visible. I ran it through a car wash and returned it a few days later. It looked like new. I decided not to make a big deal out of the fact that it had not been able to turn left at the end of an icy driveway.

52

The (Expletive Deleted)
Had An Axe!

On January 23, 1968, the North Koreans captured the U.S.S. Pueblo, which was engaged in the collection of electronic intelligence. The North Koreans claimed the ship was in its territorial waters and was "spying" on it, and that they thus had every right to seize it. The United States countered that the ship was in international waters, had every right to be there and demanded the return of the ship and crew. The North Koreans remained unmoved. In a conference call with Digest CEO and Editor-in-Chief Hobart Lewis, it was decided that David Reed and I both should be on hand when the U.S. Navy in all its majesty swept into the North Korean port of Wonsan and recovered the ship and crew; we were to provide an article, perhaps a book-length feature, detailing the dramatic recovery and all of the attendant diplomatic wrestling.

We made appointments at both the State Department and the Defense Department for briefings on the current political atmosphere of the region. We listened to people who allegedly had expertise. The substance of the briefings seemed insubstantial; we were told that Kim Il Sung, then the dictator of North Korea, was a bad guy, and that Park Chung Hee, then President of South Korea, was a good guy whom Kim Il Sung had recently tried to assassinate. We were also told that the U.S.S. Pueblo had been seized illegally in international waters, where it had every right to be, and that the United States had demanded the return of both the ship and her crew forthwith. We knew all this. We had read it in the newspapers.

We repaired to David's house in the Washington suburb of Bethesda. We had a couple of beers and then a nice dinner prepared by David's first wife, Marie. During dinner, David said that we dare not enter East Asia unarmed.

"Be sure to bring your gun," he said.

"I don't have a gun," I said. "Why do we need guns? We aren't going to war, we're going on a journalistic assignment."

"Listen," he said, "what do you mean, you don't have a gun? We can't run around Asia without guns."

"Why not? I never run around anywhere with a gun."

"Asia is very unpredictable."

"I predict that we don't need guns."

In the end, as I was leaving his house, he came out of his study with a .38 caliber pistol, complete with shoulder holster and all kinds of harnessing and insisted that I take it. "I have another one I can use," he explained.

"On what or whom do you plan to use it?"

"Just pack the thing in your suitcase and bring it along," he said, impatiently. We agreed to meet a week later in the Ocura Hotel, in Tokyo.

I climbed into my rented car and laid the holstered gun atop my briefcase, which lay in the passenger seat beside me. I began driving back to the Jefferson Hotel, where I sometimes stayed when in Washington because it was close to the Digest's Washington Office. I was on Wisconsin Avenue, in downtown Bethesda, when a police car behind me signaled me with his flashing lights to pull over.

Oh, my God! I hadn't been speeding. What to do with this gun? I had to hide it before the cop reached the car. If he saw it he would be bound to think I had done something awful, or was up to no good. I didn't pull over right away, I kept on moving, slowly, as I leaned way over and tried to get the gun and the holster and its spider web-like straps under the front seat, out of sight. He turned on one of those blaring "whoop whoop" things. The damnable holster and its straps kept fighting me; the straps seemed unmanageable as I tried to shove them out of sight underneath the driver's seat. I bent over, while trying to pull over. I was shoving and kicking at the straps, finally got them under the seat and finally pulled over, slamming on the brakes. My briefcase flew off the passenger seat onto the floor. Within the briefcase a tape recording I had earlier made at a memorial service could be heard playing taps. I opened the window to talk to the policeman.

I forced myself to grin, wanted to look pleasant, innocent. "Is there a problem, Officer?" My voice sounded squeaky to me, and I knew that I was disheveled, all sweaty, obviously nervous, and the bugle kept on playing taps. The policeman stared down at me. He stuck his head inside my window and listened to the bugle.

"Sir," he said, "would you please step out of the car?"

I did so.

"Where have you been this evening."

"I had dinner at a friend's house, here, in Bethesda."

"Were you drinking?"

"A couple of beers. No more. Then we had dinner."

"Where are you going now?"

"Back to my hotel, in the District. The Jefferson."

"Please get back in your car and follow me."

I followed him into an underground garage in the Montgomery County police station. There, I was instructed to park the car, get out and follow him I made sure before I got out that the straps of the holster were as far underneath the driver's seat as I could get them. I took my briefcase and followed the policeman upstairs. He told me to be seated on a bench where a few other criminals were sitting. He asked for David's telephone number, which I provided. He went into an office and talked to another cop, obviously a senior officer. I prayed they would not search the rented car; if they did, they surely would find the holstered gun under the driver's seat! I was probably headed for some hard time in the Maryland state penitentiary.

The cop came out of the senior officer's office, went to a desk, picked up a telephone and talked for what seemed quite a while. I wondered if he was talking to David, and if so what Reed could be telling him – probably that he had never heard of me, or that he thought I was up to no good. No! David loved practical jokes and was constantly inventing them, but he wouldn't go that far. Finally, the officer came back to me.

"Mr. Reed confirms everything you told me," he said. "He said you are a Roving Editor for The Reader's Digest. He said that you are a very important writer. He mentioned some of the stories you have written. I read your story about the missing H-bomb. That was a great story. I'm very sorry to have detained you, Mr. Hubbell. The only reason I pulled you over was to warn you that one of your tail lights is broken, but I thought your behavior was odd...."

"Hey, listen..." I said, relieved, magnanimously waving off his apology, letting him know that there was nothing to apologize for, "glad to know the police are doing their job. This car is a rental; they shouldn't be renting out cars with broken tail lights. I'll let them know when I turn it back in, tonight."

The next morning I packed the pistol between layers of clothing in my suitcase; there were no security inspections at airports in those days. At home, I buried it deep in a dresser drawer, beneath layers of clothing, and forgot about it for years.

A few days later I kissed Punkin and the kids goodbye; Katie, our eighth child and third daughter was less than three months old[11] I had not had much chance to get to know her and I was not overjoyed about leaving on what could be an extended trip. But the North Koreans had left me no choice. I left for the Far East.

---

[11] In addition to growing up to become a beautiful woman, she is an accomplished artist and writer; people have been known to pay thousands of dollars for her portraits of their grandchildren; and readers of the Chicago Tribune's Redeye have enjoyed her side-splitting satire.

In Tokyo, Dennis McEvoy, who had been so helpful to me and David in various places, greeted us and saw that we met the right people. I wanted to know what he was doing in Tokyo. He muttered something about writing a book, but the important thing was to get us to a cocktail reception at the American Embassy. There, he introduced us to his good friend, the U.S. Ambassador to Japan, U. Alexis Johnson. We had a pleasant drink together, then Johnson took David and me aside and told us to talk to the Skipper of a Japanese merchant ship who had been on the scene when the North Koreans had seized the Pueblo. The next day we found the Skipper, who had plotted the whole event, and his plot demonstrated that Pueblo had been 21 miles east of Wonsan, in international waters, well clear of North Korea's territorial waters, when the North Korean navy pounced.

We boarded a Northwest (now Delta) Airlines flight for Seoul. We took seats way up front. David opened his portable typewriter, I opened my notebook. I began reading aloud notes of my interviews in both Washington and Japan with intelligence officers and various U.S. Naval officers, all of whom were involved with the investigation of the Pueblo incident. David listened and typed. Then, I took the typewriter and David began reading his notes of interviews with various people in the State Department in Washington, and the American embassy in Tokyo. Almost as quickly as I began typing a Flight Steward came by and instructed me to put away the typewriter, that I was disturbing the other passengers.

I looked around. This was a giant of an airplane, a DC-10 or a Boeing 747, one of those. The only other passengers aboard were approximately a city block behind us, paying no attention to us and engaged in animated conversation. I pointed out to the steward that they did not appear to be at all disturbed by us. "Sorry," he said, loftily, obviously not a bit sorry, "you'll have to put it away." He walked on.

David continued reading his notes to me, and I continued typing. Minutes later the steward was back. "I told you to put that typewriter away!" he said, nastily. "Now, put it away."

"I don't think so," I said. "We have work to do, and we are not disturbing anyone"

"Yes, you are."

I gave David the typewriter and got up and walked back to where the other people were seated. They smiled as I approached, and greeted me. They were German, but spoke fluent English. "We are using a portable typewriter," I told them. "Does it bother you? Do you find the noise objectionable?"

They looked puzzled, looked at each other quizzically, then back at me. "Of course not," one man said. "We didn't know you were using a typewriter. We couldn't hear it. And even if we could, it wouldn't bother us."

"The steward said we were disturbing you."

"You are not disturbing us. He is imagining things." I thanked them, returned to my seat.

David began reading again and I typed. Shortly, the steward was back; he was furious. "You're either going to put that thing away or you are going to be put off of this aircraft."

"The hell we are!" Reed said, angrily. "Where's the pilot? We want to talk to the pilot."

"The pilot is busy. He's preparing...."

"Tell the pilot we want to see him," I said. *"Now!"*

"Who are you?" Reed demanded of the steward. "I want your name."

The steward stuck his chest out at us, defiantly, so that we could read the name tag on his jacket. We both wrote it down. He stormed away.

We seethed.

"Wish we had that gun I gave you," Reed said.

"We can't shoot the (expletive deleted). I said. "By the way, where's your gun? Didn't you bring a gun?"

"No, I forgot."

"You *forgot? After forcing a gun on me? After insisting that we couldn't 'run around Asia without guns'? After I was arrested with the gun you gave me?* And I meant to ask you, where did you get that gun you gave me? It looked old and used."

"I bought it in New York, from a cab driver."

"A New York cab driver?" I used some bad language, trying to keep my voice down. I pointed out that for all he knew it could be traced to a lot of gangland hit jobs.

A few minutes later the pilot came back. He was a big, nice looking fellow, probably in his middle 50's. He dismissed the steward, then turned to us and spoke in a very low, soft voice. "Gentlemen, I apologize, I'm very sorry about this. This guy is a terrible jerk. There have been a lot of complaints about him, and the airline has been trying to get rid of him for years. The problem is that it's a union thing; there has to be a hearing, a sort of trial, and no one has ever been willing to take the trouble to travel to the Twin Cities, at our expense, and testify as to his behavior, so it has never been possible to make a case acceptable to the union. Would you be willing to do that?

"I live in Minneapolis," I said. Minneapolis was then the airline's headquarters. "It would be no problem for me to do that. I would joyfully testify against this (expletive deleted)."

"I would come from the end of the world to testify against this (expletive deleted)", David said.

"I'm going to ask you to do the airline a great favor," the pilot said. "Would you each *please* write a letter to the President of the company and describe in detail what has happened here? And let the company know that you would be available to testify at a hearing?"

We agreed, enthusiastically.

The pilot pointed out that it was only a short flight to Seoul and wondered if we could put the typewriter away, "to keep the peace," and to *please* write our letters to the company as quickly as was convenient. He said that he would make a report of his own, and would be there to testify with us.

Some months later we all were at company headquarters, in Minneapolis, testifying in detail. The pilot was there, and so was the (expletive deleted), swearing under oath that despite his gentlemanly suggestions, we had thought nothing of savaging the ears of other passengers with our noisy typewriter, and he lied that we had been extremely and profanely disagreeable when asked to desist.

We heard nothing. A few months later I called Northwest's customer relations department and found someone who knew about the case. I wanted to know if the airline had freed itself of the (expletive deleted). The answer was no; the union had refused to go along with a dismissal, and had threatened to call a strike if it happened.

This was very frustrating.

Then, it got worse.

A few months later the (expletive deleted) was in headlines all over the world: A crazy radical had attempted to hijack a Northwest Airliner flying out of Manila. The (expletive deleted) had hit him in the head with an axe, and had saved the aircraft and its passengers! Airline officials were expressing pride in his courageous behavior.

In the eyes of much of the world, the (expletive deleted) was a hero!

"How can this be, Reed?" I asked David on the telephone. "Whatever has become of justice?"

"I have no idea," David said. "Just be sure that if you go Northwest again that the (expletive deleted) isn't working the flight. As you have noted, he is handy with an axe."

53
Lyndon Was No Teddy

I n Seoul, we interview everyone who will talk to us in the American embassy, the U.S. Army and the government of the Republic of Korea (ROK).

We attend meetings at Panmunjom, on the 38th parallel, which divides North and South Korea, between representatives of the United States and the Republic of Korea (ROK), and representatives of the so-called Peoples Democratic Republic of Korea (PDRK) and their mentor-partners from the Peoples Republic of China (PRC). The meetings are not cordial; in fact, they seem constantly to verge on violence; every few minutes, an American or a ROK person will say something that brings the Chicoms and the PDRKs to their feet, shouting angrily, almost hysterically, using language that we do not understand but surely must contain large numbers of expletives deleted. They are always shouting, baring their teeth, snarling, threatening. They pick up heavy ashtrays and threaten to throw them at their counterparts across the table. Sometimes they jump up and pick up chairs and threaten to throw them. We learn from the ever calm American representatives that this is standard behavior, typical of the meetings that have been taking place here for 15 years, ever since the alleged end of the Korean War; and that no progress whatever is being made concerning the Pueblo and her men.

This was an especially tense time in the American and South Korean relationship with North Korea; it would have surprised no one, at least, no one in the Far East at the time, should hostilities that had ended 15 years earlier resume. Only weeks earlier a 31-man team of North Korean commandos had been intercepted on a mission to assassinate the President of South Korea. North Korea's "Dear Leader," Kim Il Sung, had ordered his commandos to, "Bring me the head of Park Chung Hee."

Early one evening David and I sat in the Officer's Club in the Army's Advance Camp in the DMZ, only yards below the 38th parallel. It was not a swanky place, but the best relaxation spot in the neighborhood. The commanding officer, an Army colonel, sat with us, and we all imbibed martinis. At length, a clean cut young lieutenant in battle dress approached and spoke to the colonel.

"Sir," he said, "I'm going to inspect the guard posts." He was the Officer of the Day, and this was his responsibility.

I won't name the colonel, because he'd had a number of martinis, and at this moment was in no condition to lead anything resembling a sturdy defense against an invasion should the North Koreans mount one. Furthermore, I was sitting across from him and had matched him martini for martini, and so had David, sitting between us – in fact, David might have been one or two up on us.

"Lieutenant," I said, rising, "may I accompany you?" I was intrigued; I wanted a look at the sentry posts, and at the young Americans who manned them.

"Me, too," David slurred, "I wanna check out the garpis."

I hoped my voice wasn't as slurred as David's, and God forbid that it should sound anything like the colonel's; the colonel rose to his feet slurring really badly, "By God, I'm not askin' my men to do an'thing I woodn do!"

The lieutenant looked doubtful. "There are six posts," he said, ignoring the colonel and speaking directly to me. "It will take about an hour. Sometimes, North Korean troops sneak close and whisper threats at the sentries and throw rocks at them. Sometimes it gets a little hairy…"

"C'mon," the colonel slurred, struggling into his jacket, "les go check the garpis."

The four of us piled into the lieutenant's jeep and checked the guard posts. Nothing untoward was happening. The sentries all were young fellows, appeared to be in their early and mid-20's. I took all their names and addresses in case we wrote anything about them. The lieutenant talked to each of them, and quite obviously tried to shield them from their commanding officer, who kept draping an arm around their shoulders and breathing the echos of his martinis upon them, telling them what fine boys they were and how proud he was of them.

The last post we visited was at a place called The Bridge of No Return. It was small footbridge that led across a gorge into

North Korea. The colonel said that the name derived from the fact that no one who crossed into the earthly hell that is North Korea ever returned. Ever. No one seemed to know how often or if ever this had happened, or even why the bridge was there; the colonel said it was there so that North Koreans who wanted out could sneak into South Korea. The sentry said that some rocks had come his way earlier, but that nothing had happened in the past hour.

David indicated that he needed to relieve himself, and said, "I'm goin' over there." He nodded at The Bridge of No Return. He said, "I wanna micturate on North Korea."

With that, and against all sorts of dire warnings, he lurched, a bit unsteadily, toward the bridge. The colonel and I were far too relaxed to be concerned. The Officer of the Day and the Sentry stopped him, and persuaded him that it was okay to relieve himself on South Korean soil.

Days passed, and nothing continued to happen concerning the Pueblo. We went back to Seoul and began interviewing American and ROK officials as to North Korea's behavior since the 1953 armistice. We found a long history of outrageous depredations that continued. Only a few months earlier North Korean troops had sneaked below the DMZ to a hill just above a U.S. Army camp and raked a chow line with automatic weapons, killing three American soldiers and wounding 25. In the previous year alone Kim's agents had intruded into South Korea 566 times. Time and time again North Korean troops had, in blatant violation of the armistice, crossed into South Korea and killed and wounded American and South Korean troops.

We learned, Kim Il Sung recently had been taking all kinds of ominous steps: Food supplies, essential materials and much of his military and industrial facilities had been moved underground. Factories were being dispersed, people were being moved away from population centers. Kim had asserted that, "War may come at any minute," and it surely looked like he was preparing for war.

Little of this had appeared in the Western press; Western leaders had not been making much noise about it. David and I went in different directions, interviewing, gathering complementary information. We produced an article entitled, "Korea: The War That Never Ended," detailing North Korea's continuing violations of the armistice agreement and the behavior of their representatives at the Panmunjom "peace talks." The piece was well received in Pleasantville.

Since the United States had angrily denounced North Korea's seizure of the Pueblo as "an act of war." We remained confident that our government would not allow this situation to stand, any more than President Teddy Roosevelt in 1904 had allowed a Barbary pirate named Raisuli to get away with kidnapping an American citizen named Perdicaris. "Perdicarus alive or Raisuli dead," Roosevelt had warned, as he sent a squadron of U.S. Naval vessels into the harbor at Tangier. Perdicarus had been returned forthwith, very much alive and healthy. We were confident that Lyndon Johnson, a rough, tough Texan, would emulate his long ago predecessor, that a carrier battle group, many times more powerful than the Naval squadron that had gone into Tangier, would soon enter the harbor at Wonsan. I called the American embassy in Seoul and spoke to the Naval attaché, told him we wanted to be aboard any such battle group. He claimed to be unaware of any such plan. Doubtless, I thought, because he didn't feel he could reveal a military secret.

Over a period of weeks our confidence dissipated. The United States took no action. The North Koreans made a museum of the Pueblo, mooring it in the harbor at Wonsan and taking visitors from allied countries, like China, the Soviet Union and other communist utopias on sightseeing tours of the "spy ship" they had wrested from the Americans. The Pueblo's officers and crew remained imprisoned, and their captors spent the next year brutalizing them.

We investigated other excitements that had been roiling the neighborhood. Only one of the 31 North Korean commandos who had been sent to collect the head of the President of South Korea had survived. "We need to talk with him," I told Kim Sung Eun, Minister of Defense for the Republic of Korea.

He said, "That might be difficult."

I said, "Make it happen anyway. No one knew these killers were coming, and you stopped them. Get your story in front of 100 million people around the world."

The following Sunday I persuaded David, a professed nonbeliever, to accompany me to mass in a Catholic cathedral in downtown Seoul. It was a bitterly cold February morning – Seoul is at about the same parallel as Minneapolis. For some reason several doors of the cathedral were left open, and strong winds kept rushing through the place. All the seats were filled, and we stood in a side aisle and shivered as a Korean priest sang the high mass in his own language. Two or three times I thought I heard David muttering expletives deleted. At one point he leaned over to me to whisper, "Last time you're dragging me to one of these jam sessions, Pal."

We breakfasted afterward at the Eighth Army mess, at the time one of the better eateries in Seoul. There, I was surprised and delighted to encounter a gentleman named Dan Herget, who had been one of my high school basketball coaches and now was a high ranking official in the American embassy. We reminisced briefly, and I accepted his invitation to lunch with him and his wife at their residence the following Tuesday.

David and I had rooms at Walker Hill, an upscale hotel compound a few miles out of Seoul. On Tuesday morning I was just leaving for lunch with the Hergets when suddenly a couple of Army trucks rolled into the compound and disgorged a large number of troops. Some surrounded the building, and others came inside and evacuated all of the other guests and all of the hotel's employees. David and I were invited to sit at a table in the dining room. Kim Shin Jo, the sole survivor of the North Korean commando team raid on the Blue House, was marched in; the Blue house is the resident of the President, South Korea's White House. Kim was seated before us and instructed to answer all of our questions. An interpreter was provided.

Before we began, I excused myself, called Dan Herget, explained the situation, and that it would not be possible for me to come to lunch. Certain that his wife had arranged a lovely table, I apologized profusely, but there was nothing I could do about it. He sounded most unhappy, and I couldn't blame him. I tried to contact him later but was unsuccessful, and I never saw him again.

David and I interviewed Kim for nearly eight hours. He gave us a lot of detailed, blood curdling information about the attempt on Park's life, and the training of North Korea's commandos, which rivaled that of the U.S. Navy's SEALs.

Having done all we could think of to do in Korea and by now aware that the Johnson Administration was determined to take no for an answer to its demands – no, its *pleas* – for the return of the Pueblo and her men, we returned to Tokyo. I wanted to get Kim Shin Jo's story written. David said, "Let's go to Saigon."

I said, "I don't want to go to Saigon. Let's write Kim Shin Jo."

"We can do that later, when we get home," he said. "C'mon, let's go to Saigon."

"Listen," I said, "I have a new daughter back in the City of Lakes. All I know about her is that her name is Katie. I am going to Minneapolis and get reacquainted with my wife and get to know Katie, and spend some time playing with her siblings. That sounds a lot better to me than Saigon."

"Well, then," David said, "you go ahead home and write the Kim Shin Jo piece, and when I get home I will make the necessary corrections and do all the necessary rewriting and get it in acceptable condition, and I'll meet you in Pleasantville."

"I will write the piece," I said. "I have your notes and mine, and if you presume to do any rewriting whatever I will certainly let everyone know that you spent the whole interview sucking down martinis, and you must know that no one will have any trouble believing that."

"And do me a favor," he added, "call Marie (his first wife) and tell her I went to Saigon."

This information did not please Marie. On the plus side, I was happy, getting to know my newest daughter, Katie, and playing with her siblings.

A few weeks later David and I reconvened in Pleasantville. He could find no reason to make any corrections or do any rewriting of the Kim Shin Jo piece, which I had entitled, "Mission: To Murder a President," and which already had been well received by Editorial.

A year later Lyndon Johnson sent a formal letter of apology to North Korea's "Dear Leader", Kim Il Sung, agreeing that the United States had indeed been spying on his country and promising to do so no more. The North Koreans kept the ship; they still have it. But in return for Johnson's confession the officers and crew of the Pueblo were released across The Bridge of No Return into South Korea. From there, they were returned to the United States. The Navy convened a Court of Inquiry in Coronado, California. David and I attended, hoping to finish researching the story we had set out to do a year earlier.

54
A Court Of Inquiry

The Court was a fiasco. Several admirals sat at a table on a stage, looking like a group of medieval judges, seeming to glare at Pueblo's Skipper, Commander Lloyd Bucher, as he was interrogated by a Commander, an attorney representing the Navy's Judge Advocate General's Office.. There was a large audience of media. The scene was red meat for cartoonists and newspaper wordsmiths, who were able to describe gold braided Navy top brass focused accusingly on a little guy who had been given an impossible job and then captured, imprisoned and cruelly tortured for a year, and now found his own character being severely questioned. But after all, he had done the unforgivable; he had given up the ship, surrendered it without a fight.

It was awful. The media made the most of it.

The telephone in my hotel room in Coronado rang me awake in the middle of the night. CinCPac Jack McCain was upset. The Navy was getting a terrible press over "this Pueblo thing," and did I think the Navy captain who was dealing with the media should be fired? I said that I had known the captain for a long time, that he was a good man, conscientious and competent.

"He's doing the best that can possibly be done, Admiral," I said. "This is a lousy story. It makes the Navy look terrible, but there is nothing he can do about it. One thing he had better *not* do is to try to influence what any of the media thinks or says about it. Leave him alone. Stay out of it. Don't fire him, and don't say anything. Eventually, it will disappear from the public consciousness,"

He stayed out of it.

The court of Inquiry recommended that Bucher be court-martialed; its case was *prima facie*. There was no question that he had given up the ship, had offered no resistance when the North Koreans attacked. In fact, he had thrown his sidearm over the side and ordered his officers to do the same. His behavior was nowhere close to what Naval tradition calls for, which is that if all you've got left to fight with is your fingernails, you fight with your fingernails. You die trying. You don't give up the ship.

Bucher's counterargument was that his ship was no man o' war, which is to say, it was not a combatant vessel; and that to say that it was "lightly armed" was an absurd overstatement, that for all practical purposes it was defenseless, that there was not the slightest possibility that it could withstand capture, much less prevail. He pointed out that the North Koreans had fired 15 heavy shells at Pueblo and thousands of smaller rounds; that that one of his crew had been killed and several others, himself included, had been wounded. He said that prior to capture he and his officers and crew had been able to destroy all of the secret documents and equipment aboard. He also reminded the court that a U.S. Navy carrier battle group had not been far away, that he had called for air support that could have reached him in minutes, but that no air support had been sent. He insisted that the North Koreans, who had an overwhelming advantage in numbers and firepower had made it clear that he must surrender the ship or they would kill everyone aboard, that he deemed them crazy enough to do so, and that his ship was an old rust bucket that should never have been sent to sea, that it certainly should never have been sent into such a dangerous area, and that he did not believe it was worth the lives of his officers and some 80 enlisted men.

Considering the embarrassingly weak reaction of the Administration, guided no doubt by its foreign policy "experts," to what was, without question, an act of war against the United States, the failure to send available air support to a U.S. Navy vessel under attack, the failure to make any attempt in a timely fashion to retrieve the crew or ship, indeed, allowing the North Koreans to hold the crew in vile captivity for a year, the abject apology to North Korea a year later – it was disgusting; and it left one wondering if perhaps some others should be court-martialed, or dismissed from government service.

The Navy was indeed suffering a very bad press from the Pueblo affair. Finally, Secretary of the Navy John Chafee set aside the recommendation for court martial, and Bucher was allowed to continue his career. He retired in 1973, and died in 2004 at the age of 76.

David and I decided there was no story to be told that the public did not already know. Before leaving the area, we took the occasion to call retired Admiral U.S. Grant Sharp, who had preceded Jack McCain as Commander in Chief Pacific, and whom we both had interviewed several times during the Vietnam War. He now lived in nearby Point Loma.

55

A Sharp Disagreement

Sharp sounded delighted to hear from us, and invited us to his place for a visit.

During our visit, Sharp, who had never told either of us nor any other media people of his disagreements with the Johnson Administration's conduct of the war, commented that, "We should have won the war long ago." We leaped on that assertion, and he expanded. He told us that every week for four years he had recommended to the Joint Chiefs of Staff that we destroy the enemy's capacity to make war, that we take the air war to the seat of the enemy's government, Hanoi, to his military facilities in and around Hanoi and throughout North Vietnam, and to mine the harbor at Haiphong, where Soviet ships continued to deliver mountains of war materiel, that we stop of the flow of Soviet supplies through Cambodia, and block the Ho Chi Minh Trail at its entry point, in Laos.

All these things could have been accomplished easily at the outset, he said, but none of them had been done. Instead, we had watched passively, while the Soviets had equipped North Vietnam, which previously had had no air defense system worthy of the name, with what was now inarguably the most formidable air defense system in the world, with the result that a great many lives had been sacrificed, hundreds of American airmen now languished in North Vietnamese prisons and billions of dollars of worth of aircraft had been lost. A war that should never have become a war had been turned into a horrific disaster by politicians and amateur advisors who had insisted on closely controlling every aspect of the American combat effort. He knew that his recommendations had been conveyed regularly by the Joint Chiefs of Staff to the then Secretary of Defense, McNamara. He did not know what became of them thereafter. He did know that none were ever put in play.

We ghost wrote an article he signed for the Digest entitled, "We Could Have Won in Vietnam Long Ago." It lit off a furor.

For one, Paul Thompson was furious. He was the executive vice president of the Digest. A graduate of the military academy at West Point, Paul was an impressive gentleman, perhaps six feet tall, his dark hair streaked with silver, handsome, well put together, and a hero of World War II. He had been charged with the training of all the assault troops for the June 6, 1944, D-Day invasion at Normandy, had been in the thick of it on Omaha Beach, and had been shot in the shoulder and the jaw. His lasting regret was that he had not lasted long enough to see the men he had trained move inland.

A powerful personality, Paul had retired from the Army as a general officer himself. He was not connected with editorial matters at the Digest, but at a luncheon in the Guest House he seemed determined, at least today, to influence them. He was livid, with me, David Reed, and Admiral Sharp. He angrily demanded to know if we were all crazy to even contemplate publishing such a piece. Did we really want to challenge the knowledge and expertise of the Secretary of Defense, the brilliant Robert McNamara, and his advisors? Did we think the Pentagon was full of fools? Did we really think that President Lyndon Johnson would have agreed for even a moment with the stupid war fighting policies Sharp had described to us? Were we that dumb?

My co-conspirator, David Reed, was elsewhere that day, so it fell to me to respond: Yes, I said, with all due respect, we were that dumb. We did believe what Admiral Sharp had told us, that there was every reason to believe it and not a single good reason not to believe it. I pointed out that there must be very few people on the planet who did not know that the United States was the strongest military power in the history of the world, and that it was inconceivable that it could be held at bay all these years by a little backwater country like North Vietnam unless its war fighting policies were as wrongheaded as Admiral Sharp wanted publicly to insist they were. Those policies, I added, had already resulted in the deaths of scores of thousands of young Americans, had cost many billions of dollars, had bitterly divided the country and had done nothing to bring about an end to hostilities. We held the Administration's war-fighting policies to be responsible for these results, we held Defense Secretary McNamara's brilliance, at least where war-fighting policy was concerned, to be a myth, and I said that David Reed and I felt privileged to be able to place Admiral Sharp's judgment before the Digest's readers.

Paul glared at me and snapped, contemptuously, "That judgment is what I would *expect* of the *Navy!*

Then we had lunch.

Sharp's arguments were convincing because they were facts. The article was published just as we had written it. Arkansas Senator J. William Fulbright was as furious as Paul Thompson. He appeared on at least one morning network television show waving a copy of the Digest and wishing that "these admirals and generals would shut up," insisting that every time they shot off their mouths this way the enemy in Vietnam got mad and intensified his efforts. I had no memory of any other flag officer having had the courage Admiral Sharp had displayed.

Not long thereafter I met Sharp again, at the Naval War College, in Newport, Rhode Island. He wanted me to know how much strong support he had received for the article, from both his military contemporaries and many ordinary citizens. He sought my advice as to how to put together a book on the subject. I was delighted to be of assistance. The book was entitled, "Strategy for Defeat: Vietnam in Retrospect." He sent me a copy. He had inscribed his gratitude in a lengthy note on a flyleaf. I loaned it to a friend, and never saw it again. That is my only regret about my relationship with Admiral Sharp.

56

"You Are Not Welcome..."

"**W**e cannot grant you a visa to visit our country, Mr. Gilmore," the man said. "You are not welcome in the Soviet Union. None of you. Not you. Not Edward T. Thompson. Not John G. Hubbell. A visit by any or all three of you would only result in another round of anti-Soviet stories in The Reader's Digest. You continue to slander us all over the world, and yet you expect us to welcome you. You are none of you welcome in the Soviet Union."

The man was a minor functionary in the Soviet embassy, someone Ken Gilmore, then chief of the Digest's Washington bureau, had never seen during his previous several visits to the embassy. He had applied for visas for each of us weeks earlier. He recalled that the people he had dealt with at the time had seemed agreeable enough, that they had merely instructed him that all of the air fares and hotel charges must be paid before visas could be granted. He had seen to it, and had been assured that he could pick up the visas on this date.

Ed Thompson was now a very senior Senior Editor at the magazine's editorial headquarters. I was a Roving Editor whose work was focused on military affairs. Ed and I were waiting in the Washington office, and Gilmore brought us the bad news. We were all disappointed. We had planned to embark that day on a ten-day trip that would take us first to Moscow, then Leningrad (now St. Petersburg) then Tashkent and out through Central Asia. We wanted to see whatever we could see, talk to whomever would talk to us and just generally get a firsthand feel for the U.S.S.R. But it wasn't going to happen.

This was in the autumn of 1969, at approximately the midpoint of the Cold War. Ed suggested that it probably didn't help that the then current issue of the Digest included a piece entitled, "A Bold New Plan for National Defense." It pointed out that we were witnessing in the U.S.S.R. the most enormous nuclear arms buildup in history, and that the primary target of this buildup could only be the deterrent nuclear firepower based in the United States, the Strategic Air Command's bombers and its Intercontinental Ballistic Missiles (ICBMs) loaded into underground silos across the Great Plains. The article argued forcefully for a plan developed in response to the Soviet buildup in the Navy's Office of Offensive and Defensive Strategic Systems, headed by the innovative Rear Admiral George H. Miller.

I had authored the piece following many discussions concerning the idea with Admiral Miller. He had ascertained that it was now possible for the United States to confront the Soviets with a virtually impossible targeting problem, one certain to nullify any plans they might have for a nuclear first-strike that could eliminate our retaliatory forces.

Miller proposed removing the continental United States from the Soviets' line of nuclear fire. He would accomplish this by taking the American ICBMs out of the underground silos in the United States and sending them to sea; I had been made privy to extensive studies proving that they could just as easily be fired from the surface of the sea as from holes in the ground. Miller insisted that many ICBMs could go to sea immediately, on aircraft carriers and large auxiliary vessels. He argued that we should also start immediately on the design and construction of as many as thirty fast-moving surface ships capable of carrying hundreds of ICBMs. His plan called for widely dispersing such a fleet over the seas that cover some seventy percent of the earth's surface, keep the ships moving constantly and at high speeds on constantly changing headings, making it impossible for an enemy to target them with any degree of certainty.

Not only would such a deployment deprive the Soviets' of the fixed targets they were now able to pinpoint in the United States, but it would also immensely complicate their defensive problem: they knew that as things stood an American retaliatory strike would have to come through a narrow northern corridor that formed a 32-degree arc, only nine percent of their total perimeter. Thus, they only had to concentrate their defensive systems against a limited sector. A full-fledged American nuclear-armed sea force would require them to construct defenses around the full 360 degrees of the compass.

The technologies for building such ships had long been in hand, Miller said, and estimated that a completed force could be at sea in four years.

No expensive, time-consuming research and development would be necessary. We already had developed the Polaris and Poseidon missiles that could be fired directly from our undersea fleet. But there was no question that ballistic missiles could also be fired from the surface of the sea; in fact, we knew that the missiles carried on Soviet submarines were designed to be floated to the surface and fired from there.

Across the second and third pages of the article was a global projection, with most of the world in muted tans and browns, the seas blue, but the U.S.S.R. in a brilliant red, stretching from East Berlin nearly to Alaska. On the projection the American ICBM fleet was deployed in the seas all around the world, and flight trajectories had been imposed to indicate the arcs the seagoing missiles would follow into targets all over the U.S.S.R. The proposal had been advocated strongly before Congress by the then Chief of Naval Operations, Admiral Thomas H. Moorer.[12]

A footnote to the article described me as, "one of the nation's most respected writers in the field of military affairs." And only a year earlier the Digest had featured as a lead article a piece I had

---

[12] There was never a chance that Miller's proposal would come to fruition. The deterrent systems then in place, The Strategic Air Command's bomber and ICBM forces and the Navy's ballistic missile submarine force, had huge bureaucracies supporting them; many thousands of careers and many billions of dollars were involved, as were large numbers of jobs in many Congressional districts. But it seemed worth thinking about as the years passed and the nation's strategic posture kept evolving.

written calling the world's attention for the first time to "The Rising Threat of Soviet Strategic Power."

I could understand the Soviets antipathy toward me.

And I could understand their dislike of Ken Gilmore, whose Washington Bureau had produced a great many anti-Soviet articles; in fact, one of his writers, John Barron, had written a book entitled, "KGB: The Secret Work of Soviet Secret Agents," a definitive and damning expose of the Kremlin's secret police. Several chapters had appeared in the magazine, and in the Digest's foreign editions.

Ed Thompson, of course, was Gilmore's liaison in Pleasantville, his consultant and advisor, and involved in all of the material that came out of the Washington office as well as my typewriter, the editor who made sure it all was solidly researched, well written and worthy of presentation to the magazine's readers.

I had another thought as to why our visa applications had been denied:. I had arrived in Washington early the previous evening and checked in at the Jefferson Hotel, not far from Gilmore's Rhode Island Avenue office. Almost immediately the telephone rang. It was Editor-in-Chief and CEO Hobart Lewis, down from Pleasantville for some reason. He was calling from a well attended Georgetown watering hole, a meeting place where a lot of the government's movers and shakers drank and dined. He was having dinner with Hanson Baldwin, the Military Affairs Editor of the New York Times, Charlie Murphy, of Fortune magazine, and "some other fellows" whom he wanted me to meet. Baldwin and Murphy were friends of mine; I enjoyed their company. I agreed to be there as quickly as I could find a cab.

By the time I arrived they had had some drinks, and the aura was pleasantly jovial. The group included two gentleman I did not know. I don't remember the name of one of them, who was seated at the other end of the table, but the one I was seated next to was introduced to me, and I was told that he was a retired businessman. He was slightly built, wore horn-rimmed glasses and had wavy dark hair parted on the side. He smiled pleasantly and shook hands, saying, "I'm very glad to meet you. I understand you are leaving tomorrow for the Soviet Union."

"Yes," I said, "three of us."

"I envy you," he said. "I wish I were going with you. I have always been very interested in the country. I keep trying to under-stand the Soviets, but every time I think I do, they do something that confuses me. I would really like to talk with you about your visit when you return. What you see, whom you talk to, what they say, just what you feel about them and the country. I'm retired, but keep an office here, in the District." He handed me his card; it was clear that this was very important to him. The card was inscribed with the address of his office, his telephone number and his name: Jim Angleton.

I was puzzled. I had never heard of him. My first impulse was to say that hopefully he could read everything worth the telling in a future issue of the Digest, but decided that would sound rude. Since he was so friendly with my friends, I simply assured him that I would call.

At the time, of course, James Jesus Angleton was a major secret, Chief of Counterintelligence for the Central Intelligence Agency (CIA). A few years later there was a nasty squabble at the Agency as to whether or not it was honeycombed with "moles," phony defectors from the U.S.S.R. and Americans who had sold out and were working for the other side. Angleton insisted that the Agency had been infiltrated, that moles were providing it with a lot of disinformation and misdirection. The squabble spilled into the public prints. When I read Angleton's name it occurred to me that secret though he had been when I met him, the Soviets surely knew who he was. In those days they certainly had plenty of their own "secret" people around Washington, who spent a lot of time in the city's elite watering holes, watching people who knew things, drinking, dining and sometimes talking too much. I assumed that they kept a close watch on Angleton. I wondered if they saw me talking, drinking and dining with him the night before our visas were to be granted, and we were to leave to leave for the U.S.S.R. I wrote Hobe a note asking if he had known who Angleton was the night he had introduced us. I never got a response. I assumed he was embarrassed, so I never mentioned it again.

57
"What To Do With All This Money...?"

A t this stage of DeWitt Wallace's life the magazine that he had invented had made him wealthy beyond the dreams of Croesus. He and Lila were two of the most generous people in the world and had no heirs. First and foremost they thought of their employees and all of their employees' progeny as their family, and treated them as such. Their payroll was unmatched anywhere else in the world of magazine journalism, and the rates they paid their authors were legendary – every aspiring writer in the world yearned to be struck by the kind of lightning that would bring them to the Digest.

Wally often handed out substantial bonuses. On the morning of June 2, 1956, I was walking with my father and my sister out of the house I had bought in Minneapolis to the car that would take us to the church where, in an hour or so, I would be married to the love of my life. Just then a postman pulled up in a car and emerged to hand me a special delivery airmail envelope. I opened it to find a congratulatory note from DeWitt Wallace and wedding present, a check in the amount of $3,000. That wasn't the only bonus I received in the years that followed. Other writers and editors who worked in the office sometimes got hefty bonuses for what Wally deemed a superior perform-ance. He saw to it that every employee and contributor, even those who worked out of their own homes, received the gift of a turkey at Thanksgiving.

Wally's generosity had long been legendary. To make sure his in-house employees, editors and everyone else, were able to work in a pleasing atmosphere he and his wife, Lila, had hung about $100 million worth of art in offices and hallways all over the build-ing, original works of such as Renoir, Manet, Monet, Van Gogh, Gauguin, Chagall, et al.

Once, several senior editors, intent on serving his best interests, warned him about a writer they knew to be taking obscene advan-tage of his generosity. The writer happened to be a particularly obnoxious person, and was widely loathed; editors hated having to work with him, wanted him banished and had acquired conclusive evidence that the man was blatantly misusing his expense account. He had set himself up in a plush apartment in Paris, was treating himself to a great life in the City of Lights and was charging almost all of his extravagant living habits and entertainment costs to the Digest.

"Get him on the phone and tell him to get over here," Wally said, grimly. "Tell him I want to see him."

The man was soon in Wally's office, where the Editor-in-Chief chatted amiably with him for a while, then told him, "If those fellows down the hall give you any trouble, let me know. I'll take care of it." And the writer returned to the good life in Paris. He was industrious, had produced many articles that Wally had liked, and had told him of some interesting projects he had planned.

For the most part those of us who traveled a lot tried to be sensible with the company's money. It wasn't always easy. Once, just as I was preparing to leave Minneapolis for Pleasantville, I received a memo, sent from someone who dealt with the corporation's finances to all Digesters whose jobs involved travel, that if the trip was one of less than four hours, it wasn't always necessary to fly first class, and that rented Fords and Chevrolets could take one anywhere rented Cadillacs and Lincolns could.

I complied. I flew coach class to New York's LaGuardia Airport, rented a small car, drove up to Pleasantville, got my suitcase and golf clubs stowed aboard the company jet and four of us flew south for a few days of golf at the Augusta National, where Hobe Lewis had become a member.

One day when I was at editorial headquarters, DeWitt Wallace waved me into his office. He closed the door, invited me into a comfortable chair and took a comfortable chair opposite me. I could not imagine what this was about.

He said, "I would like you to do a little personal research for me: Talk to some knowledgeable people in the financial field and write me a memo explaining how I can go about financing college educations for all of the children of everyone who works for me.

"The children of *all* of your employees?"

"Yes."

"All your employees *worldwide*?" (The Digest had many international editions.)

"Yes, all of them."

"There must be a lot of them; I have nine children myself."

He smiled. "Didn't Punkin have something to do with that?"

"Oh, yes. I keep forgetting that."

"And I'm sure that she and you want them to be able to go to college," he said

"Yes, we do.".

"Well, that's what I want to do; the children of all the people who work for me, and I want to know how best to go about doing it."

I had not the slightest idea how much he was worth. All I knew was that it was a lot more than a lot. He had contributed hundreds of millions of dollars to Macalester College, in St. Paul. His father had been President of the school, and DeWitt, his son, had been expelled for his youthful enthusiasms. It was alleged that one day, he and a friend had taken a horse to an upper floor of one of the school's main buildings, where it had emptied itself of its day's intake. Macalester had been dear to his father's heart, and by the time Wally had achieved his enormous wealth he was determined to honor his father's memory by making Macalester "the best small college in the world." He had spared no expense on buildings or in the hiring of distinguished faculty.

He had given many other millions to many other worthy causes. I had once written a piece on Outward Bound, the outdoor program designed to convince young people that they are better than they know, that they can achieve more with their lives than they ever dreamed possible. The story had so impressed him that he gave Outward Bound a million dollars that year, and in each of several years thereafter.

He had supported colonial Williamsburg, in Virginia, with many more millions.

And had infused more millions into many other things.

There was no question that he really wanted all of his employees to know that if their children wanted college educations there was no need to worry about the expense, that college educations would be available to them.

I said. "This is the most generous thing I have ever heard."

"What else am I going to do with all this money?" he said. He grimaced. It was as though he was offended at the notion that he should have "all this money." Then, with a certainty that I was not certain I shared, he assured me, "*You'd* do it."

"I will talk to people in the financial field," I told him. "I will find the advice you need."

"Good. There isn't any reason why anyone you consult would have to know that I'm involved. And I don't want you to breathe a word about this around here. I don't want *anyone* around here to know. If the lawyers find out they'll find a way to stop me."

"No one will hear of it from me," I said.

"Good. I'll look forward to hearing from you."

I got all the necessary advice from bank bigwigs and other financial executives who knew how to do these things. I gave no hint to anyone that my inquiry had anything to do with DeWitt Wallace. Most were curious, and I'm sure some knew exactly who it was for whom I was seeking answers, but questioning ended when I pointed out that in my line of work I met all sorts of people, some of them extremely wealthy, and that those involved wished to remain anonymous. All I remember about the advice I collected is that it would have been a relatively easy process to do what Wally wanted done. I sent him a detailed memo. He never responded, and never mentioned it to me again.

Apparently, the people Wally didn't want to know of his plan learned about it, but were not able to stop him entirely. In the end, a system was worked out whereby senior high school students who were the children of Digest employees would engage in some sort of competition for six college scholarships that were awarded each year. Not close to what he wanted, but much better than nothing.

One year as the Christmas holidays approached, he managed a spectacular end run around those who so zealously guarded his fortune. All the lawyers and people on the business side were engaged in some kind of conference in a swank Florida hostelry. Wally took the occasion of their absence from the office to write a news release himself and send it to the New York Times and the news services, reporting that beginning on the upcoming New Year's Day every Reader's Digest employee would receive an eleven percent increase. By the time the people in Florida returned to Pleasantville it was in headlines on every business page in the country; there was no way that decision could be repealed or changed. I read it in the Minneapolis Star Tribune and my wife and I bought eleven percent more Christmas presents for our kids that year.

But I know that it was one of his lasting regrets that he wasn't able to buy college educations for all of his employees' kids.

58
The Torch is Passed

One evening in February, 1976 I picked up the phone to hear Ed Thompson ask, "Have you heard anything on the news about the Digest?"

"No."

"Good. I'm the new Editor-in-Chief. The press release has already gone out, and I wanted you to know before you read it in the newspapers."

I am not sure of what I am hearing; it sounds like he is saying that he is now the Editor-in-Chief of The Reader's Digest, one of the most important and powerful editorial positions in the world. I make him say it again. He does so.

I am thrilled. "Ed," I shout, "this is *wonderful!* This is *terrific!* This is *great!* Tell me how and when it happened."

"This morning," he said. "Hobe came to my office and said, "Mr. Wallace wants to see you. He had a kind of funny look on his face."

"What kind of look? Angry? Pleasant?"

"Pleasant. Kind of curious. As though he was seeing me for the first time. I had no idea what this was about. Was Wally going to fire me? What had I done? Anyway, I walked down into his office. He asked me to sit down. He began talking about things I knew nothing about, charities he supported, the Wallace Trust, things like that. Then, he said, 'As Editor-in-Chief, you're going to have to deal with these things.'"

"Did you remain conscious? Did you fall out of your chair?"

"Barely. I wasn't certain I had heard him right. I said, 'Did you just say what I thought you said? Did I hear you right?'"

"He said, 'Yes, you're the new Editor-in-Chief'."

I interrupted to say, "This is the best news I've heard in a long time! This is a great thing for the magazine. Congratulations, Ed. You've earned it. You certainly deserve it."

"Thanks. I wanted to be sure you knew before you heard it elsewhere."

Then, he yielded the phone to a lot of other mutual friends, editors who all had adjourned to a gleeful celebratory party Janny and Andy Jones were hosting. I was just that evening home from researching a story somewhere; I wished Punkin and I were at Jones, helping with the celebration. DeWitt Wallace had passed the leadership to the one most likely to keep things on the upswing into the foreseeable future.

I had known for months that Wally and Hobe were agonizing over the succession, because Hobe had told me so. He had become Editor-in-Chief and Chief Executive Officer of the company 12 years earlier, in 1964 – although Wally had never left; he had remained in his corner office much of the time, looking over Hobe's shoulder, "helping" with many important decisions. Hobe had never seemed to mind. In fact, I think he felt comfortable to have Wally behind him when he made controversial decisions.

"Wally is 86, I'm 66," Hobe had told me. "Pretty soon, something's gotta give. Wally's idea has burgeoned into one of the greatest companies in the world. There is no reason why it shouldn't go on and on, but it's going to take leadership in the mold of DW, and that's very hard to find."

"Maybe not," I said. "There's a lot of leadership talent down the hallway."

"Yes," Hobe agreed, "there is."

We both were referring to five people, all in their mid- to late 40's, who recently had been named Managing Editors. All were being groomed for the executive hierarchy. "The problem is making the right choice." He ticked them off:

Edward T. Thompson, brilliant, a chemical engineering graduate of the Massachusetts Institute of Technology supercompetent – but with "a hard edge, blunt, tough, maybe a little too tough."

Fulton "Tony" Oursler, also brilliant, but maybe a little more outspoken with his conservative political views than you might want in an Editor-in-Chief.

"John Allen; everybody loves him. He's very good, a great speaker, a great representative of the company. Maybe his real field is public relations."

"Roy Herbert has made it plain that he does not want to be considered, does not want the job."

"Ken Gilmore," chief of the Washington Bureau. "But he's well connected in Washington, and doesn't want to leave."

This was a very big deal. All these candidates were friends of mine. Through the years I had often lunched, dined and partied with all of them and at one time or another had worked closely with most of them. But if Hobe wanted my opinion, I didn't feel qualified to offer one. I did not work in the office, I saw none of them on a day to day basis, and had rarely been involved in any of the inside stuff. Years earlier I had been offered that option and had declined. I had stayed in the field, doing what I wanted to do and what I was best at. I was a writer, an observer, sometimes a reporter, sometimes a humorist, sometimes an analyst and commentator. I was a Digest Roving Editor, and that was as good as it got for a writer. I did not want to be an editor who worked with and managed writers and other editors, or had to worry about getting issues of the magazine produced.

All I was willing to contribute to the conversation was to say that all these colleagues were good friends of mine, and that, "Wally and you are confronted with an embarrassment if riches," that "any one of them would be a good choice." I pointed out that I knew Ken Gilmore pretty well, and asked Hobe if he wanted me to let him know that he and several others were being considered, that the impression was that he did not want to leave the nation's capitol, but that if he was interested to let it be known, throw his hat in the ring.

"Please do so," Hobe said. "Tell him to call me and let me know."

I did so. Soon, Gilmore ceded the Washington bureau to Bill Schulz and moved into an office in Pleasantville.

But Wally had made the right decision.

It had been a quarter century since I had first contacted Hobe Lewis, and through all those years he had been my editor, my friend, my mentor, my cheerleader. He had instilled me with the confidence that was crucial to the makeup of a major league magazine writer. I would miss him. We would remain close friends until he died, 34 years later, at the age of 101. But I meant what I said to Ed. I could not have been happier with Wally's choice.

Hobe had created the conditions that culminated in his retirement. He was urbane, sophisticated, connected, a smooth personality, a *nice* man, and his friendships included lots of people in high places. He was handsome; in appearance and manner he bore a resemblance to the actor, Cary Grant, and everyone, including his lovely wife, Edie, knew that he had an eye for the ladies. And ladies found his looks and position to be most attractive. There was one lady named Adele Dillingham whom he had met somewhere in Europe. For some reason she had impressed Hobe with many of what he thought her "good ideas," and he had added her to the magazine's writing corps, although she never wrote anything that appeared in the magazine. When her "good ideas" reached Pleasantville, they were uniformly adjudged unworthy of the time it took to reject them.

In his book, "American Dreamers," Peter Canning reported that an audit of RD's expenses having to do with Ms. Dillingham revealed that she had been well financed by the magazine with a $10,000 retainer, a plush expense account and an authorization by Hobe to the Finance Department to make rental payments on a London townhouse. Canning explains that the money didn't matter to Wally so much as Hobe's continuous efforts to force into the magazine the bizarre proposals of a person who had no idea what the Digest was all about. The final straw fell when Hobe insisted that an upcoming Christmas issue – a season in which the Digest along with countless people around the world celebrated the birth of Christ -- include a Time magazine article Adele Dillingham recommended which celebrated various Eastern religions.`

Wally "killed" the article, took Hobe for a walk, explained to him how old he was and that it was time for him to retire and sent him to fetch Ed Thompson.

Ed told me that the first thing Wally asked of him was to "inform Ms Dillingham that her services are no longer required"

"Yes, Sir," Ed replied, "I'll do that right away."

He got her on the telephone quickly. "I'm the new Editor-in-Chief of The Reader's Digest," he told her. "We have never met, so this is a bit awkward. I'm calling to tell you that you're fired."

So ended Ms. Dillingham's association with the Digest. I had never heard of her before.

With Ed at the helm, the future looked bright.

59

The Most Outrageous
Person I Ever Knew

My colleague and pal, David Reed, was, in the view of many, including me, one of the world's foremost writers on foreign affairs.

He was also the most outrageous person I ever knew.

He did not appear to be outrageous. He was a nice looking gentleman. He was slightly built, perhaps five feet nine inches tall, possibly weighed 145 pounds, had straight dark brown hair which was always neatly combed. He wore spectacles, and often had a pipe in his mouth. He could easily have passed for a professor of Philosophy at the University of Chicago, where he had earned his liberal arts degree by the time he was 18 years old.

He did philosophize a lot, but his field was journalism. He was without question one of the great magazine journalists of his time. He reported from more than 100 countries. He covered every insurgency and war the world's disputatious people could arrange, from the Mau Mau insurrection in Kenya during the 1950's, to El Salvador, Nicaragua, Cambodia, wherever the action was. He spent a lot of time in the Congo during the struggle there for independence, and his book, "111 Days in Stanleyville," delivered a riveting account of the Stanleyville Massacre. On several forays into Vietnam during that war, he scrambled around the country in jeeps, helicopters, trucks, cargo aircraft and on foot, gathering material for a number of Digest articles, plus a book, "Up Front in Vietnam," which conveyed to readers what it was like to be in the combat zone.

Ernest Hemingway, physically imposing and a robust outdoorsman who presented himself as a fearless war correspondent preceded David by decades, but the professorial looking Reed was the man Hemingway really wanted to be and pretended to be.

And he was utterly outrageous.

He was also my sometime collaborator; our work for the Digest was focused on different subjects, my own on military affairs, his on foreign affairs. But two often were intertwined, and we co-authored a number of articles, one of which, "Hill 488: A Fight to Remember," was included in Ed Thompson's "Dream Issue," in which the former Editor-in-Chief, with the help of other senior editorial people, myself included, put together a single fantasy issue that included what they deemed the best of the magazine's "greatest hits" of the 30,000-odd pieces it had run during the 88 years since its founding in 1922 through 2000. "Hill 488" was ranked 15th.

It was a gripping Vietnam war story and was presented as a "Drama in Real Life." An 18-man Marine reconnaissance platoon had been surrounded on a hilltop by an immensely superior enemy force and spent a hellishly long night fighting it to a standstill. By the time relief arrived at first light, the platoon had eight rounds of ammo left., had lost six men, and each of the 12 survivors had qualified for The Purple Heart – some were substantially overqualified, having taken several wounds. The action earned four of the men the Navy Cross, the Navy's highest award for combat valor; 13 Silver Stars were awarded for "conspicuous gallantry in action;" and the Medal of Honor, the nation's highest award for a performance "above and beyond the call of duty," was awarded in a White House ceremony to the platoon leader, SSgt. Jimmie Earl Howard. The platoon thus became the most highly decorated unit in American military history.

David had attended the White House ceremony, then had to respond to an interview opportunity he had been anxiously awaiting in Managua or Mozambique or some such place. I was in Washington investigating another subject, and he asked me to take the reins on this one. He briefed me on his extensive notes, taken from interviews he had conducted with several of the survivors. I read the after action report, and talked at length with Marine Lt. Col. Arthur Sullivan, who had been in overall command of the reconnaissance effort and who judged the action that night to be "one of the great final stands in all of history." Then, I visited at length with Jimmie Earl Howard at the Marine Corps base in San Diego. I got the piece written before David returned from wherever.

David was so impressed with my effort that he conferred upon me a major award. I read about it in the Southwest Minneapolis Sun, a neighborhood newspaper with a wide readership: "Minneapolis author and historian John G. Hubbell has been named to France's Legion of Honor (Legion d'Honneur). The French embassy in Washington, D.C., made the announcement."

This was no small thing. This is France's highest honor. It was invented by Napolean Bonaparte on May 19, 1802. *The Ordre National de la Legion d'Honneur* is divided into five ranks. I was to be inducted at the very highest rank, that of Chevalier.

A Chevalier, the news story said, is entitled to wear an impressive five-armed silver cross, with an enameled laurel and oak leaf badge between the arms. It was to hang on a crimson ribbon from the left side of the chest. If one didn't want to go formal every day, one could instead wear a much smaller but also impressive pin on one's left lapel.

I had always appreciated the fact that the French, in their long quest for *liberte*, had launched their revolution on July 14, 1789, with the assault on the Bastille, 138 years to the day before I was launched in the Bronx

Now, I learned that the Legion of Honor was first awarded on July 14, 1804.

There appears to be something magical, at least in the French mind and mine, about July 14.

In any case, according to David's press release, my induction was to take place at the Embassy of France, in Washington, on March 20th in recognition of my "stalwart stand against communism," as exemplified in my book, "Stand Tall!" The book, the press release emphasized, was a call on the U.S. government to cease being intimidated by the aggressive antics of the communists, to whom Reed, an atheist, often referred as "the godless commies." I had never written such a book and had no plans to do so, but I had produced a lot of material that must have infuriated people in the Kremlin, and could imagine some luckless clerk being ordered to find a copy of my non-existent book, "Stand Tall!"

As I contemplated this I received a telephone call from a columnist for the Minneapolis Star Tribune, who wanted to congratulate me. She was clearly elated that such an honor was to be bestowed upon a Minnesotan. Fearing that she planned a column about it, I warned her off, explaining that it was a prank, a colleague's way of having fun, that I doubted that France had ever heard of me, and to ignore it. She became very angry, outraged that anyone, particularly a member of the Press, would use the Press in such a manner. I could think of nothing to say about Reed that wouldn't further incense her, so said nothing.

Reed had also sent the news release and invitations to the award ceremony to the entire Minnesota Congressional delegation, so I had to disinvite them, explaining that it was a hoax. The only response came from the then Senator David Durenberger, whom I knew. He sent a note suggesting that since I had, in fact, authored articles the communists surely detested, perhaps France could be persuaded to award me at least a *Croix de Guerre*.

Noting that I was 62 years old,[13] Reed reminded the reader that I had been the recipient of numerous awards for my reporting on military affairs, "among them, the InterAmerican Press

---

[13] I was in my mid-40's at the time,

Association's[14] Hemispheric Solidarity Award for a series of articles confronting the communist threat in Latin America."

On another occasion, and without checking with me, my home-town newspaper published every word of a Reed press release announcing that I was to receive the Homer Gunch Freedom Foundation Award, again for my strong stand against the godless commies; the last line in the release, which the Star Tribune included, was that, "Hubbell, who is 59, stays in trim by bowling seven nights per week."

I don't know whether anyone named Homer Gunch exists or ever existed, but I knew there was no Homer Gunch Freedom Foundation. I had kids in high school by then, and they spent a lot of time assuring teachers and classmates that they knew nothing about awards that were being rained upon me – I think some of the kids were denying that they knew me, or had ever heard of me.

David was imaginative and energetic in these matters. Once, at a luncheon at the Digest's headquarters, he became irate at what he thought to be the pomposity of a vice president on the business side. He later wrote him a long letter describing himself as the leader of an organization called American Women for Disease Free Future (AWDFF) and pleaded for his help in getting some supportive articles about AWDFF's efforts into the Digest. He signed it, "Sadie Zuckerman, President." He got a newsman friend to send it to the pompous one, postmarked from a rural New Jersey address, which was listed as AWDFF's headquarters.

He then got me to write an equally long letter to "the big shot," as he called him, describing myself as an avid AWDFF member, marveling at "what a fighter" Sadie was, and urging him to heed her

---

[14] There is no such thing as an InterAmerican Press Association.

pleas and to get the Digest active in support of AWDFF. I signed it, "Dorothy Baldwin," and dropped in a mailbox in Seattle.

I wrote another such letter, signed it Gloria Martin, and mailed it from Colorado Springs.

David and I made up a long list of names, affixed them to long letters to "Mr. Big Shot" about how he could help AWDFF and sent them from wherever our story research took us – New Orleans, San Diego, Tokyo, Seoul, Wichita, London, Managua, Cape Town, Abilene, wherever one of us happened to be. From the foreign addresses, we explained that we were American women temporarily living abroad, that we were thrilled at AWDFF's agenda and with the possibility that "the cause" was going to be promoted in The Reader's Digest. We always lavished praise upon him for the great articles we had read in the Digest, with which he had had absolutely nothing to do, and let him know that we were confident that he was doing what he could to advance AWDFF's cause in the massively influential magazine. We told him that we knew that sooner or later he would be successful, and that there would be a huge and well deserved benefit to AWDFF, and thus to all women.

One day, David went to Luchow's the famous German restaurant in lower Manhattan and paid a waiter $50 to go to "the big shot's" office, high in the Pan Am Building, and explain that AWDFF officials were planning a dinner in his honor and would like him to choose the menu for the affair.

The pompous one panicked. He chased the waiter out of his office and hurried to Pleasantville, demanding that someone deal with the hated AWDFF.

"Sadie Zuckerman," in rural New Jersey, received a telegram instructing, "Have no further contact with" the vice presidential gentleman, that, "all further contact with The Reader's Digest must be through me." It was signed by an editor, who told "Mr. Big Shot" that the Digest's editorial research department, which probably was the world's best fact-checking unit, could find no record anywhere of an organization entitled AWDFF, and suspected that he had been the butt of a practical joke. That was the end of the AWDFF caper. It had been a lot of fun.

David actually began his career doing this sort of thing. His first job out of college was with the Chicago City News Service. His first assignment was to man the news desk during the small hours. There was usually enough night time action in Chicago to keep him busy firing dispatches at the city's newspapers. But one night when nothing much was happening David decided to make something happen. At about 3 a.m. he found the last name in the Chicago telephone book, which began with a couple of Z's, then dialed the first number in the book, which belonged to someone whose name began with a couple of A's. A male with a very groggy voice answered. David introduced himself as the owner of the last name in the book, and what did A think of that? A did not think highly of that; in fact, he wanted to know if Z had any idea what time it was, and was he crazy? David proposed that they meet for lunch, saying that it would be "an interesting civic affair," that he was sure the media would want to cover it, that it would attract a lot of attention and probably would impress both their bosses, and by the way, where did A work?

"He began using a lot of very bad language," David told me, in sober tones. "I could not abide it, so I hung up."

Then, he called Z and warned him him to watch out for A, that he was very angry with Z. Z, he said, did not seem to understand or appreciate the warning.

David did not go unscathed. He had a beautiful 42-foot sail-boat. For a while he lived in Connecticut and sailed it in Long Island Sound. Then, he tired of Connecticut, found the waters he really loved in Chesapeake Bay, and moved to Annapolis, Maryland. Then, he got bored with Chesapeake Bay and moved to the Coconut Grove section of southwest Miami, and sailed the waters he really, really loved, in Biscayne Bay. One summer day in the Digest's Washington office he was heard to say that he had been sailing in Biscayne Bay on July 4th and had nearly collided with a yacht, that the near-miss had been the yacht's fault, that as they parted he had sent some nasty signals, then noted that it was flying the Presidential flag. The yacht, he then realized, belonged to Bebe Rebozo, one of President Richard Nixon's closest friends, and the President was aboard.

At about 2 a.m. one morning a week or so later Bill Schulz, then chief of the Digest's Washington bureau, and Ken Tomlinson, then a Washington staffer, had a friend, a Washington newspaper reporter who was good at such things, call Reed. He introduced himself as "Lieutenant Commander McKay, of the Coast Guard." He instructed David to report to the Coast Guard office in the Civic Center, in downtown Miami, on Monday morning to explain his "breach of presidential security on July 4th," and suggested that it was likely that his "boat will be impounded." He supplied David with the room number in the Civic Center to which he should report.

Despite the hour, David was instantly wide awake and furious. First, he described the near collision as "entirely the fault of the Presidential yacht." Then, loudly and angrily, he demanded to know, "Who ordered this investigation? Did Nixon order this?"

"McKay" replied, very officiously, that the Coast Guard had film showing Reed to be at fault, that the Coast Guard was obligated to see to the President's security when he was sailing, that Reed's "reckless behavior" and the "disrespectful signals" he had sent following the near collision could not be countenanced.

David noisily insisted that he had been sailing for many years, that he was well versed in the "Rules of the Road," that he always adhered to safe procedures and furthermore that the Coast Guard was wasting its time talking to him, that it should be talking to, "the *idiot* who was at the helm of the Presidential yacht!"

"McKay" interrupted to say that when Reed came in he should, "be sure to bring all documents certifying your ownership of the sailboat, that such documentation will be needed in the event the boat is auctioned off."

There arose a rumor, almost certainly true, that David consulted with an attorney. It is not known whether he and the attorney visited the room to which he had been directed in the Civic Center, which was a lavatory.

The matter came up later at a social event at a Pleasantville editor's house when David, mildly lubricated, began regaling the assemblage of "a caper" he had worked on Hubbell. One of the editors present turned on the tape recording of David's exchanges with "Lieutenant Commander McKay, of the Coast Guard." I was not present, but was given to understand that it was a fun evening.

David took revenge. One spring morning just prior to 7 a.m. Ken Tomlinson's front door bell was rung by the first of a long line of customers who were responding to a want ad in the Washington Post describing his "estate sale." The ad offered a long list of items, including electric train sets, bicycles, skis, sleds, a ping pong table with paddles and balls, golf equipment, all kinds of clothing, cookware, cutlery, dishes, books, office supplies and the *piece de resistance*, a player piano and ten roles of music for whomever bought the piano before 8 a.m.

Traffic crowded Tomlinson's street early that day.

David's victims were not unimaginative or helpless. Just before Memorial Day one year the Reed's house in Coconut Grove was advertised in neighborhood newspapers for sale at a distress price. Late in the day a friend called from Miami to say that the neighborhood could have used a battalion of traffic cops.

Once, David awakened Andy Jones at 2:30 a.m. to tell him that he was in jail in White Plains, about 20 miles from Bedford Village, where Jones lay asleep in bed. He sounded a though he had had perhaps a tad too much to drink, and pleaded with Andy to come bail him out. Jones rose, dressed and motored to the White Plains hoosegow, where no one had ever heard of Reed. He had called from a saloon somewhere in Florida.

There was always retaliation; it was always fun.

And there was always another caper.

60

The Corruption Never Ends

I n recent times the media have been full of photographs of some galoot who has been an official of the General Services Administration (GSA). He was seated in a bathtub in a Las Vegas hotel. A tray before him in the tub held two glasses of wine, and he was mugging, happily, for the camera. In case the viewer did not understand, this goofball was partying; the GSA had thrown a party for itself – correction, the GSA had allowed America's taxpayers to throw a Las Vegas party for it, to the tune of $800,000-plus.

There was an uproar, which resulted in a Congressional investigation, at which the aforementioned galoot took the fifth – he wouldn't even tell Congress what his job was.

One result was that GSA Administrator Martha Johnson resigned.

It seemed to have little effect. A few months later, GSA stunk things up again with an "awards ceremony" for hundreds of its employees at a high end Washington hotel. The conference included catered food, drink and some high-priced entertainment. Cost to the taxpayers: approximately a quarter of a million dollars.

Plans were announced to investigate 77 other GSA "conferences" and "awards ceremonies".

T'was ever thus. I was well acquainted with GSA. The agency purchases everything the government needs, from buildings to automobiles and trucks to pencils, paper and paper clips. Back in the 1970's it had been in the headlines for rampant corruption. Employees and vendors had been stealing the agency, i.e., the taxpayers, blind. Ken Tomlinson had sources who felt that the man who had exposed the rot, the "Whistleblower", had not been treated appropriately by those in power. At Ken's suggestion, I took a look.

The Whistleblower's name was William A. Clinkscales, Jr. He had retired from the Army after 20 years as an intelligence officer, a lieutenant colonel. He was burly, bespectacled and with a shock of curly brown hair. He had joined the Investigative Division at GSA and had spent much of his time wondering at the Division's obvious reluctance to do its job. There was abundant evidence of improper activity in government buying and contracting. He talked with other investigators, and found that many were itching to crack down, but had reason to believe they would not have the support of management, that they would not fare well if they objected to the thievery they were seeing. In case after case Clinkscales kept finding things that needed serious scrutiny. For example, a Maryland office supplies firm had billed GSA for 4.4 million file folders, but delivered only one million, a theft of $630,000 from the taxpayers.

GSA employees who approved payment for such bills had received substantial gifts, including color television sets and vacation, trips to Bermuda, even to China.

He found all kinds of similar transactions in GSA's Washington, D.C. and Cleveland, Ohio, operations, and got promising investigations underway in those places and elsewhere.

Eventually, Clinkscales became chief of GSA's Investigations Division and directed his 70 field offices to "improve the quality of your investigations." Those with whom he had earlier discussed his suspicions were happy that he was now head of the Investigations Division, and followed his instruction enthusiatically. Their efforts soon bore fruit. GSA's Audits Division Chief Howard Davia became an energetic Clinkscales ally. Davia told me, "We had so many rich targets for attention that that we had difficulty choosing which would have the greatest impact in terms of savings to the taxpayer."

The often spectacular findings stayed in the headlines. Morale soared in the Investigations Division. These investigators were heroes. Clinkscales recalled, "The people who were working the major cases were so excited that they had our backing that they were working 12 to 15 hours a day, and without additional compensation; they weren't being paid for overtime."

At first, he said, President Jimmie Carter had been a strong supporter of the cleanup effort. He had appointed Tennessee businessman Joel W. "Jay" Solomon GSA Administrator, urging him to urge on the investigators. Solomon did so, but as they continued to unearth more and more headline-worthy corruption Solomon's calls to the President went unanswered. It became clear there was a fear that the continuing news stories about crooked behavior in a major government agency were making his Administration look bad.

It was also speculated that a lot of big companies, big political contributors, were doing a lot of big business with GSA, and some could make offers that some politicians couldn't refuse. In any case, Solomon soon felt compelled to tell his cleanup crew, "Fellas, the White House is no longer behind us." He resigned.

The GSA scandals moved Congress to create an Office of the Inspector General (IG) for every major department of the government. The IG was to be an independent cop, on the lookout for mismanagement, fraud and waste. An attorney who had been Chief of the Justice Department's Organized Crime and Racketeering Division was named to succeed Solomon as head of GSA. A real crime fighter; seemed to be a good choice.

"What actually happened," I found, "provides a stark lesson in what often happens to those who try to expose waste and corruption in government." The new boss quickly found Clinkscales to be "incompatible" and dismissed him from the Investigations Division.

He denied to me that he went to GSA with any plan to get rid of Clinkscales. He said that he found that Clinkscales' Investigations Division "needed a lot of improvement."

Clinkscales simply pointed to his Division's results, which spoke for themselves.

Clinkscales was then appointed Deputy Director of a Division that reviewed classified documents, and was consigned to a small basement office piled high with desks and chairs – a storeroom.

There were people in GSA's ranks who were happy to talk to me in detail, and very important people in high positions who refused talk to me at all. But I learned enough to write a piece entitled, "The Persecution of a Government Watchdog." It described Clinkscales' experience in detail. One morning just prior to the article's appearance in the Digest I received calls at home from seven different attorneys in Washington, each of whom assured me that I was way out of line with my story and warned me that if such a story were published it would "destroy the career and life of a really good man." I have no idea how they knew that I was "way out of line" with my story; no one had seen it other than my editors and the tough ladies in the Digest's Research Department who checked out every line before it appeared in the magazine, The lawyers may have assumed that the "really good man" whose career and life I was ruining was one of those who had refused to talk to me, or made assumptions from the kinds of questions I had been asking. In my view, none of these people belonged in public service, and the conversations didn't last long. The article attracted a lot of attention.

During the 1980 Presidential campaign, nominee Ronald Reagan vowed that if elected he would "put the corruption fighters back in charge, and they are going to be told to clean out that agency from top to bottom." Once in office, Reagan appointed Gerald T. Carmen, a New Hampshire businessman, to head GSA. Carman named Clinkscales Director of Oversight for the Agency, and directed him and Davia to clean house.

By the end of 1985 Clinkscales and Davia had saved taxpayers many millions of dollars. Clinkscales had received annual performance evaluations of "Outstanding," along with GSA's highest honor, its Distinguished Service Award, and the Presidential Rank Award, the highest a career government executive can achieve.

Carmen left GSA after a couple of years to take a job with the United Nations, recommending that Clinkscales succeed him as head of the Agency. But Clinkscales' angry intolerance for mismanagement, incompetence and outright theft had won him lots of enemies who made sure that didn't happen. The top GSA job remained vacant for a year, and a vicious harassment campaign ensued.

Clinkscales was said to be guilty of all kinds of mortal sins. For example, his office was responsible for assigning parking spaces, but did so unfairly.

GSA complained to the Justice Department that Clinkscales had launched an illegal investigation, and demanded that he be ordered to desist. The Justice Department found the complaint to be baseless.

A high ranking GSA official said that he wanted Clinkscales fired, or that he be forced to retire; he even suggested that it might be a good idea to induce such anxiety in Clinkscales, who had high blood pressure, that he would die.

Carmen had been gone a year when an assistant Treasury Secretary was named to head the Agency. Within a month, Clinkscales' office was abolished, its investigative functions assigned to another department and its staff scattered throughout GSA. All without a word to Clinkscales. Finally, Clinkscales was told that he would now become Deputy Regional Administrator in Philadelphia. It was a deliberate insult, and a warning to any other would-be whistleblowers in our ever sprawling government as to the fate that awaits those who dare to speak out.

Those who thought the Reagan White House would rectify matters, as it should have, were disappointed. Clinkscales' demotion and transfer were set aside, but instead of returning him to a position where he could keep cleaning up GSA he was named to a nothing job, Director of the Selective Service System.

Bill Clinkscales, Howard Davia and their corruption fighters are long gone, and several Presidencies later, during the Obama Administration, GSA was found to be awash in a new series of scandals. In an increasingly enormous government one wonders if it's possible to keep the thieves at bay.

The GSA story was the last I ever worked on with Tomlinson. He was soon gone. He had maintained serious political connections in Washington. The Reagan Administration was looking for someone to run the Voice of America, and so there Ken went. Eventually, he would rejoin the Digest, in a way that stunned everyone.

61

The Kid on the Playground

I now worked with Frank Devine, one of the most pleasant experiences of my career. Frank was an especially personable and delightful New Zealander, slim, bespectacled, with graying reddish hair and equipped with enormous talent, a quick, sparkling wit and a beautiful wife named Jacqueline and several beautiful daughters. Frank was Editor-in-Chief of the Digest's Australian edition by the time DeWitt Wallace discovered him and imported him to Pleasantville to become one of the U.S. edition's four Issue Editors; these were powerful positions, and alternating four different Issue Editors ensured that the magazine, while it always stood fast on its fundamentals, was always new. Issue Editors also worked with individual writers. Devine worked with me, David Reed and some others.

My work with Frank included a number of articles about someone I had known since the autumn of 1939, when we met on a playground at Christ the King grade school, in Minneapolis, when his name was Bob and mine was Jerry. One day in late 1976 I found myself reading about him in Look Magazine, one of the leading mass circulation picture magazines of the era.

Bob had been in the eighth grade when we met, and I was in the seventh. We both were sports lovers, and played a lot of football, basketball and baseball together. We had become good friends, but had gone to different high schools and colleges. We had remained friends, but had seen each other few times and usually by accident in the years that followed. Now, I met him again, in Look Magazine's pages, where he was Dr. Robert J. White, M.D., Ph.D, and read of his fantastic work in the Brain Research Laboratory of Cleveland's Metropolitan General Hospital. It was an incredible story.

A day or so later I was enjoying a reunion with him in his office in Cleveland. He seemed almost to bubble with enthusiasm for what I was doing, "running around the world, writing about all the interesting things that are going on," was, "the most exciting thing" he could imagine. I expressed the view that high up on the list of interesting things that were going on were the things he had been doing, and let's talk about them.

He had long been convinced that from a physiological stand-point the human body was mainly a platform to support and enable its owner to do the things that the brain wanted it to do; all the brain needed to survive was a compatible blood supply. After all, he reasoned, one could survive the loss of any other of the body's organs, the limbs, eyes, ears, even the liver, stomach, appendix, prostate and bladder, but the one thing no one could survive was the loss of the brain; when the brain died, one was dead. Period. But no one knew whether the brain could survive without the body, either; no one ever had been able to isolate the living brain, separate it from its cranial vault and keep it alive indefinitely. But on January 17, 1963, White had proved it could be done.

After months of intense experimentation and in an exquisite eight-hour surgery he had placed the brain of a rhesus monkey on a small platform of bone; it was still connected by four major arteries to a reservoir containing a donor monkey's compatible blood. Prior to isolation tiny electrodes had been installed in the brain in the hope that it would signal that it remained alive and functioning by sending out electrical activity. The vertebral arteries were cut, the spinal cord was severed and the new circulation was switched on. Strong electroencephalographic (EKG) tracings were recording. For the first time in history, the brain of a highly developed animal was being kept alive outside of its own body by the compatible blood of another such animal.

This triumph of medical research brought us a gigantic step closer to the possibility of developing substantial improvements in the ways the ills and accidents that occur in the brain are treated – tumors, cancerous growths, meningitis, stroke, encephalitis. In the fullness of time a better understanding of how and why these things happen should lead to more effective preventive programs and treatments.

Bob was a neuroscience pioneer. A certainty had been growing in him for a long time that hypothermia, deep cold, was the key to many problems having to do with the brain. He had wondered, for example, if the brain could survive deep cold; and could it be returned to its normal temperature with no ill effect? Or might damage be done to intelligence, memory, personality? Emboldened by his success in isolating the brain, he and his staff spent a year training 13 monkeys to perform a number of complex tasks. Complete profiles were made of each animal's intelligence, memory and cognitive ability. Then, each monkey's blood was routed from the femoral artery, in the groin, through a heat exchanger that reduced blood temperature. The cooled blood was returned to the brain When brain temperature reached 50 degrees Fahrenheit, blood flow was cut off for half an hour, then resumed and normal brain temperatures were restored. Tests revealed no impairment in intelligence, memory or cognition.

He now tried it with a small number of terminally ill cancer patients whose families understood that the experimental surgery offered their loved ones at least a chance to spend some of their last days in relative comfort and in touch with them. Typically, he brain-cooled a 54-year-old man with a massive brain tumor that had kept him in a coma for a month. An earlier attempt to excise the tumor had failed; it had developed its own circulation system and was impossible to extract in the time available to the neurosurgeon to work in the brain, usually, three- to five minutes. But after cooling the patient's brain White had half an hour, time enough to remove the huge tumor. And for several days before the demise of his cancer-ravaged body, the patient was able to sit up, feed himself and visit with loved ones.

White's research successes seemed almost magical. His thinking had been evolving for years, ever since he was a young Fellow at the Mayo Clinic. He had spent many nights attending to young highway accident victims who had suffered spinal injuries. Too often

412

these kids, in the prime of life, would never be able to move again. Yet, as he stood over operating tables where they lay, the damage to their spinal cords did not appear to him to be that serious; only rarely was he able to see anything that in a pathological sense would seem to explain the paralysis. Like the brain, the spinal cord is nervous tissue, and in many cases destruction was not immediate and total – there *must* be a way, he thought, to arrest and reverse the process of destruction.

He set out to prove or disprove it: Identical injuries were inflicted on the spinal cords of 14 monkeys. They received no medical treatment, and remained completely and permanently paralyzed. Then, the same injury was inflicted on 14 more monkeys. After four hours – the average time it takes to get a spinal cord injury victim from an accident scene to an operating room – these monkeys were treated: At the injury sites two tubes were inserted into the dura, the tough membrane that surrounds the spinal cord's fluid jacket, and ice cold saline water was circulated around the damaged areas for three hours. Then, the tubing was withdrawn. Within three days seven of these treated monkeys were running, jumping and climbing as though nothing had happened. Six others were weak in both legs at first, but fully recovered within two weeks. After three months only one showed a slight inability to perform as before, but even he was a good climber.

That was in 1968. It electrified the medical world, which had all but given up on spinal cord treatment. Soon, spectacular successes were being reported: A doctor in Verona, Italy advised that a woman three months pregnant had been in an accident that had paralyzed her from the waist down. Two weeks after he treated her with cold she had walked away from the hospital on her own. But White remained cautious, pointing out that while cooling had worked with some patients, it had not with others, and there remained a need to find out why.

Really interesting stuff. What I also found hugely interesting was the man who was making it happen.

He recalled that he had only been attending the University of Minnesota's medical school for a short time when his counselor told him, "You belong at Harvard Medical, and I have arranged for a scholarship." He was surprised, thrilled that he had been scholarshipped into the prestigious institution. But while the education was on the house, food, shelter and travel were not. Organizing his time, he had studied hard, found odd jobs around campus during the school year, had worked on a railroad during vacation periods and hardly ever squandered money on travel between Minneapolis and Boston, often hitchhiked and found rides.

Graduating from Harvard Medical, he trained in general surgery at Boston's Brigham and Women's Hospital. There, not incidentally, he met, courted and married a lovely young nurse named Patricia Murray, who, over time and to his delight, gave him ten children. Patsy proved herself not only a competent mother but also the active wife of a world class neurosurgeon, often accompanying him on his travels across the world, joining him in visits with Popes and political leaders. Additionally, she was among the Cleveland Indians baseball teams' most loyal fans; she rarely missed a home game, and was known to show up in other cities to support the team when it went on the road.

Bob was awarded a six-year Fellowship at the Mayo Clinic, in Rochester, Minnesota. He used what little spare time he had there to earn a Ph.D in Neurosurgical Physiology at the University of Minnesota.

Then, recruited by Case Western Reserve University's Medical School, he became co-director of neurosurgery at Cleveland's Metro General Hospital and had remained there ever since. In addition to performing some 10,000 neurosurgeries, he had organized and presided over what became one of the world's preeminent brain research laboratories.

"We learned," he said, "that the brain is much tougher than anyone suspected. There is on hand enough successful experimental work with animals to justify the design of an emergency brain-cooling system for human beings."

I asked why, in view of so much of his successful experimental work, such a system was not coming into common usage. He explained that his research had led him to the conclusion that in an accident involving the spine, destruction is progressive, that cooling must be applied within four hours to have any chance of success. He lamented that no one had followed up on his work, explaining that the main reason was what he called "the enthusiasm for malpractice lawsuits. If a new surgical technique is used and is not successful," he explained, "chances are good that the physician and the hospital both will find themselves in court; it could cost them everything. Even if they successfully defend themselves they acquire crippling attorneys' fees.

"Practitioners are seriously vulnerable," he said. "Suppose a physician judges that an incoming patient is never going to move again no matter what – perhaps too much time has elapsed since the injury occurred and there can be no question that total, irretrievable destruction has occurred; or perhaps the results of the injury were far too devastating, totally ruinous, so he knows that it would be a waste of time and resources to cool the site of the injury. He could be sued for not doing so. On the other hand, if the patient is cooled and it doesn't work, a lawyer could argue that the patient would have been better off if left alone."

I visited him often after that, and wrote several Digest articles about him and ghost-wrote pieces for him. One of the latter, "The Meaning of Jason," was a heart-wrenching piece about his failed struggle to save a two-year-old boy who almost literally sparkled with personality who was afflicted with a massive brain tumor. Just when it appeared that Bob had won the battle, the little boy died. He could not have been more anguished had it been one of his own children, but the case taught him that he couldn't win every time, but that every such fight was worth all of the skill, discipline and determination that he had. Entitled," The Meaning of Jason, the article resulted in a landslide of mail to the Digest, and Bob himself received more than 2100 letters and phone calls.

Another, entitled, "Thoughts of a Brain Surgeon," explained his unshakably devout Catholic faith; a conviction not found in many scientists.

His habit was to give himself over to intense prayer before, during and after every one his surgeries. Many of his successes had the look of miracles, but he would not agree that he ever had been involved in a miracle. He insisted that Divine help was there for the asking and that he always asked for it, but also insisted that success could not have been achieved without the combined skill, dedication and determination of his entire surgical team.

Bob explained his feeling about the human brain: "From a purely scientific standpoint it is far beyond anything that science has ever developed or will develop; the most sophisticated computer that will ever be devised will never match the complexity, efficiency and performance of this gelatinous mass of tissue weighing approximately three pounds. With its topography of small hills and valleys laced with red and blue streams, one brain looks much like any other. But somewhere in there is what makes each of us unique. For the brain contains the mind, the essence of us. And of this brain-mind linkage, the relationship between the container and its contents, science knows very little. I am compelled to believe that all this had an intelligent beginning, that a superior Intellect-Creator must have devised this magical system. Simple logic requires me to believe that *Someone* made it happen. I can't accept the proposition that at random points in time such substantial entities as intelligence, personality, memory and the human body all just sort of fell together.

"This is sharply at odds with the thinking of great and good men among my colleagues," he continued. "They seem satisfactorily to explain things to themselves in terms of mathematics and chemical formulas, and are comfortable in assuming that what is not explainable today will come clear as science continues to progress. But the notion that life is nothing more than a chance confluence of complex molecular biology and electrical activity strikes me as a defiance of logic."

He had an abundance of honorary doctorates, Visiting Professorships and Papal Knighthoods, and the 1997 Humanitarian of the Year Award from the American Association of Neurosurgery. Appointed to the Pontifical Academy of Science, he became an advisor to Popes Paul VI and John Paul II, and founded the latter's Committee on Bioethics. He described to me a walk he once took with Pope (now Saint) John Paul II in his office:

"It was about the size of a gymnasium," he said, "and his desk was about the size of a card table. Almost as quickly as I sat down in a chair beside his desk, he got up and started pacing. I got up and walked with him, up and down the length of the room. He walked at a rapid pace, with his hands clasped behind his back. I had trouble keeping up with him while explaining my theory that the brain is the repository of the human spirit, the soul. I told him that I found it unreasonable to think that at brain death those powerful entities, intelligence, personality and memory simply cease to exist, that it made much more sense to me to believe that at death the essence of us escapes from a container, the brain, and finds support in another dimension."

"How did the Holy Father respond?" I asked.

"He smiled and said, 'That's very interesting.'"

The kid I met on the playground in 1939 had, indeed, become an interesting man, had lived a life very much worth living. And I had been privileged to tell much of his story.

And the privilege of working with Frank Devine ended when Frank's Australian friend, media megamogul Rupert Murdoch, lured him away to become Editor-in-Chief of the New York Post, then Editor-in-Chief of the Chicago Sun-Times, then back to Sydney as Editor-in-Chief of the Australian, the country's biggest newspaper.

62

Beginning of the End

One day I was on the phone with Andy Jones when suddenly he said, "I think Wally's losing it."

"What do you mean? Why do you think so?"

"He called me seven times yesterday and asked me the same question.

Shortly, I was in the office in Pleasantville and hearing similar things from others.

Apparently, there was no question that Alzheimer's Disease was overtaking DeWitt Wallace.

Everyone who knew him was concerned about his well being. And to be sure, we all wondered what would be the consequences for his magazine.

Wally had long believed and assumed that:

1) The magazine that he had invented would last and prosper as long as people could read.

2) That the Editor-in-Chief of the magazine would always remain the corporation's supreme leader, the one who made all the final decisions affecting the company. And

3) That The Reader's Digest would always remain a privately held corporation, that it would never place itself in a position where it was required to explain itself to shareholders.

His assumptions were not shared by others. Others dreamed of the money to be made, for the company and themselves, if the famous entity were taken public.

Titles and positions meant little to Wally. When he named Ed Thompson to succeed Hobart Lewis, the title "Editor-in-Chief" meant all that was important to him about the company: Ed was the boss. But when Wally named Ed Editor-in-Chief he had not named him CEO, as he had Hobart Lewis. But even when he named Hobe CEO he had remained in his own corner office, next door, looking over Hobe's shoulder, staying involved in the important decisions; I don't think Hobe ever was uncomfortable with the situation. I think he liked having Wally at his back. But now, in handing the editorial reins over to the new generation, Wally apparently was anxious that Ed be able to keep his attentions focused on the only thing that really mattered to him, his beloved magazine. He did not want him distracted with all the extraneous things with which the corporation was now involved.

A businessman, Jack O'Hara, was named President. He was in charge of the business side. In addition to promoting circulation and selling advertising space in the magazine, the business side operated a sort of company store that produced and sold a lot of Digest products: Reader's Digest Condensed Books sold millions of books, indeed had become the biggest book club in the world. The record club had become the biggest purveyor of music in the world; the company had produced and sold millions of copies of the Digest's own condensed version of the Bible, as well as millions of copies of anthologies, millions of copies of Atlases and sometimes stuff that was available in hardware and department stores. All of which kept tidal waves of money gushing in. And none of which Wally cared much about, including the money; the only thing thst really mattered to him was his magazine.

Ed now occupied Wally's corner office, and the founder was spending more and more time at home. But he tried to keep up with what was going on. In "American Dreamers" Peter Canning recalls that when a financial magazine reported a rumor that the Digest was considering going public, offering shares of itself on the New York Exchange, Wallace sent memos to both Thompson and O'Hara reiterating his oft-expressed insistence that the Digest never go public, that it must always remain a privately held corporation.

Thompson and O'Hara got along well, but no one, themselves included, knew who was the final authority. Wally himself remained the final authority, and it never seemed to occur to him that he would not live forever.

In "American Dreamers" Peter Canning relates that George Grune, then head of The Digest's Books and Records Division, and Dick McLoughlin, then head of Magazine Operations, were unhappy with O'Hara's leadership; they deemed him overly conservative, unwilling to make decisions they believed would increase the company's financial strength. They approached Ed with their dissatisfaction, saying that they felt they could persuade the Board to unseat O'Hara if Thompson would agree to become CEO. At the time, Thompson and O'Hara both were proceeding in accordance with what they knew to be DeWitt Wallace's desires, which was that the Digest should continue to perform a valuable public service, and not simply focus on the pursuit of more and more money. Ed declined to associate himself with an effort to unseat O'Hara. Had he become CEO under such circumstances his support certainly would have been expected for the business side's schemes, which included ideas Ed knew to be anathema to DeWitt Wallace.

Ed and O'Hara each argued their own cases to Wally. O'Hara was well aware that the Editor-in-Chief's thinking had always ruled. He wrote a memo to Wally suggesting that he and Ed be named co-CEOs.

In turn, Ed argued strongly that the Editor-in-Chief alone should always be CEO. He pointed out that while he and O'Hara understood their separate roles and were working well together, he worried about the future; he could imagine a time when an Editor-in-Chief and his co-CEO on the business side were not in agreement, or on good terms. The way to ensure that the Editor-in-Chief always had the final word, Ed believed, was to name him CEO and the President, O'Hara, Chief Operating Officer.

At this end stage of his life, unable to think clearly, Wally turned to two older friends for advice, a banker named Harold Helm, and Laurance Rockefeller. Both thought they knew what was best. In January, 1977, Wally followed their recommendation and named the businessman, O'Hara, CEO.

Ed Thompson continued to report only to DeWitt Wallace, but Editorial was now just another branch of the company.

Thus began the disintegration of The Reader's Digest as DeWitt Wallace had conceived it.

63
Shock and Change

DeWitt Wallace died on March 30, 1981, a victim of colon cancer complicated by Alzheimer's Disease.

It took three years for the tsunami of change to overwhelm the Digest. On a March day in 1984 a bewildering shock was delivered to Editorial: Ed Thompson was fired. Canning points out that only a year earlier – and after seven years of Thompson's editorial leadership – the Columbia Journalism Review noted that "enthusiasm quotients" for the Digest remained high, that "subscription renewals remained at an impressive 70 percent".

In other words, under Thompson's editorial guidance the magazine had continued to be hugely successful.

Thompson was undone by non-editorial people who, whether or not they convinced themselves that they knew better than he the secret of DeWitt Wallace's success, knew what they had to do to get control of the corporation and the Wallace Estate, then valued at several billions.

Simpatico with George Grune and his cohorts on the business side were Al Cole, a businessman who had helped Wally build the Digest's enormous circulation, and Laurance Rockefeller, who had become a close friend of the Wallaces. They were in Cole's winter home in Hobe Sound, Florida, angrily disliking some recent Digest articles and issues as too liberal, agreeing that Thompson was "taking the magazine in a direction that Wally would never have countenanced", and that, "Ed Thompson has to go".

Hobe Lewis, by this time long retired, was in the room. "I warned them," he later told me. "I told them that if they started interfering with Editorial they would bring down the company. But I was no longer CEO. They were not interested in what I thought."

Cole and Rockefeller badly misread Thompson. In truth, Ed's political bent was conservative, but his professional creed was to remain open minded, to listen closely to all arguments and make decisions favoring those he deemed most sensible. But like DeWitt Wallace, he sometimes thought it appropriate to provide the reader with all sides of contentious issues. And, as it had under the leadership of DeWitt Wallace, this occasionally meant articles that raised conservative temperatures.

But Ed was gone.

Soon, Jack O'Hara was gone.

And George Grune was CEO.

Editorial morale had never been higher than it was on the day in 1976 when Thompson became Editor-in-Chief. It had remained high and the magazine had continued to improve and prosper. It was never lower than on the day in 1984 when he was ousted and replaced with Ken Gilmore. I was not aware of any antipathy for Gilmore; he was a long time good friend of mine, a competent editorial executive and a very nice fellow. I also thought that he and Ed Thompson had been good friends; I had never detected any rivalry between them. But Gilmore was no match for CEO George Grune. Ed Thompson had warned Wally that a time might come when the heads of the editorial and business sides were not in consonance. The time had come; there was little doubt as to who was in command.

Grune was a big man, powerfully built, armed with a powerful, outgoing personality and strong ideas about how to make money with The Reader's Digest. He had little interest in the editorial magic that had made the magazine the world's most popular publication. He was infamous in Editorial for once wondering aloud why "all these high priced editors" were needed, "we could hire high school teachers to do what they do".

Bill Schulz told me that Gilmore had confessed to him that he was afraid of Grune. That was dismaying. Thompson had not been afraid of Grune, or anyone else. But many of us assured ourselves that somehow the magazine would muddle though.

Never having been involved in management, I knew nothing of the financial shenanigans that were driving the action. Against Wally's wishes the company was taken public. Shares were on the New York Stock Exchange and available to anyone. Canning found that soon "nearly two-thirds of the ownership of The Reader's Digest had been transferred from Wallace Funds to Rockefeller charities, and these charities, naturally, were interested in all the money the

427

company could deliver to them. And this fit right in with the business side's ambitions.

I had no idea that such an earthquake was underway. I was preoccupied with an assessment of the future. I was 57 years old, still several years from retirement. I had a wife, nine children, a dog and a cat. I had behind me more than 30 successful years as a Digest writer; I had reason to believe that Editorial deemed me to be one of its premier writers.

My best option seemed to me be to continue to do what I had been doing and hope for the best.

64
Nina

David Reed and I remained close, and apprehensive about the future. Hobe Lewis was gone, Wally was gone, Frank Devine was gone, Andy Jones had retired and now Ed Thompson was gone. We shared forebodings as to what lay ahead. Years earlier we had seriously discussed partnering a column for possible syndication: few writers, if any, were plugged into the diplomatic world more comprehensively than David, and I was well connected throughout the Defense establishment and to a lot of people on Capitol Hill and throughout the Defense industry. We both had salable reputations and rich sources, and were confident we could produce a regular column on national and world affairs that should do well in syndication. We saw no reason why such a column would not work to the Digest's benefit as well as our own.

But the more we talked about it the more we agreed that we were happy with our lives the way they were. The kind of column we contemplated would have required us both to live in the Washington area, which neither of us wanted to do. In fact, David, who was then living in Annapolis, only a short drive from Washington, was now intent on moving to Florida. And the more I thought about it the more it seemed a poor idea to uproot my family and move it to Washington. We dropped the idea of a column and decided to be optimistic about the future of the Digest.

But our forebodings were prescient; the best was behind us, and it wasn't coming back.

When Frank Devine departed Gilmore suggested that I work with Assistant Managing Editor Nina Bell Allen. I liked the idea. Nina was an old friend, and special. She had started at the Digest as an assistant to Dorothy Kavanaugh, who had been Hobart Lewis's secretary. Nina was dark-haired, pretty, outgoing, armed with plenty of intellectual firepower and had made herself a factor in Editorial. Plus, she was fun. She had escaped the clerical ranks, worked hard and come far. We got a number of good stories into the magazine, including a number of highly successful family humor pieces. Once, she called to say, "We need something funny. Write something funny, John." By this time I had written a number of humor pieces for the magazine which had gone over well with readers. It so happened that at the moment I was looking at some of the preposterous messages my kids kept leaving each other on those little post-it notes that some genius had invented, that have a light sticky substance along one edge so that they are easily affixable to prominent surfaces, like the kitchen cupboard doors above the telephone;

"Your car ran out of gas.," one of my progeny had written to another. "It's on 46th near Grand. I don't know anything about it." It was signed, "Anonymous."

And a message to me, unsigned: "Dad, some guy in Washington called. He said it was really important. I ferget his name."

The notes usually were angry complaints about one thing or another, but always ended with, "Love." Or, "Billy, you majer lege dork, your headed for a frackjured spine," and signed, "Your frend, Andy."

I asked the reader, "Who says American kids can't write?"

It filled the bill. Nina entitled the piece, "Stickum Up, Love," and it reached the magazine's pages quickly.

Once, five years after Wally's death but still adhering when it seemed appropriate to his initial instructions to me, I went to the Palm Harbor Yacht Club, in Florida without a word to anyone in Pleaantville to talk with Jack Nicklaus about his 1986 victory at the Masters Tournament, an unprecedented sixth Masters Championship and an unprecedented 20th major tournament win.[15] Nicklaus was 46 years old at the time, an old man in terms of major championhip golf, and his performance in the first three rounds of the Masters had every "older" golfer in the world on the edge of his seat in front of his television, praying every Nicklaus drive down the middle of every fairway, every Nicklaus putt into every hole. It was one of the most dramatic moments in the history

---

[15] Nicklaus is generally credited with 18 major tournament wins. The two National Amateur championships he won prior to turning professional are not counted, but they were considered majors at the time, so the number actually is 20.

of the game, one that had captured the attention of the world. But I didn't write a proposal; by then, all proposals were going to an assignment committee, which always seemed to include some editor who would argue that a proposal for a sports story was a bad idea. I knew this was a great, inspirational story, so I simply wrote it, from the perspective of a fan who knew and loved the game.

I entitled it, "One More Time, Jack!" I sent it to Nina. She called to say, "You just scored an ace." She immediately called it to Gilmore's attention, and he sent me a bonus for what he called "a masterpiece of magazine journalism." It appeared in April, 1987, the first anniversary issue of Nicklaus's win. I was out playing at the Minneapolis Golf Club one day when someone in Nicklaus's office called to tell one of my daughters, "Tell your Dad that I said that was a great article." My daughter didn't "know who the guy was".

Nina was terrific! We got on well.

65
Teller

He looked stern, a bit disgusted, as he entered his study in his home, in Berkeley, California. He was of average height, trim, dark haired and with heavy, dark eyebrows, and a longish face. He was condescending. "Our meeting," he explained, somewhat haughtily I thought, and in Eastern European accents, "was scheduled for ten o'clock. It was not scheduled for four minutes before ten or four minutes after ten, but for ten o'clock."

"I understand," I said, looking at my wristwatch. It was four minutes past ten. I had pressed his doorbell four minutes before ten, because I didn't want to chance being late for a very important interview – important to *me*, anyway. Since I had arrived four minutes early, he had rectified matters by making me wait four minutes.

This was Dr. Edward Teller, the Hungarian physics genius who had had much to do with the success of the Manhattan Project, the development of the atomic bombs that had so abruptly brought about the end of World War II; and whose thinking thereafter had resulted in the creation of the notion that he was, "The Father of the Hydrogen Bomb."

"I reject that identification!" he snarled. "I am *not* the father of a bomb. Do not publish that about me." I assured him that I would not. The appellation derived from the fact that it was Teller who had first recognized the possibility of producing a thermonuclear weapon, a hydrogen bomb, many times more powerful than the atomic bombs that had destroyed Hiroshima and Nagasaki. Whether he liked it or not he was widely regarded as "The Father of the H-bomb." But I wasn't here to argue with him.

I was here to talk about the Strategic Defense Initiative (SDI) – ballistic missile defense. A month or so earlier, on March 23, 1983, President Ronald Reagan had proposed in a speech to the nation and the world that rather than continue to depend on the doctrine of Mutual Assured Destruction (MAD), the theory that the United States and the Soviet Union, both of them then well armed with fleets of bombers and intercontinental ballistic missiles (ICBMs), the United States would embark on development of a ballistic missile defense system, one that would destroy Soviet missiles before the latter could get anywhere near their targets in the United States.

Reagan's proposal had set off a national uproar. Obviously, such a system would cost vast amounts of money, and a great many loud voices on Capitol Hill, in the media, in Academe's scientific precincts and some in the Military insisted that the idea was fantasy, that it couldn't be done, that the money would be wasted, that no such system was possible, that MAD was the only answer. The opposition mantra had been established by Senator Ted Kennedy, who called it "Star Wars," likening the idea to a popular George Lucas 1977 movie about intergalactic warfare. Editorialists generally subscribed to Kennedy's mockery. Reagan, the Hollywood actor who had become President, was proving that he was a "reckless cowboy" who really belonged back in Hollywood.

The American people didn't know what to think.

I set out to ask the people who ought to know what we should think; people like Teller.

Teller advised me, somewhat testily, that it was a stupid question. Was it possible, he asked, that I thought that the current policy, MAD, made sense? "A policy that requires us to sit and wait for a missile attack to be launched against the United States that will kill scores of millions of people and destroy much of America, and then launch a retaliatory attack that will kill many millions of Russians and destroy much of Russia?" He wondered, "Do you think *that* a sensible policy?"

I ignored the impulse to point out that MAD had been working for 30-plus years, that the Soviets had shown no inclination to test our resolve to retaliate overwhelmingly if they struck first. Then I remembered that in 1962 they had tried an end run around our retaliatory force, attempting to install nuclear ballistic missiles in Cuba, whence they would have been able to launch a no-warning nuclear strike against us. Instead, I noted that the President seemed to be saying that we were going to build a system firing bullets capable of knocking down incoming bullets, and wondered if this were a realistic possibility?

"Do you *really* think," Teller asked, a little more testily, "that the President of the United States would propose such a thing on national television, before the whole world, without having first consulted competent scientific authority? Has it *occurred* to you that this is a country that was able a long time ago to send a man to walk on the moon? Of *course* it is possible, of *course* it is a realistic proposal, of *course* it can be done, of *course* it *must* be done."

He said that yes, SDI would indeed require a great deal of time and money, but that the safety of the nation, indeed the safety of humankind was at stake. What did I think *that* might be worth? The opposition to the President's proposal, he said, "consists mainly of fools who do not know what they are talking about", or "politicians, like Kennedy, who not only do not know what they are talking about, but do not have the best interests of the nation or the world at heart, who want the money to squander on social programs that would help to cement themselves in power."

I left, somewhat chastened at the implied insults in his responses to my "stupid" questions, the same questions that were being raised by the President's political opponents and by many of the nation's pundits, many of whom were also Reagan's political opponents, as I was not. But regardless of the rude manner in which Teller had couched his answers, I was happy to have them. What he had told me was that Reagan's proposal made sense, that it could and *"must"* be done.

I drove down the glorious Monterey Peninsula to the Hoover Institution on War, Revolution and Peace, on the gorgeous campus of Stanford University. Founded by Herbert Hoover, an alumnus who became President of the United States, it is one of the world's great "think tanks," a haven for brilliant and original thinkers. The brilliant and original thinker I wanted to talk to was Stefan Thomas

Possony, a Viennese historian-economist-political scientist, a 1930's anti-Nazi idea man who had escaped to the United States, worked in Military Intelligence, took a Professorship at Georgetown University and became a consultant to the Defense Department – among other notable achievements, he had accurately predicted the first Soviet nuclear tests. Along with his colleague William Kintner, a star at a University of Pennsylvania think tank, Possony had many years earlier informed and guided my thinking in the production of a 1968 Reader's Digest lead article, "The Rising Threat of Soviet Strategic Power," the first major treatment of the subject in a popular publication. It was Steve Possony who actually conceived the notion of Reagan's Strategic Defense Initiative.

Possony laughed when I told him how Teller had beaten me up. "He talks that way to the people with whom he deigns to talk," he said. "Don't worry, you can be sure that he knows who you are, and he certainly knows how much clout The Reader's Digest has. Don't hesitate to call him back if you have any more questions; he'll talk to you."

That made me feel better. Added to that was Possony's reassurances on the whole idea of SDI.

I visited with other big thinkers, ending with Dr. Harold Agnew, who by this time was President and Chief Executive Officer at General Atomics, in La Jolla, California. He agreed with Teller and Possony.

Agnew was a chemical engineer who was enlisted by Enrico Fermi for the team he organized which accomplished history's first controlled nuclear chain reaction, under the football stadium at the University of Chicago. Agnew had been a key figure in the

Manhattan Project throughout;, he eventually became Director of Weapons Development at Los Alamos. I found him to be a man of great good humor, and he delighted in recalling history.

He greatly admired Teller. "I sometimes wondered about his connections," he said. "One day at Los Alamos, several of the world's leading scientists were trying to solve a problem, and had spent hours staring an equation about 20 yards long they had constructed on a blackboard. They were right on the cusp of the answer, but something crucial was missing, and no one could figure out what it was. They had been focused on it for hours, not getting anywhere. Teller was not involved. He happened to be walking through the room, he stopped, looked at the blackboard, walked to it, picked up a piece of chalk, inserted a symbol in the middle of the equation, and that was it! It made the whole thing make sense. It was as though someone had thrown a light switch. It was amazing.

"This sort of thing happened often. I asked him, 'Edward, how do you do these things? How do you *know*?' He said, 'God tells me'." Agnew laughed again. "I don't know where else he could have gotten some of the answers he came up with."

I asked him about reactions to the first atomic explosion, at Alamagordo, when it was learned that an atomic bomb would actually work. I thought it must have been a sobering moment for everyone involved. I referred to a famous photograph of J. Robert Oppenheimer, the theoretical physicist who had directed the Manhattan Project to its successful conclusion, holding his head in his hands and lamenting that, "I am death, the destroyer of worlds."

"What actually happened," Agnew said, laughing again, "was that Oppie danced around cheering and shouting, 'Hot damn! Now we've got the sons of bitches'."

Agnew also told me that with the successful construction of the two atomic bombs, nicknamed Fat Man and Little Boy, a great debate had raged among the insiders who knew about them. One faction, appalled at what it would cost in Japanese lives, argued for a "demonstration" drop on an uninhabited island on the Pacific, close to Japan, so that the leadership there could see it; surely, this would lead quickly to surrender. Teller was the foremost voice for this faction.

The other faction pointed out that we only had two atomic bombs, and could not afford to waste either on a "demonstration" drop; furthermore that the Japanese were demonstrably fanatical, determined to defend to the death the home islands. And that if the United States had to invade many hundreds of thousands of young Americans would die, so a direct nuclear assault on two important military targets in the Japanese homeland stood the best chance of eliciting a surrender. The foremost voice for this faction was Oppenheimer, who finally and firmly instructed Teller to "stay out of it, and stick to science".

On August 6, 1945, Agnew was aboard the B-29 bomber *The Great Artiste*, which dropped the second atomic bomb, over Nagasaki; his task was to measure the yield of the nuclear blast. "When I returned to Los Alamos," he recalled, "I went directly to Oppenheimer's office to give the boss a report. When I walked in he jumped up, ran around his desk and hugged me. He said, 'You really gave it to the bastards!'"

In Pleasantville, I may have discovered a reason for Teller's disdainful treatment of me when I met with him: He had sent some manuscripts of his own to the Digest, and all had been rejected because they had been written in language that readers who were not well versed in high level physics could understand. But Steve Possony had been correct with his assurance that Teller would be available to me whenever I called. In the years that followed I called him a number of times and he always provided the information I needed, all the while, of course, muttering dire assessments of my intelligence.

Things ended unhappily for both Oppenheimer and Teller. At Congressional hearings in the late 1940's and early 1950's Oppenheimer's security clearance was called into question for what he had never denied, having long had close associations with many communists; but he insisted that he had remained a loyal American – which should never have been questioned. Teller testified against him, not, he emphasized, because he ever doubted Oppenheimer's loyalty, but that in his experience with him he felt that he had made "too many confusing...complicated...poor decisions," and that he would feel more comfortable with the country's vital secrets in other hands.

Oppenheimer's security clearance was revoked. He died in 1967, at the age of 62.

Following his testimony, Teller was ostracized by his colleagues; they would have nothing to do with him. Prior to his death in 2003 at the age of 95 he said that if he had it to do again, he would never have testified as he did against Oppenheimer, that he deserved better.

They both did.

66
The End

Ken Tomlinson completed his service at the Voice of America. Editor-in-Chief Gilmore, who had hired him in 1968 in Washington, now brought him back to the Digest in 1985, this time as the magazine's Executive Editor. By now, Gilmore had Parkinson's Disease, and it was steadily eroding his ability to function. He was going to have to step down, and had put Tomlinson in position to succeed himself as Editor-in-Chief.

This was stunning. One senior editor pronounced it "grotesque!" Things seemed chaotic: George Grune, a businessman who knew and cared little about Editorial had become CEO. A group of people on the business side who had little or no understanding of the Digest's core values had, with the help of some aged millionaires who could claim to be close friends and advisors to Wally, seen to Thompson's removal and Gilmore's appointment as Editor-in-Chief. Out of the blue and obviously with the approval of the CEO

Gilmore had chosen as his successor someone who had not been around for years, had spent very limited time in editorial management and who was much younger and much less experienced than many accomplished editors who were now subordinate to him.

Gilmore retired in 1989, and Tomlinson ascended. Gilmore remained a close advisor to Tomlinson. He also continued to represent the Wallace Trust. In the latter capacity he periodically visited Macalester College, in St. Paul, which was included in the Trust. We lived only a short drive from the school, so during these visits Ken usually would visit and dine with us. On one such visit he advised me that he and Tomlinson felt that I should not continue to work with Nina, that they both thought I should be working with someone else.

I was amazed. I could not get a coherent explanation for this thinking, and objected strongly to it. I pointed out that it was Gilmore himself who, when Frank Devine departed, had suggested that I work with Nina, and that we had been working well together. Then I learned that it wasn't a proposal but an accomplished fact. Nina had already been told. She had no more idea than I did why this had happened.

I found myself working with a new editor. All I knew about him was that he stood high in Gilmore's and Tomlinson's favor. I had seen him around the office, but did not recall ever having exchanged a word with him. He didn't thrill me when we first sat down together and he told me what he *didn't* want from me: Any more of those family humor pieces. I was dumbfounded. Fifteen had been published. Readers had always placed them at or near the top of the Digest's reader polls, surveys the magazine took to keep itself apprised of its readers' tastes. I had been advised by four Editors-in-Chief, including Tomlinson, and other senior editors that such "high quality family humor" was "very hard to find," and to please "keep it up", that it "struck a chord with everyone who had a family or had grown up in one", that it was "golden".

My new editor explained to me that "Our readers are serious people," that "we are not going to waste their time or ours with such stories," and that he intended to be "a strong gatekeeper... etc."

Nothing funny ever happened at my house again – which is to say, nothing that anyone read about.

No one ever explained to me why this particular editor-writer rearrangement was necessary.

As Editor-in-Chief, Tomlinson was up against it. Some older editors had resented Gilmore, who some believed had helped engineer Ed Thompson's ouster. Now, having spent years in Editorial's trenches, searching the world for articles of "lasting interest and enduring value," reading and cutting, finding ideas, discovering and nurturing competent writers, they had to suffer Gilmore's protégé, who, in the view of many, had not paid his dues. There were attitudes which did not endear them to Tomlinson who, after all, was now the boss. I was never in Pleasantville on a sustained basis, but I was in touch all the time, and what I kept hearing of Tomlinson's relationships with longtime editors and writers was disconcerting. His judgment was questioned, and he was characterized as something of a martinet. An unhappy atmosphere prevailed, disappointed anger and a desperate wonder as to what the future held, and even if there was a future. Everyone continued to do his job, but it became increasingly difficult for some editors to get approval from Tomlinson's Assignment Committee for their writers to act on what they deemed good proposals.

David Reed called me one day to say that over an extended period of time none of a number of what he knew to be strong proposals had been accepted, and that he meant to retire forthwith. This was a shock, and it was soon followed by another: He was diagnosed with liver cancer. It took him in November, 1990. He was 63 years old. Someone in Washington arranged for a funeral service in a church. David's ashes were there. A female minister officiated. David had long been a devout anti-feminist and atheist, I'm certain that if he'd had anything to say about it a memorial service would have been held in a saloon, with a bartender officiating. Some months later a memorial service was held in a saloon, in Virginia's Tidewater area; before contracting cancer David had become bored with Florida, and decided that this was a better place to sail. Ed Thompson, Bill Schulz and I were in the saloon, to render a final salute to our outrageous friend.

I was having my own troubles with the assignments process. More than once in my career I had written pieces which I knew no one else was working. I had judged that any editor who knew about the story would want it written. I had had a lot of success with such articles. I learned the hard way that that kind of spontaneous production wasn't going to happen again.

444

Example: I found and wrote a dramatic story of a ground breaking approach to surgery at the Mayo Clinic that demonstrated that the best medicine, including surgery, in the world could now be made available to people anywhere in the world. Knowing that I had written a winner, I was stunned when an editor on the Assignment Committee kept posing nonsensical objections. I kept answering them until finally it became obvious that the piece was not going to be published, and it never was.

I wrote two proposals for stories that I thought were so good that when Tomlinson's Assignment Committee rejected them I wrote them anyway and sent them to The Catholic Digest. The Editor called me each time with effusive thanks, and sent me nice checks.

My new editor and I got a couple of articles into the Digest, but we didn't really mesh. One day he called me to say, "Ken wants to know why you're writing these good stories for other magazines."

I explained why. He had no response. It was our last conversation.

I was angry and frustrated. Then, suddenly, I realized that I was several months past my 65th birthday, the milestone at which Wally had insisted that anyone who wasn't DeWitt Wallace retire, where one went fishing, or played golf, or went to afternoon baseball games, or do whatever else one felt inclined to do, but one stopped working. More than four decades had passed since my first contact with Hobe Lewis, and my first sale to the Digest I certainly didn't feel old; I still felt full of energy; I could not understand why writers should retire while they still had the energy to research and write. It seemed to me that the older a writer became the more wisdom he could bring to his work.

No matter. One spring morning Tomlinson's secretary called to say that Ken wanted to see me. At lunch at the Guest House my former legman and I were old and good friends. He was Editor-in-Chief now, but he was not the Chief. The Chief was CEO George Grune, and Tomlinson was doing as he was told, trimming the masthead of a lot of those expensive editorial people. Ken pointed out that I had a nice pension awaiting me, and in addition to it he had arranged for a very nice cash settlement; plus, he said, if I saw any good stories that I wanted to write would I be good enough give the Digest first look? I said that of course I would, but I was sure we both knew that it wouldn't happen, that my life with Wally's brilliant idea was over.

It seemed such a short time since I had first walked, awe-struck, into the rotunda of the lovely building Wally had built in 1939, since the first time I was greeted so warmly by DeWitt Wallace himself, heard him invite me to join the Digest, heard him saying, "...*If you have to go to Timbuktu to get a paragraph to make a story right, you don't have to ask anyone's permission...*" I had made the most of his incredible charter, but he was gone, and the magazine's glory years were gone, too. What was left for me was the immense satisfaction of having been a major participant in the acquisition of the glory

But it was time to go. This wasn't The Reader's Digest I had been so thrilled to reach as a young writer, but it had been a wonderful career. There were a lot of memories to cherish. But I had had enough of the long downhill slide that had begun with the dismissal of Ed Thompson; enough of trying to work with editors who didn't know a good story until it appeared in another magazine;

446

enough of a so-called Assignment Committee whose primary purpose seemed to be to keep good stories out of the magazine, and much too much of an editorial leadership that had to take its guidance from the business side.

A few months later Tomlinson brought Punkin and me back to Pleasantville to honor us at a farewell dinner at the Guest House. The party included Hobart Lewis and his wife, Edith, Nina Bell Allen, Ken Tomlinson and his wife, Rebecca, and Ken Gilmore. There was even a nice goodbye letter and a gift from CEO George Grune. The party did not include Ed Thompson and his wife, Susan, with whom we would remain good friends for the rest our lives. Even so, it was a lovely evening.

Since the day I made that stupid decision in the summer of 1949 I have been more than comfortable with it. If I had it all to do over again I surely would, and exactly the same way. What a great life I've had, what a great family and what great editors and friends, and what a great privilege it had been to participate in the making of Wally's brilliant idea into the great American institution that his Reader's Digest had been.

Epilogue

y the time I joined the Digest and during the four-plus decades I spent with it, it was the most popular print journalism entity in history. It is still difficult to believe that the
magazine, as DeWitt Wallace conceived it, failed. It failed, in my
view, because Wally fell victim to Alzheimer's Disease before preparing properly for the succession; I am confident that had he remained
in full possession of his faculties he would have named Edward T.
Thompson Chief Executive Officer, and that had he done so the
Digest, notwithstanding the devastating impact of the internet on
print journalism, would remain today one of the world's significant
journalistic enterprises.

But what happened is what happened. Wally's magazine evapo-
rated in a miasma of arrogant ignorance and overweening greed.
The company failed exactly as Hobart Lewis had warned Al Cole
and Laurance Rockefeller it would fail if they started "interfering
with Editorial."

There was a lot of interference, and indeed it was fatal. Wally's advice was ignored, and the company was taken public. Some in management made themselves very wealthy. The quantity and quality of editorial content declined, as did circulation and the value of the stock. In 2006 corporate raiders extracted several billions of dollars in loans from various banks, took control of the company and took it private again. By 2009 the new owners couldn't service the debt, and the company entered into bankruptcy, at considerable cost to the retirement incomes of many who had helped to make the Digest the great magazine it had been.

The company was reorganized, but in February, 2013 was again taken into bankruptcy. Its newest leadership has expressed an earnest intention to focus on the Digest's "core mission."

I wish them success, hope for it and believe that it is achievable. I believe that there always will be a large audience for a high quality pocket-size magazine that can be held in one's hands and which offers closely researched, interesting, valuable information.

In other words, DeWitt Wallace's brilliant idea is still a brilliant idea.

Made in the USA
Las Vegas, NV
21 November 2020

11275662R00256